Eco-House
Manual

Acknowledgements

This book would not have been possible without help and co-operation from many people and organisations.

For their comments on the early drafts I am indebted to Jan Metcalf, Martyn Sawyer, Martyn Gittins, Corina Reay and Desmond Kerr.

For technical review I am grateful to the Energy Saving Trust, the Water Demand Management Team at the Environment Agency, the National Energy Foundation, Natural England and the Association of Environment Conscious Builders.

For information, photo locations and other assistance I would also like to thank Bradfords Building Supplies, British Hydropower Association, City Electrical Factors, Wellington Waste, Kensa Engineering, South West Water, Lime Technology, Solalighting, Plumbase, Dr Kirk Semple, Dr Robin Curtis at Earth Energy, Whispergen, David Moore, Garden Organic, Dr Rebecca Wade at the University of Abertay Dundee, The Green Shop, Imagination Solar, The Green Building Store, Recovery Insulation, Plantlife International, Electrisave, EcoTech Recycled Products, Trada, EDF Energy, Powergen, The Heat Project, The Concrete Centre, The Wool Marketing Board, Ian Constantinides, Ian Rock, Neil May, Geoff Stow, David Holloway, Ian Moore, Mark Johnston, Julian Brooks, Matt Hill, Caroline Barry, Liz Clark, Jim Carfrae, Gary & Cy Lane, Dan Dix, Patrick Stow, Elisabeth de Veer, Alison Henry, Sue Lilleman, Bob & Dorothy Griffiths, Joyce Westwood, Tom Worthington, Alex Carter, Phoebe Gange, John Tuer, Katie Bond, Amy Plumridge, Ted Gange and Darren Gray.

Unless credited otherwise, most photographs are by John Peters. Thanks John.

Haynes Publishing would like to thank the Energy Saving Trust for its contribution to the Eco-House Manual

energy saving trust®

© Nigel Griffiths 2007

Nigel Griffiths has asserted his right to be identified as the author of this work.

Published in July 2007

British Library Cataloguing in Publication Data:
A catalogue record for this book is availablefrom the British Library.

ISBN 978 1 84425 405 7

Published by Haynes Publishing, Sparkford, Yeovil, Somerset BA22 7JJ, UK
Tel: 01963 442030 Fax: 01963 440001
Int. tel: +44 1963 442030 Int. fax: +44 1963 440001
E-mail: sales@haynes.co.uk
Website: www.haynes.co.uk

Haynes North America Inc.
861 Lawrence Drive, Newbury Park, California 91320, USA

Printed and bound in Great Britain
by J. H. Haynes & Co. Ltd, Sparkford

This book is printed on Greencoat Velvet paper, which comprises 80% recycled post-consumer fibre, 10% TCF (Totally Chlorine Free) fibre and 10% ECF (Element Chlorine Free) fibre.

While every effort is taken to ensure the accuracy of the information given in this book, no liability can be accepted by the author or publishers for any loss, damage or injury caused by errors in, or omissions from, the information given.

Eco-House
Manual

Nigel Griffiths

CONTENTS

INTRODUCTION

This manual is designed to help homeowners alter or renovate their properties in ways that will reduce their impact on the environment and, ultimately, benefit themselves.

Some of the strategies outlined in this book will cost money, some are cost neutral and some will save money. There is no attempt on the part of the author to suggest to anyone what they should be doing – the manual merely attempts to provide the necessary information so that the reader can make an informed judgement.

If there is one shorthand way of summarising the approach which this book advocates, it would be to think carefully and in the broadest possible terms before starting work. We all do things in ways which are familiar to us, without bothering to challenge convention. However, unscrupulous business practices and careless governmental control at all levels have meant that the consumer has unwittingly participated in wholesale ecological destruction and pollution, much of it occurring since the Second World War.

Eco-renovation gives us an opportunity to put right some of the mistakes of the past by removing the bad and replacing it with something better. The consumption of energy and water by our existing housing stock can be reduced by making changes to the building fabric, to the services systems and to our lifestyles. By using non-toxic materials, we have the opportunity to make a difference to our future well-being. Houses which are refurbished with healthy materials and which achieve low running costs may also command a higher price in due course.

This manual reflects where we stand at the time of writing. The subject is constantly evolving as we come to understand the impact of our actions upon the health of the environment and each other. Older buildings and techniques have stood the test of time, whereas the long-term effects of many modern substances are not yet fully known. It will therefore be necessary to keep up to date and to research the materials and technologies which may be useful or relevant to your own property.

Not all subjects covered in this book are appropriate for all properties or lifestyles. However, doing a little is more beneficial than doing nothing at all and even small gestures can have surprisingly positive consequences.

For details of any updates and for links to suppliers see:
www.haynes.co.uk/ecohousemanual

Photo: Alamy.com

1 PRINCIPLES OF ECO-RENOVATION

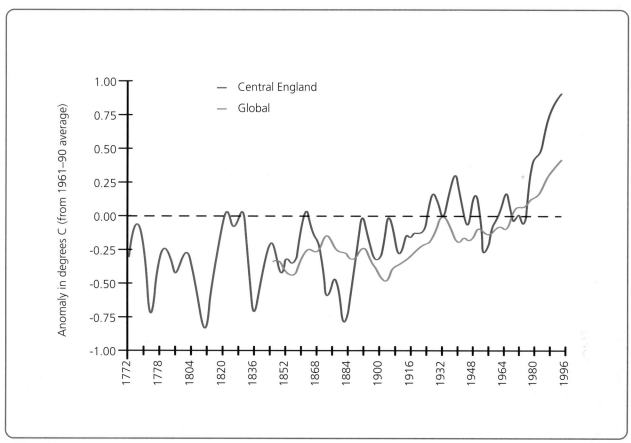

The threat to the environment

Mankind has damaged the planet, in some cases beyond repair. Irreplaceable natural resources are approaching exhaustion and the environmental effects of industrial and post-industrial development are increasingly plain to see.

GLOBAL WARMING

The greatest source of concern at present is the potential effects of global warming. Mean UK temperatures rose during the last century by two thirds of a degree and this rise is reflected by global temperature records. The period from 1993–2002 was the warmest decade in the UK since records began over 300 years ago. If this does indeed constitute an upward trend in global temperatures, there is a risk that sea levels will rise as a consequence of thermal expansion and of a net reduction in ice cover in the polar regions. This rise could, in turn, render large areas of the planet uninhabitable, particularly low-lying areas which are some of the most densely populated.

In addition to causing sea levels to rise, global warming is also contributing to climate change. Extreme weather events such as floods, droughts, hurricanes and heat waves are thought to be more common in the UK and snow is already less frequent. We may be experiencing a change in the intensity of rainfall, with more frequent spells of heavy rain and a shift in the distribution pattern which means that dry places will become drier and wet places will become wetter. Wildlife ranges are already altering and it is feared that diseases once confined to warmer climates will spread further north.

Climate is a notoriously complex subject and there are many factors which influence climate from one decade to the next. Some scientists argue that observed climate change is a result of natural fluctuations which have occurred many times in the earth's history and that human impact on these cycles is negligible. It appears that the majority of climate scientists are of the opinion that human activity is contributing to climate change, largely through our emissions of 'greenhouse gases'.

The earth is kept at a steady temperature by the delicate balance between the incoming heat of the sun and by the radiation of heat back out into space. The radiation of heat is slowed down by gases in the atmosphere (including water vapour) which form a necessary warm blanket around the planet. These gases admit short wavelength energy from the sun but some of the longer wavelength energy reflected back from the surface of the earth is

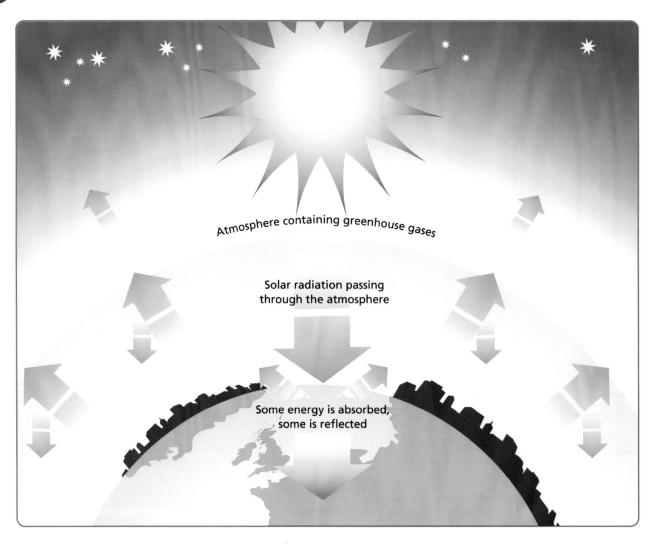

prevented from escaping. This is known as the 'greenhouse effect'.

Carbon dioxide, in particular, has increased in concentration in the atmosphere from 280 parts per million (ppm) in 1750 to 367ppm in 1999. The rise in CO_2 levels mirrors the pace of industrial development over the same period which has led scientists to conclude that this rise is caused largely by burning fossil fuels and in part by deforestation. Carbon dioxide is thought to contribute approximately 63% of the greenhouse effect.[1] The available ice core data does not suggest that CO_2 is a primary driver of climate change but it is possible that once global warming has begun, excessive CO_2 in that atmosphere could amplify the rate of temperature increase and therefore contribute to climate change.

CO_2 is an essential part of life on earth and it is only an excess of CO_2 which might be problematic. Other gases contribute to the greenhouse effect – methane is thought to contribute significantly – it is many times more potent

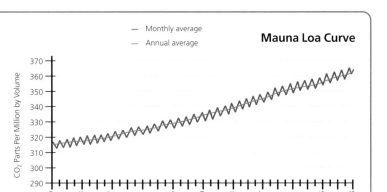

Kyoto gas	Global Warming Potential
Carbon dioxide (CO_2)	1
Methane (CH_4)	23
Nitrous oxide (N_2O)	296
Sulphur hexafluoride (SF_6)	22,200
Perfluorocarbons (PFCs)	4,800–9,200
Hydrofluorocarbons (HFCs)	12–12,000

Source: Scripps Institution of Oceanography, University of California.

than CO_2 as a greenhouse gas but currently it occurs in much lower concentrations in the atmosphere. The 1997 Kyoto Protocol identifies 6 greenhouse gases which signatory nations are now committed to reducing.

The science which underpins the concept of man-made global warming is steadily gaining acceptance, although it is not without its detractors. What is undeniable is that by burning fossil fuels at an unprecedented rate we are adding many millions of tonnes of CO_2 per annum to the earth's natural cycle. By simultaneously reducing the vegetation cover on the planet we have reduced its ability to soak up this additional carbon dioxide, compounding the problem.

DEFORESTATION

Photo: www.worldlandtrust.org

Forests are the green lungs of the planet. If we continue to reduce lung capacity at the present rate we will suffocate, but forests have a much wider function in the eco-system than simply the absorption of carbon dioxide. Tropical rainforests contain over two-thirds of the earth's living species and their store of plants and other organisms may yet hold the key to treating a wide variety of diseases for which there is currently no cure in conventional medicine. Continued logging in many parts of the world reduces the habitat available to species for whom the rainforest is their only home and threatens the very existence of indigenous peoples.

RESOURCE EXHAUSTION

Recent concerns about global warming have overshadowed the dominant ecological issues of the 1960s and 1970s, which included the inevitability of exhausting supplies of fossil fuels and other materials. Conservation was focussed upon prolonging the life of these resources while alternative sources of power were developed. However, the fact remains that the supply of fossil fuels is finite so our present rate of consumption cannot continue indefinitely.

There is also an ultimate limit to the amount of metals

and aggregates at our disposal. Substitution with alternative and preferably renewable materials is essential if our enjoyment of a wide variety of goods and building products is to be sustained. A reduction in consumption and an increase in recycling will both be required as supplies of virgin aggregates and metal ores are steadily depleted. Quarrying for some materials has a substantial environmental impact in certain areas and ultimately this is also unsustainable.

WATER RESOURCES

Despite the increasing incidence of heavy rainfall, we may start to face water shortages more often as this is the 'wrong kind of rain'. If it continues, climate change will also redistribute

Photo: ecoscene.com (Tony Page)

existing rainfall and on a global scale this may require massive population movements, as human settlement only exists where there is adequate water supply. Even within the UK, the South and East will receive progressively less useful rainfall, so we will have to reduce our water consumption or adjust our housebuilding programmes accordingly.

HEALTH AND WELL-BEING

The environment in which we live can have a profound impact upon personal health. Materials with which houses are constructed, decorated and furnished contain a variety of toxic chemicals, not to mention those that are contained in sprays and disinfectants in everyday use. This chemical soup weakens the immune system; some substances merely cause allergic reactions or headaches, whereas others are now known to cause cancer. Many modern houses are hermetically sealed and lack sufficient ventilation, leading to air quality which can be far worse than that on the average urban street.

Houses constructed and refurbished with natural materials greatly reduce this 'sick building syndrome', while adequate levels of daylight and ventilation contribute towards a more comfortable internal environment and have significant health benefits. Gardens also have an important role to play in improving quality of life, and can do much to reduce the impact of modern housing upon the eco-system.

POLLUTION

Construction is not the only culprit when it comes to polluting the environment as transport, mass food production and many other forms of commerce have caused enormous pollution. However, the production of materials for construction is directly responsible for damage where mines pollute rivers or factories release chemicals into the air and soil. Some synthetic materials present in buildings are now regarded as pollutants – asbestos is a good example, as it has now been spread widely throughout the UK. Construction also contributes to transport pollution, so careful choice of materials can reduce this problem. On the positive side, new construction provides an opportunity to clean up brownfield sites after centuries of contamination as a result of industrial processes. When building or refurbishing a house, many opportunities arise to embrace a lifestyle which generates less pollution.

General principles

When extending, altering or renovating domestic property, the environmental impact can be reduced by one or more of the following means:

- Using natural, renewable and locally-sourced materials
- Repairing rather than replacing where practicable
- Using recycled materials
- Avoiding materials whose production causes damage to the environment
- Employing local companies and local labour
- Reducing heat loss
- Maximising natural light and heat gain
- Using energy-efficient heating systems
- Reducing electricity consumption
- Introducing renewable energy, if possible and affordable
- Reducing water use
- Reducing and recycling waste
- Treating the outside space with the same care as the house itself

None of these principles amounts to anything more than the exercise of common sense. If we are running out of something quickly, we have to reduce our consumption of that resource, by finding a renewable alternative or by reducing consumption overall. On the other hand, if we have a problem with waste, we need to find ways to reduce the amount that we discard and then learn to treat the waste stream as a resource rather than as a problem to be buried.

However, the environmental consequences of certain building materials are not always obvious. The damage is frequently done far from the place of eventual sale and use of the product, and the consumer is not encouraged to find out how, or even where, the raw materials were produced. The effects of habitat destruction, or chemical spillage, or the long-term difficulties of disposing of certain materials, are all invisible to the consumer. However, these effects are already being experienced acutely in many other countries and may affect later generations in the UK.

From time to time, situations will occur when these principles conflict with each other. For example, when substituting a naturally produced material for a synthetic and non-renewable material, it may be found that the natural item is produced thousands of miles away and there is a significant energy cost in transporting it to the UK. This partly reflects a market in transition and more local alternatives are likely to become available as demand increases and producers take advantage of the opportunity. The UK manufacturing capacity for a wide range of recycled and renewable materials is already expanding every year in response to consumer demand.

In the rush to combat climate change by altering our housing stock to reduce CO_2 emissions, we are in danger of losing sight of all the other issues which are important if we are to live and build sustainably. Eco-building recognises that human quality of life depends upon the health of the whole environment, and that wildlife, ecology and aesthetics must all be considered when making choices about how to refurbish property.

Approach to old buildings

"These old buildings do not belong to us only…they have belonged to our forefathers and they will belong to our descendants unless we play them false. They are not…our property to do as we like with. We are only trustees for those that come after us."

William Morris 1889

Great damage has already been caused to the fabric of many old buildings by misguided attempts to modernise and improve them. Speculative restoration, repair with inappropriate materials, subdivision, unsympathetic extension, the introduction of services, and even regulatory intervention have all contributed to this process. It is crucial to ensure that any attempt to make ancient buildings more 'efficient' in energy performance terms does not add to this list of miscreants. An understanding of how traditional materials perform is essential before making any alterations to a historic building.

Even buildings which are not listed or considered significant or ancient can be a vital part of the visual fabric of our society, so considerable thought is needed before deciding to alter the appearance of our Edwardian, Victorian and Georgian housing stock in the name of eco-renovation. Much can be done to improve these buildings without ripping out irreplaceable historic fabric and inserting materials which may not last as well or which cause damage to the original building.

Technology is constantly evolving and some advances are actively helpful. For example, the advent of wireless communication systems may reduce the number of cables which need to be threaded through the fabric of houses and thus reduce the damage often inflicted during installation.

Regular maintenance and conservative repair with original materials are the first principles of conservation. Although the knowledge and skills necessary for the repair

uPVC replacement windows and timber originals.

Photo: Alison Heavy

Lime repointing.

Photo: Alison Heavy

of old buildings were once commonplace, nowadays this is a specialist area and professional advice should always be sought from a builder genuinely experienced in historic building repair, or possibly an architect or surveyor.

In terms of sustainability, old buildings have already performed well simply by being there for so long. Their embodied energy is extremely low because they were generally constructed with locally sourced labour and unprocessed materials. However, old buildings are not as easy to keep warm as modern insulated dwellings. It is usually possible to super-insulate at least the ceiling or roof without hiding historically interesting features, in order to compensate for the lack of insulation in walls or solid ground floors.

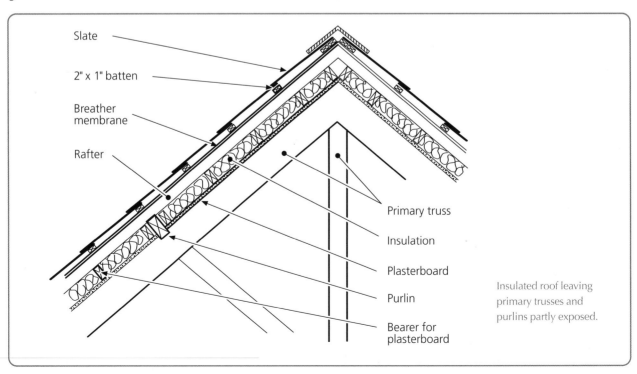

Slate

2" x 1" batten

Breather membrane

Rafter

Primary truss

Insulation

Plasterboard

Purlin

Bearer for plasterboard

Insulated roof leaving primary trusses and purlins partly exposed.

Most historic buildings which survive today have done so because they are well-ventilated. It is important to understand water vapour movement through a building before considering any alterations or reducing the existing ventilation in any way. The potential effects of adding any impervious insulation material to walls, floors or roofs in all older buildings (not just historic buildings) should also be researched and assessed.

Well-detailed modern roof windows are watertight, unlike their earlier prototypes. They admit good quantities of daylight and conservation roof windows blend in well with the appearance of many old buildings. Solar water heaters designed to look like conservation roof lights have now become available, so it may become possible to take selected steps towards energy efficiency without adversely affecting the character of a building.

The eco-renovation of old buildings thus represents a

Above: Solar water heater. Below: Conservation rooflights.

Photo: www.aranservices.co.uk

trade-off between the need to conserve energy and the need to conserve historic fabric. Energy is, in some senses, renewable, but historic fabric is not, so it is always necessary to err on the side of caution. Ironically, many of the techniques employed in eco-building and described in this book are similar to those used during the 19th century and earlier. It was only in the 20th century that many common-sense principles of construction were abandoned.

There are methods of space heating which do not involve burning fossil fuels and it may be that this is the answer to the particular needs of older buildings, rather than making wholesale alterations to the structure as a response to climate change. Perhaps we should not expect old buildings to be able to perform to the thermal standards required of new construction. Living in an old building has been compared to the experience of driving an old open-top car – it may require a different kind of lifestyle and possibly a different kind of occupant:

"If you really want to live in an old building then you have to come from the kind of culture whereby you are prepared to make a mad dash from an open fire to a hot water bottle with no prospect of any succour in between."

Ian Constantinides 2006

For further information see: Survey and Repair of Traditional Buildings – A Sustainable Approach *by Richard Oxley, Donhead (2003); Society for the Protection of Ancient Buildings (SPAB),* **www.spab.org.uk***; and English Heritage (Interim) Guidance Note on Part L,* **www.english-heritage.org.uk**

REFERENCES
[1] Energy Saving Trust Climate Change Briefing Note.

2 CONSTRUCTION MATERIALS

Selecting materials

EMBODIED ENERGY

Energy is used to extract raw materials, to process them and then to transport them. Once the materials have reached their destination, further energy is then required to fit or fix them. The sum of all this energy is known as the 'embodied energy' of a particular material.

This is a difficult subject as the economy and the environment are both so complex. It is possible to calculate the energy required to extract coal at the coal-face, but practically impossible to calculate the energy consumption of the communities whose main reason for being there is the work which the pit affords. The energy required to produce the mining machinery must then be added and it rapidly becomes apparent that the calculations are very open-ended and it is difficult to know where to draw an arbitrary line.

However, it is necessary to make an estimate of the embodied energy of various materials, if only for comparative purposes. Having done so, it is then necessary to take into account the volumes in which differing materials are used. For example, concrete has a much lower embodied energy than aluminium, but aluminium is only used in small quantities in house construction (and renovation) while concrete is currently used in very large quantities.

This table is useful when faced with a choice between two materials which will do substantially the same job. For example, a suitably sized hardwood lintel will perform similarly to a steel lintel at a fraction of the embodied energy cost. In general, materials which are used in a form which is as near as possible to their natural state will have the lowest embodied energy, in contrast to materials which are highly processed.

Material	kWh/m³
Lead	157,414
Copper	133,000
Steel (iron ore)	63-80,000
Aluminium	55,868
Plastics	47,000
Steel (recycled)	29,669
Glass	23,000
Fibre cement slate	12,783
Cement	2,860
Aluminium (recycled)	2,793–3,910
Clay tile	1,520
Brick	1,462
Plastic insulation	1,125
Gypsum	900
Autoclaved bricks	800
Concrete 1:2:4	800
Imported softwood	754
Foamed glass	751
Concrete tile	630
Concrete 1:3:6	600
Clinker blocks	600
Local slate	540
Local stone	450
Sand/cement render	400
Mineral fibre	230
Local green oak	220
Crushed granite	150
Cellulose insulation	133
Local air-dried softwood	110
Sand & gravel	45
Sheepswool	30

Source: Green Building Bible (Vol 1)

LOCAL MATERIALS AND LABOUR

The energy required to transport goods and people constitutes a large percentage of the embodied energy of a building. Historically, most buildings were constructed from natural materials which could be obtained as close as possible to the site. Transport and communications systems were undeveloped and large or heavy materials could not be moved without considerable difficulty and significant cost.

Photo: Jackie Abey

The farmhouse in this picture, for example, was constructed almost entirely out of materials sourced within a few hundred yards of the site. The walls are built of cob dug from the adjacent field, the roof is thatched from locally grown reeds and the timber for joists, rafters, floorboards and joinery would have been harvested from the wood surrounding the farmhouse.

It is extremely difficult to assess the environmental impact of obtaining construction materials, even down to the number of trips made to the local suppliers to collect them at the end of their journey. Complex computer programmes are available to calculate CO_2 emissions costs but a simple rule for householders would be to buy locally wherever possible, to be prepared to ask where things come from, and to expect an answer.

In just the same way as materials used to be sourced locally, in the past it would have been unthinkable for small construction projects to utilise anything other than the most local labour. The craftsmen would have been familiar with the available materials and, just as importantly, would understand the local methods of building. There would have been little concern over guarantees when the builders still lived in the same village. Large construction projects are a somewhat different matter and not the subject of this book.

In addition to the benefits of the experience and implicit guarantees provided by using local labour, there is a benefit to the community as a whole. Money spent within the community can be recycled several times, increasing the prosperity of the whole area, which benefits everyone – if only indirectly. This is known as the local economic multiplier and it is most keenly felt in more isolated communities.

LIFE-CYCLE ANALYSIS

Assessment of embodied energy does not stop with the fitting of the material. An estimate needs to be made of the energy cost of any future maintenance which may be required and ultimately the costs of disposal once the building (or that element of the building) has reached the end of its life. Certain materials are difficult or impossible to recycle, especially when combined with other materials and bound together with adhesives.

Life-cycle analysis (LCA) looks at all the issues which arise during the life of a building material, through to the demolition of the building. This is often referred to as 'cradle to grave' analysis, but the term increasingly used is 'cradle to cradle'. This reflects the use of waste as a resource and the need to design materials so that they can be recycled at the end of their use. LCA also takes into account embodied pollution, resource depletion and the expected life of the material or product.

SUPPLIERS

Where a number of suppliers sell apparently similar materials, it is sometimes worth checking on the environmental policies of the suppliers to discover whether there are any significant safeguards in place. Policies regarding transportation and embodied energy, pollution or resource degradation may help in deciding between potential sources of supply.

Masonry

Masonry comprises bricks, blocks, stone, concrete and mortar. Masonry is employed everywhere in buildings, from

foundations to floors and walls and even in some cases for roofing. Its stability and longevity make it ideal for use in construction; but there are some environmental issues to consider.

Firstly, the main drawback to masonry is that it is heavy. The embodied energy needed to transport products from a quarry or brickworks to a builders' merchant or direct to site is the primary environmental cost of masonry.

Secondly, quarrying has a destructive effect at the quarry face and considerable environmental impact in the surrounding area. While some quarrying is obviously economically and practically necessary, measures to reduce its impact and to return spent quarries to areas of ecological diversity do go some way towards reversing the process of destruction.

Thirdly, local supplies of sand, gravel, clay and stone will run out eventually. These materials were laid down by geological activity thousands or millions of years ago and cannot be replaced. The more slowly we consume the local resources, the less energy will be needed in the future to transport alternative supplies over longer distances. The dredging of marine aggregates also has a significant environmental impact and measures have already been introduced to control and reduce the effects of this kind of extraction.

Above: Active quarry. Below: Restored quarry.

Photo: Quarry Products Association

Photo: Quarry Products Association

19

RECYCLED AGGREGATES

Recycled aggregates are steadily gaining acceptance in the construction industry. Rather than digging up virgin aggregates, recycled hardcore is commonly used for road base material, blinding, granular fills, temporary working platforms for heavy plant, oversite concrete and a variety of precast concrete products. Recycled asphalt planings and other reclaimed hardcore are now being used, for example, in asphalt pavements.

STONE

Stone is a natural and extremely versatile building resource. The majority of stone buildings in the UK were built from the most locally available stone, as it would have been impossible to move stone over anything more than a short

 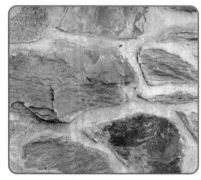

Above left: Flint. Above right: Morte Slate. Below: Hamstone.

distance except where water-based transport was readily available. This accounts for the wide variation in colour, texture and style of stone-built property throughout the country.

As transportation is such a high proportion of the cost of heavy materials, especially aggregates, it should make economic as well as environmental sense to use local materials wherever possible. It is not uncommon to find stone in DIY stores and builders' merchants which has been imported from the other side of the world. Although the UK has a great variety of natural stone, the internal supply chain at present is weak. However, if a more locally sourced product can be found which is affordable, equally attractive and performs just as well, the embodied energy of the stone will be far lower.

MORTAR

Mortar is simply sand (or other fine aggregate) mixed with a binder such as cement or lime. Cement is the most common binder now in use in the UK but there are considerable advantages to using lime in some situations. In like-for-like mortars, lime is responsible for slightly lower CO_2 emissions.[1]

Both lime and cement can cause burns to the skin but it is worth noting that the supply or use of cement (or cement products) which has a chromium VI concentration of more than two parts per million was prohibited after July 2005. Chromium VI was responsible for the contact dermatitis which many people report after touching wet cement. This is one example of how the construction industry is, very belatedly, cleaning up its act.

Lime is softer than cement and more permeable to both air and water. Many forms of green construction require the use of a weathering skin which can flex and breathe, so lime render is greatly preferable to cement render in this application.

Most houses constructed in the UK before 1920 were built with lime mortar so repair (or renovation work) is best achieved with similar materials. Repairing brickwork with lime mortar also prolongs the life of the brickwork, which makes it inherently much more sustainable than cement mortar.

Cement repointing leading to brick decay.

NORMAL DECAY

CAN OCCUR AFTER CEMENT RE-POINTING

Strong cement pointing

Water vapour

Lime mortar

CONCRETE

Concrete consists of aggregate, sand and a binder, usually cement. Due to the high energy cost of producing cement and the energy required to transport the aggregates, the production of concrete accounts for between 5 and 10% of the world's man-made annual CO_2 emissions.

Although, by volume and weight, concrete has a relatively low embodied energy compared to steel and plastics, so much of it is produced – over 14 billion tonnes are poured every year – that there is great potential to reduce energy consumption by using concrete more efficiently. Most of this concrete is used in new construction but domestic renovators can still make a difference by avoiding the use of concrete or concrete products for external surfaces where other, less energy-intensive, materials would work just as well (see section on 'Hard landscaping' in Chapter 10).

When building an extension, the use of concrete can be reduced by pouring concrete pads to underpin post-and-beam foundations rather than the 'trench fill' technique commonly used to create strip foundations.

'Oversite concrete' refers to the slab which is usually poured to form the ground floor of a dwelling. Oversite concrete is unnecessary where it is possible to build a highly insulated suspended floor rather than a solid

floor resting on the ground. It is worth noting that most of the older housing stock in the UK was built without the use of oversite concrete. On the other hand, where insulation has been fitted underneath the concrete, the concrete acts as 'thermal mass' (see section on 'Passive solar design' in Chapter 4). Together with underfloor heating, this can form part of the thermal strategy for a building.

Mortar needs to be of similar strength to (or slightly weaker than) the materials which it binds together. When water enters lime masonry as a result of driving rain, it will eventually find the easiest way back out, which is generally via the joints. With the added action of frost, over many years the joints will tend to weather back a little, which leads to the need for repointing. If repointing is carried out with cement mortar, it prevents the water from flowing out through joints. As cement mortar is so much harder than most stone or old bricks, the water then seeks the next easiest way out, which is via the edges of the bricks or stone. In exposed locations, such as chimney stacks, this in turn leads to weathering of the brick edges and to the eventual loss of the face. Once a brick has lost its hard face the softer core rapidly decays, leading to substantial and costly repairs.

In terms of embodied energy, it is generally better to repair than to replace. This is particularly true of heavy items such as masonry, so good conservation techniques have an important role to play in reducing our consumption of materials and energy.

Lastly, since lime mortar does not adhere as firmly as cement mortar, materials which have been bound together with lime mortar are much easier to clean and reuse at the end of the life of the building.

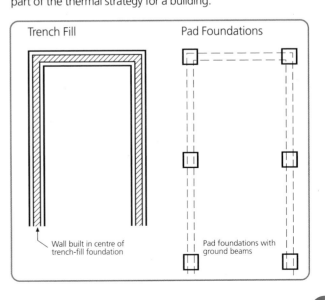

Trench Fill

Pad Foundations

Wall built in centre of trench-fill foundation

Pad foundations with ground beams

BRICKS AND BLOCKS

Bricks are made from clay which is fired in a kiln to bake it hard and give it a weatherproof outer surface. Although clay is a naturally occurring material, the firing is obviously an energy-intensive process. To reduce the transport cost of the operation, brickworks were originally built near housing developments, taking advantage of the locally available clay. This accounts for the variety of colours of older bricks.

Most of these brickworks have now disappeared and bricks are now mass-produced in a much smaller number of factories, which means that the transportation (thus energy, CO_2 emissions, pollution) costs are now much higher.

Concrete blocks are made with cement. The energy required to produce the cement is greater than the energy required to fire the equivalent volume of bricks so, generally speaking, blocks have a higher embodied energy than bricks. Blocks vary from dense to lightweight, depending on their load-bearing characteristics and thermal performance. For some years, concrete blocks have been manufactured using recycled aggregates such as fuel ash and, more recently, glass. Some blocks may contain up to 80% recycled material (by volume). Recycled aggregates are also used in paving slabs and any cement-based product could in theory make use of recycled aggregate.

For further information see: WRAP – Waste and Resources Action Programme, **www.wrap.org.uk**

Thermalite blocks.

Photo: Oak Apple Frames

Sustainable timber use

Timber is the most versatile building material of all. It can be used for structures, cladding, joinery, flooring and decorative purposes.

In contrast to most other materials, timber absorbs CO_2 as it grows. Some energy is required to log, mill and transport the timber, so the same principles of local sourcing and waste minimisation apply as with all other materials. However, there is a serious downside to timber production: illegal logging is responsible for the destruction of forests world-wide, together with the resultant loss of wildlife habitats, biodiversity and, in some cases, traditional lifestyles. Soil erosion and downstream river sedimentation add to the damaging effects of deforestation.

CERTIFICATION SCHEMES

Contributing to this type of environmental destruction can be avoided by insisting upon timber which is certified as having been produced from a sustainable source. This generally means that the impact of the logging has been minimised and that replanting is replacing the harvested timber – although not necessarily in the same place.

The following certification schemes are currently recognised by the Building Research Establishment as acceptable proof of sustainability:

FSC	Forestry Stewardship Council
PEFC	Program for the Endorsement of Forest Certification
MTCC	Malaysian Timber Certification Council
CSA	Canadian Standards Association
SFI	Sustainable Forestry Initiative

FSC
Mixed Sources
Product group from well-managed forests, controlled sources and recycled wood or fibre
Cert no. TT-COC 1519
www.fsc.org
© 1996 Forest Stewardship Council

It is worth noting that the FSC standard is widely recognised as the

serves to separate – which is why an I-beam is the shape it is, discarding the parts that do less work. The strength of a beam increases in relation to the distance between the top and bottom flanges, so the deeper the beam the stronger it becomes.

The timber I-beam works in exactly the same way. By taking out the middle section of the joist and replacing it with a separating web, the I-beam can be engineered to accept the same loads but with a greatly reduced consumption of timber and a more reliable bearing capacity. Timber I-beams are also lighter to handle than equivalent solid joists, which makes construction easier. The separating web is usually constructed from oriented strand board (OSB) or structural board manufactured from wood

Photo: Jackson Moulding

most environmentally rigorous of these schemes and it is the only one which is entirely independent of the forestry industry. It is encouraging to note that some builders merchants and DIY stores have already decided to obtain some or all of their timber from certified sources.

In addition to these schemes, timber may be available which is harvested from local gardens or woodlands which are then replanted. Together with reclaimed timber, this is the most sustainable supply of all. Most timber used in the UK construction industry is imported but the embodied energy cost of shipping timber from Sweden is a fraction of that used to transport timber from the Far East, so not all imported timbers are comparable.

Many tropical hardwoods are non-renewable. Reducing or eliminating demand for tropical hardwoods may eventually reduce the speed at which the remaining forests are being destroyed. Remaining tropical rainforests cover approximately 2% of the land surface of the earth but 1.5 acres are lost every second.[2] Rainforests play a vital role in absorbing CO_2 and also help to maintain the climate elsewhere as most of the rain which falls there is later returned to the atmosphere via evapotranspiration and is then conveyed to other parts of the world.

For further information visit **www.savetherainforest.org**

waste – see the next section for more information on these products.

A similar concept is also used in modern timber frame construction for walls where an inner and an outer skin are joined together by a series of connecting plates. This is particularly useful where a building is designed to be superinsulated, as the separation of the inner and outer skins allows for an almost complete thermal break between the two and for thick walls to be constructed without having to use deep timber studs, which are prone to warping or twisting. This type of construction also allows for reclaimed timber of varying sizes to be used if available.

EFFICIENT TIMBER PRODUCTS

Timber I-beams are the timber equivalent of the steel I-beam. Most of the strength in a steel beam is provided by its top and bottom sections, which the centre section mainly

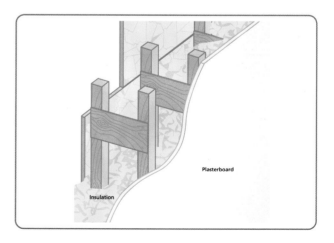

Plasterboard

Insulation

Photo: Nick Spollin

Splice repairs.

REPAIR RATHER THAN REPLACE

In old buildings, decayed beams can be cut back to sound wood and structural repairs carried out while minimising the loss of original timber. Certain types of repair can be achieved purely by well-designed carpentry joints, but other situations may require the addition of steel plates or splicing with steel rods and epoxy grouts.

The environmental impact of the materials used to carry out these repairs far outweighs the impact of replacing the entire section of timber, even if this is technically feasible. The added advantage is that the maximum amount of historic fabric is retained and the disruption to the building is reduced.

Timber treatment

PRE-TREATED TIMBER

During the last 50 years, the pre-treatment of structural timber has become commonplace. The long-term effects of these chemical treatments on human health cannot yet be fully known. The most commonly used preservative for many years was CCA – copper chromated arsenic. This was finally banned for domestic use in 2004, a good example of

Untreated softwood (below) and treated softwood (below right).

how the government is responding to public pressure for healthier buildings.

For further information see: Toxic Treatment, *London Hazard Centre (1989).*

A well-detailed timber building may have no need of treatment for the great majority of its structural members. The converse is also true – where the conditions exist for rot or other forms of timber decay to commence, as a result of poor detailing and lack of maintenance, timber treatment will only slow down rather than prevent the onset of decay. Some species of timber can survive for centuries even when exposed to the elements, irrespective of timber treatment.

Any timber which may come into prolonged contact with damp will still need to be protected – for example, base-plates in some wooden buildings. In the garden, fence posts, decking bases and any garden buildings should be treated, although larch, cedar and local hardwoods may be used as cladding with no necessity for treatment at all. Oil-

based treatments for decking surfaces work by nourishing the wood rather than trying to seal it and can be an effective and non-toxic alternative to chemical treatment.

NON-TOXIC TIMBER PRESERVATIVES

Alternative timber treatments are available which are potentially less harmful to the environment. The relevant British standard for timber treatment is BS 8417. If the need for treatment has been established, builders' merchants should be able to supply timber which has been treated with chemicals such as Tanalith-e (based on copper triazole), Naturewood, or Boron.

Boron is a naturally occurring mineral which already exists in the environment and has a toxicity to humans similar to that of common salt. Plant and aquatic toxicity is also relatively low. Inorganic borates are also water soluble which eliminates the need to use solvents and gives them a much better penetration into the wood than many conventional preservatives.

REMEDIAL TIMBER TREATMENT

When there has been an outbreak of dry rot or woodworm, it is common practice to treat the affected timbers and any surrounding timber with chemicals. There are potential risks to human health associated with chemical woodworm eradication treatment in domestic property. The most common chemical in use at the present time is Permethrin, which is a suspected endocrine disruptor and possible carcinogen.[3]

However, there should be no need to introduce toxic chemicals into the living environment. Wood-boring creatures only flourish in a damp, dark, unventilated environment, perhaps arising as a result of defective rainwater fittings or incorrect ground levels. Failure to maintain joinery and the seals around frames is another common cause of damp ingress and timber decay. Sometimes, woodworm damage is treated long after the woodworm have done their work and disappeared, so it is best to check for signs of fresh activity (clean wood dust) before taking remedial action.

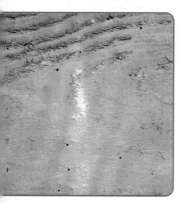

Experts on old buildings recommend locating and eliminating the source of the moisture which has caused the problem before resorting to chemical remedies. However, the necessity to use chemical treatment against apparent or actual wood decay frequently arises at the

Above left: Old woodworm damage.
Left: Dust produced by active woodworm.

suggestion of surveyors and at the insistence of mortgage providers. Either party may still need convincing of the efficacy of alternative approaches to timber treatment. Furthermore, treatment with toxic chemicals will not necessarily prevent the recurrence of decay if the original source of moisture is not eliminated.

Most buildings, if properly maintained, function perfectly well indefinitely without the need for any chemical treatment but where it is unavoidable there is a range of products based on boron which are effective against dry rot, wet rot and woodworm, while having a greatly reduced environmental impact.

For further information see: Society for the Protection of Ancient Buildings, www.spab.org.uk; and Pesticide Action Network, www.pan-uk.org

Composite/ particle boards

STRUCTURAL BOARDS

A variety of composite sheet materials is used for flooring, kitchen worktops and other structural purposes. They fall into three basic categories – particle boards such as chipboard, fibre boards such as MDF and laminated boards such as plywood.

Five issues arise when deciding which board to choose:

- Where does the raw material come from?
- What is used to bind it together?
- How much energy is used in its manufacture and transportation?
- Does it last well?
- Can it be recycled at the end of its useful life?

Source of the raw material

The small size of particles and fibres in composite boards means that they can be manufactured from the waste generated in the processing of raw timber, although this is not always the case. Some manufacturers use raw material produced from non-sustainable sources so, as with unprocessed timber, it is necessary to look for the FSC or PEFC label on sheet materials. OSB was designed in part to use smaller logs which could not be processed into plywood. It thus represents a more efficient use of raw materials than some structural boards.

Binders

The most common binders used in laminated boards, particle boards and fibre boards are urea-formaldehyde and phenol-formaldehyde. Even at relatively low levels, exposure to formaldehyde causes irritation to eyes and to

MDF.

Plywood.

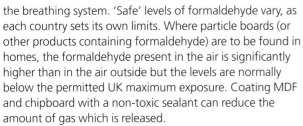

Chipboard.

OSB.

the breathing system. 'Safe' levels of formaldehyde vary, as each country sets its own limits. Where particle boards (or other products containing formaldehyde) are to be found in homes, the formaldehyde present in the air is significantly higher than in the air outside but the levels are normally below the permitted UK maximum exposure. Coating MDF and chipboard with a non-toxic sealant can reduce the amount of gas which is released.

The International Agency for Research on Cancer (IARC) – part of the World Health Organisation – has evaluated the available evidence on the carcinogenicity of formaldehyde and concluded that it is carcinogenic to humans.[4]

The Wood Panel Industries Federation (WPIF) states that: "The UK's Building Research Establishment has tested the air quality in typical British homes and found the average concentration of formaldehyde is less than one-quarter of the guideline limit from all formaldehyde emitting sources in the home."[5] However, it is acknowledged that off-gassing reduces over time and that these figures are averages, so it is easy to envisage a scenario where a newly refurbished house might have a range of products present leading to levels of formaldehyde which significantly exceed the permitted exposure levels.

OSB is commonly bound with phenol formaldehyde, considered to be more stable than urea-formaldehyde. Formaldehyde-free chipboards and MDF (European E1 grade) are now starting to become available in the UK.

Alternative structural sheet materials with much lower formaldehyde content could be Birch plywood, HDF (high density fibreboard) and OSB.[6]

For further information on the risks of exposure to dust arising from working with wood products see: COSHH and the woodworking industries – *Woodworking Sheet No 6 (rev) – Health & Safety Executive (2003).*

Embodied energy
Most man-made boards have a high embodied energy in comparison to natural timber due to the processing needed to create the board and the embodied energy of the binders which are added. It appears that hardboard, medium board and softboard have a somewhat lower embodied energy than MDF and chipboard, if no synthetic resin binders are used. Medium board is made by steaming wood into fires and adding water to form a slurry. When it is finally pressed, it is bound together by the natural lignin in the wood. Medium board should not be confused with MDF, where the fibres are allowed to dry before the binder is added, as with particle boards. The raw materials for OSB and plywood are less processed than those in particle board or chipboard.

Many plywood products are imported from Brazil or the Far East, giving them a high embodied energy and increasing the risk that illegally logged timber has been used as raw material. European-sourced plywoods are generally available as an alternative.

Durability

The durability of fibre boards and particle boards is their main downfall as most will swell up and lose their strength when in prolonged contact with water. Even moisture-resistant boards will fail in the long run but a laminated board such as plywood generally has a better strength and durability than the alternatives.

Disposal

Advice from County Councils is not to burn MDF or particle boards such as chipboard as they contain toxic glues; there is often a separate skip at the municipal site for such 'man-made wood'.[7] This would not apply to the wet process fibre boards described above.

PLASTERBOARD AND ALTERNATIVES

Plasterboard is composed of gypsum which is processed into a board and faced with paper. Natural gypsum is a mineral – calcium sulphate dihydrate ($CaSO_4 2H_2O$) – which is mined in Sussex, Lincolnshire and Yorkshire. A large source of gypsum for plasterboard is flue gas desulphurisation from power plants – a good use of a waste material.

Working with plasterboard inevitably generates offcuts. These used to be added to general hardcore, but recycling schemes are commencing in various parts of the UK. Moisture-resistant plasterboard cannot presently be recycled.[8] Environment Agency policy on waste minimisation and reduction of landfill, introduced June/July 2005, states that a mixed skip can contain up to 10% plasterboard and still be landfilled in non-hazardous landfills.[9] Higher concentrations than this now require specialist disposal.

Photo: Haldor Bjornson

Wall boards can be made from renewable material such as hemp or recycled newspaper, the latter containing some gypsum. Some are stronger than plasterboard but none are as cheap. For small renovation projects or extensions the additional cost will be relatively minor compared to other build elements.

Fermacell.

Photo: Construction Products

Clay board.

At present these boards have the slight disadvantage that the supply chain is weak and for small projects it is often useful to be able to pick up a couple of extra boards from the builders' merchant. It is also worth noting that the fire-resistant properties (plus sound attenuation, thermal mass, thermal conductivity and moisture conductivity) of gypsum plasterboard are well known, and that standard details for their use are familiar to the trades. Alternative products may perform equally well or better but it is important to seek expert advice when using alternative products in critical locations.

Flax board.

Insulation products

Environmental assessment and comparison of insulation products is a complex subject and includes the following considerations:

- Thermal performance (R-value) of any particular material
- Energy (per kg) required to manufacture the material
- Whether the material is produced from a recycled, sustainable or renewable source
- Where the material is manufactured (road miles)
- Potential to cause irritation
- Whether toxins are released during manufacture, use or disposal
- Whether the material can be recycled at the end of its use

Natural products score better in most of these categories but there are still some situations where a 'conventional' product may be preferred and in most cases it will be necessary to comply with the new part L of the Building Regulations. Fire resistance and sound insulation properties of the various products mentioned are not addressed here, although it is worth noting that in critical locations rockwool is the most effective firestop.

There are three main types of insulation – loose, semi-rigid and boards. Loose insulation is designed to be filled into cavities or placed over flat ceilings. Semi-rigid insulation is useful over ceilings but can also be fitted into wooden walls as they are built. Rigid boards can be used within walls, under floors or fixed directly to the rafters in pitched roofs.

CELLULOSE

Recycled newspaper insulation – cellulose – is a loose-fill product which is ideal for use in lofts. UK-manufactured Warmcel 100 is designed for DIY use and is pre-treated with inorganic salts against fire and rodent attack. This is in stark contrast to the toxic fire retardants and pesticides found in many other insulation products. Cellulose uses very little energy to manufacture, it is non-toxic and non-irritant.

Warmcel 100 is supplied in bags which can be simply emptied out into the loft space. The current target U value for a loft ceiling is 0.16 W/m^2K (see section on 'Insulation values' in Chapter 3), which can be achieved by adding 225mm of Warmcel to an uninsulated loft, or less where there is already some insulation present. Warmcel 500 is also used in new construction but must be blown into a closed structure by specialist contractors or sprayed while damp into an open structure.

SHEEPSWOOL

Sheepswool is a natural fibre from a renewable resource with low embodied energy as it requires very little processing. Natural wool can absorb and release water vapour rapidly, which increases its effectiveness as an insulant. It is simple to fit and does not irritate the skin in the way that mineral products do. An initial smell of lanolin quickly dissipates.

The majority of sheepswool insulation sold in the UK is supplied in batts which contain a very small amount of a recycled polyester binder to give them sufficient rigidity. They can be built into walls, placed over ceilings as a loft insulator, or used to insulate suspended timber floors. The batts are available in a range of thicknesses which can be used to build up to the required amount, and in a range of widths to suit most joist or rafter spacings. Wool is naturally fire resistant, melting away from an ignition source rather than igniting. However, the batts are also treated with inorganic salts (such as borax) to provide further resistance to fire or insect attack.

Loose sheepswool is not quite as simple to handle but it is much cheaper. It should be treated with borax (and thermally verified) in order to conform to Building Regulations and wool from sheep which have recently been dipped is best avoided.

HEMP/RECYCLED COTTON

A highly efficient insulation has been produced by combining hemp fibres with recycled cotton fibres. A small quantity of thermoplastic binder is required to give it the required stability for use in vertical applications. Hemp-based insulation is treated with inorganic salts to provide fire and pest resistance. Like sheepswool, it is easy to handle, simple to install and does not irritate the skin.

Photo: Natural Building Technologies Ltd

Isonat

OTHER RENEWABLE INSULATION PRODUCTS

A variety of other natural and non-toxic insulation materials is available, such as Strawboard, Flax, Hemp, Cork and a batt form of cellulose, but at present all of these are imported into the UK, thus increasing their embodied energy in comparison to locally-produced alternatives.

One product for which there is no locally-produced alternative is extremely useful and versatile. Pavatex boards, manufactured in Switzerland, are made almost entirely from waste softwood which effectively 'locks up' CO_2 in its production. They can be used for external insulation (see 'Improving wall insulation' in Chapter 3) and either clad with a timber rainscreen or rendered directly.

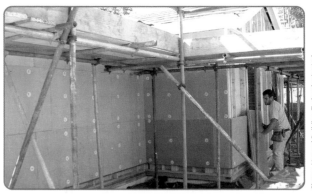

Photo: Natural Building Technologies Ltd

Above: Pavatex boards for external insulation.
Below: Finished house after external insulation.

Photo: Natural Building Technologies Ltd

For further information visit
www.greenspec.co.uk/html/materials/insulation.html

MINERAL WOOL

Mineral wool is a generic term which covers rockwool, glasswool and slagwool. Rockwool is spun from volcanic rock, which is a plentiful resource. Fibreglass, like other glass products, is derived from silica, which is also abundant; some manufacturers use recycled glass. Many people report that they suffer from skin irritation and rashes after coming into contact with glass wool. Slagwool is made from one of the waste products (slag) of the steel industry and so constitutes a good use of a waste product. Mineral wool is also available loose, normally for cavity wall insulation.

All mineral wool has a far higher embodied energy than natural and renewable materials such as those described above and it cannot presently be recycled. Given that the aim of insulation is to reduce energy use, it is preferable to use materials which need minimal processing – sheepswool is believed to have 14% of the embodied energy of mineral wool.

POLYSTYRENE

Polystyrene is a closed-cell product derived from oil. It is expanded or extruded by the use of pentane, a gas that does not contribute to global warming or to ozone depletion. Polystyrene does not degrade when in contact

with moisture so it is particularly useful in those parts of a dwelling where this is a risk. It can also bear spread loads so it may be used on the ground floor under screeds or under timber floating floors in some instances.

Expanded polystyrene-backed plasterboard allows builders to insulate and provide a finished surface at the

Polystyrene beads being injected into cavity.

Image: The Insta Group

same time. However, as the amount of insulation required by Building Regulations has increased in recent years it should be noted that this product alone may not be sufficient to bring a structure up to modern thermal standards.

Expanded polystyrene beads are used as an alternative to loose mineral wool in cavity wall insulation. They are blown in by specialist contractors, together with a bonding agent to provide long-term stability.

Both expanded and extruded polystyrene are toxic when burned and they do not biodegrade in landfill, although they can be reclaimed and recycled. Polystyrene reacts with the plasticisers used in some electrical cables, causing degradation in the cables. It may therefore be necessary to prevent the two coming into contact with each other.

POLYISOCYANURATE/ POLYISOCYANURATE-MODIFIED POLYURETHANE FOAM

Polyisocyanurate boards are also closed-cell plastic-based products, ultimately derived from oil and they are widely used in the construction industry. For many years the blowing agents used in their manufacture were CFCs or HCFCs but these have now been banned in the UK due to their damaging effect on the ozone layer. Hydrofluorocarbons (HFCs) are now used instead. Although they do not have the same ozone depleting potential as CFCs, HFCs are potent greenhouse gases which have significant global warming potential. Care must be taken when disposing of old stock which may have been expanded with CFCs or HCFCs.

Facings are aluminium foil or fibreglass-based. In addition to their use in wall and roof construction, specific products exist for use under compression in floor slabs.

Polyisocyanurate has a relatively high thermal resistance compared to most other products so it is particularly useful where space is at a premium. Polyisocyanurate boards emit fine particles when cut, are toxic when burned and do not biodegrade.[10] [11]

MULTI-LAYERED FOIL INSULATION

Multi-layered foil insulation consists of several thin layers of reflective and insulative material bonded or sewn together. It is generally supplied in wide rolls, the joins being lapped and taped together when it is installed. It has a number of advantages, principally that it is very thin – often not more than 25mm – so is extremely useful in refurbishment projects where space is at a premium, although it does require an air gap to achieve its optimal thermal performance. Foil insulation also acts as an effective reflector of solar energy in hot weather and as an impermeable membrane. It is easy to handle, simple and safe to cut and attracts no dust.

Test results differ as to the exact thermal properties of this insulation so it is wise to check with the local building inspector if a specific thermal performance must be achieved. Multi-foil insulation does not breathe so it should not be used in old buildings where it is critical that breathability is maintained.

Photo: Actis Insulation Ltd

Photo: Actis Insulation Ltd

INSULATION SUMMARY

Insulation embodied energy

Material	Embodied Energy (MJ/kg)
Fibreglass	18
Mineral wool	16
Cellulose batts	21
Wood fibreboard	16
Cork	4
Expanded polystyrene board	75
Extruded polystyrene board	72
Phenolic foam board	48
Foamed glass	11
Cellulose loose	21
Polyisocyanurate board	110

Source: Recovery Insulation

Material	Green Guide Rating
Expanded polystyrene (EPS)	A
Extruded polystyrene (XPS) with CO_2	C
Polyurethane (PU) with pentane	A
Foil-faced polyurethane (PU) with pentane	A
Polyurethane (PU) with CO_2	A
Polyisocyanurate (PIR)	Not yet assessed
Foil-faced polyisocyanurate (PIR)	Not yet assessed
Polyester fibre	Not yet assessed
Phenolic foam (PF)	Not yet assessed
Foil-faced phenolic foam (PF)	Not yet assessed
Mineral wool (glass) [$\leq$ 160kg/m^3]	A
Mineral wool (glass) [> 160kg/m^3]	B
Mineral wool (glass) [$\leq$ 150kg/m^3]	A
Mineral wool (glass) [> 150kg/m^3]	B
Sheep's wool	Not yet assessed
Cotton	Not yet assessed
Cellulose fibre (recycled)	A
Cork	B
Vermiculite	Not yet assessed
Perlite (expanded) board	Not yet assessed
Wood fibre (WF)	Not yet assessed
Cellular glass (CG)	B
Straw bale	Not yet assessed

Source: Energy Saving Trust

*An update to the Green Guide ratings is shortly to be published by the Building Research Establishment, including the assessment of more materials. This data was not available at the time of going to print.

Roofing

The key environmental questions to address when choosing roofing products are durability, embodied energy and recycled content. It may also be necessary to check with the local planning department when replacing a roof with a different material from the original.

NATURAL SLATE

Natural slate is a very durable and attractive roof covering. When renovating a roof, the most energy-efficient approach is usually to repair. Slate roofs tend to be replaced when the bearings or fixings have rotted but it is normally possible to reuse most of the slates once the battens and nails have been replaced. A breather membrane is normally added during the process.

This requires sourcing reclaimed slates of the correct size and colour to match the existing slates. The chances of

achieving this are greatly increased if there is a local reclamation yard, but it may be worth knocking on doors locally to see if anyone has held on to original slates when their roof was replaced with composite slates, as has so often happened. There is an active second-hand market for significant quantities of natural slates in good condition. The majority of new slate available today is shipped in from Spain,

Portugal, China and Canada but it is still possible to source new UK slate – for example from Wales or Cornwall – although it is rather expensive. The decision therefore rests on a compromise between cost, quality and embodied energy.

RECONSTITUTED SLATE

Approximately 90% of the material quarried for natural slate is waste. This waste can be crushed and reprocessed to make a reconstituted slate. The proportion of recycled material varies between different manufacturers but can be as high as 80%. The riven pattern is similar to a natural slate.

Britlock slates.

Photo: Sandtoft

RECYCLED PLASTIC/RUBBER

At present there are two 'slates' available in the UK made from recycled plastics and rubber, one with the addition of kaolin, a fine clay material. Both have an excellent riven pattern which makes them almost indistinguishable from natural slate. These slates are lightweight and durable, simple to cut and easy to nail. Both types are currently imported but they still represent a good use of a waste material. For durable products such as roof slates the embodied energy of the product is less important than that of a product that may only have a useful life of a few years.

Photos: EcoTech Recycled Products Ltd

COMPOSITE 'SLATE'

Composite slate consists of fibre held together with a binder such as cement. Composite slates are not as durable as natural slates, although the worst offending brands which failed after ten years have now been withdrawn from the market. Early slates also contained asbestos and these have also been withdrawn. Composite slates generally do not have the 'riven' appearance of reconstituted or recycled slates and they also have a relatively high embodied energy due to their cement content.

The main advantage of composite slate is that it is somewhat lighter than natural slate, although the same is true of recycled plastic slate. Sometimes in Victorian or Edwardian housing the purlins were slightly undersized and will have sagged under the weight of the slate, so replacing natural slate with composite slate is one way of reducing the load. This can be important if considering adding insulation and a finished surface while undertaking a loft conversion. Building Regulations apply to loft conversions and no significant weight should be added to a roof structure without consulting a structural engineer.

CLAY TILES

Clay is a plentiful and natural resource. Clay tiles have a high embodied energy due to the firing process. However, like natural slate they are very durable as millions of roofs throughout the country still have their original tiles, manufactured well over 100 years ago. Although tiles can lose their outer surface and then decay rapidly, deterioration is usually due to failure of the support structure, especially the battens, rather than the tiles themselves.

Above: Zinc roof.

Above: Copper roof. Below: Stainless steel roof.

New clay tiled roof. Old clay tiled roof.

METAL ROOFING

Zinc, copper, lead, stainless steel and especially aluminium all have a high embodied energy. There are numerous ecological issues concerning the extraction and processing of metals but they are durable and recyclable and have a high 'material efficiency', so they cover a large area of roof in relation to their weight, which partly offsets their high embodied energy.

TIMBER SHINGLES

Common in the USA and elsewhere, timber shingles are a very environmentally friendly roofing material as they are lightweight and sustainable, if harvested from certified forests. Usually of oak, sweet chestnut or western red cedar, the natural oils present in the wood serve to protect them from the weather and make them durable. Western red cedar is normally imported from the USA or Canada so the embodied energy rises due to the transportation cost. Timber absorbs CO_2 as it grows, so timber shingles have a neutral environmental impact if the timber can be sourced closer to home.

The main downside to timber shingles is that, in areas prone to wildfires, fire has been known to 'jump' from roof to roof but this is unlikely to be a concern for one-off projects in the UK.

THATCH

Thatch has perhaps the lowest environmental impact of all roofing materials. Reed lasts longer than straw – say 60 years as opposed to 30, although ridges need attention more regularly than this. If the raw material is harvested locally, the embodied energy is negligible. There are no toxic chemicals, no treatment is needed, and of course thatch is an excellent insulator. Using reed also helps to conserve natural habitats.

FLAT ROOFING MATERIALS

Currently there are no easy and environmentally friendly solutions when it comes to flat roofing. Due to their design, flat roofs need replacing far more often than pitched roofs and the damage to the substructure is usually greater than the localised damage that can occur in older pitched roofs. All of the available products are derived from petrochemicals and cannot presently be recycled at the end of their life, although synthetic rubber seems to have a lower environmental impact than the alternatives. Perhaps the best advice for the eco-renovator is to use products that have the longest possible lifespan, as this reduces the environmental (and financial) cost and to avoid using flat roofs wherever possible.

For current information on available products visit:
**www.greenspec.co.uk/html/design/materials/
flatroofs.html**

Photos: Blackdown Horticultural Consultants

Above: Sedum roof. Right: Turf roof.

GREEN ROOFS

A green roof is simply a vegetative covering over a sealed weatherproof layer similar to flat roofing, although green coverings can be installed on pitched roofs up to a certain angle. There are several reasons for planting a green roof:

- To provide a habitat for plants and wildlife
- To improve the appearance of roofs at low levels
- To reduce rainwater run-off as part of a SUDS strategy
- To absorb CO_2

The two most common types of green roof are grass and sedum – sedum is often used because it requires very little maintenance as the plants are low-growing and form a thick matt in a short time. Alternatively, a 'blanket' of ready-grown sedum can be laid to provide an instant green roof.

The additional insulation provided by a green roof is unlikely to have any significant effect in a well-insulated building. A wide variety of green roofs have already been installed in the UK and there are companies which specialise in this area. Grass roofs are heavier than sedum roofs but either will add significant weight, so not all roofs will be suitable without strengthening the underlying structure.

RAINWATER FITTINGS

The most commonly used rainwater fittings in the UK are made from PVC. They are quick to fit and standardisation means that sections can usually be replaced without having to discard the whole system. However, after a few years many PVC gutters tend to become brittle as a result of exposure to ultraviolet light. Cracking can sometimes occur when roofers are obliged to lean ladders against the building to gain access to carry out roof repairs.

The fact that some cast iron rainwater fittings may still be seen on old buildings shows that it is possible to specify rainwater fittings which last far longer than PVC. Cast iron is expensive, difficult to work with and heavy to fit, but alternatives do exist. Galvanised steel guttering is steadily gaining popularity in the UK.

In addition to lasting much longer than plastic, galvanised steel can withstand ladders and has an undoubted visual appeal – a worthwhile consideration, as rainwater fittings constitute such a strong feature of many buildings. It can be ordered through some builders' merchants and its longevity outweighs the additional cost of

Lindab galvanised steel guttering.

the system in comparison to PVC. Copper rainwater goods do the same job and look and last even better but they are prohibitively expensive for most project budgets.

Reclaimed and recycled materials

RECLAIMED MATERIALS

Reclaimed building materials are in a sense the most eco-friendly materials available. For years we have been dumping millions of perfectly serviceable Victorian bricks into landfill rather than storing and reusing them, although attitudes are at last beginning to change.

Unlike recycled materials, reclaimed materials require no energy for reprocessing and only minimal energy for transportation as they tend to be reused near their original location. Of course, this does not apply so much to high value decorative architectural salvage, which is even traded internationally.

In some cases the quality of reclaimed products is considerably higher than that of newer products. For example, timber used a century or more ago was harvested from trees which had been allowed to grow more slowly and to a greater age, so the grain is tighter, the appearance is better and the wood is more rich in resin. Consequently, the strength and durability are higher than modern fast-grown timber.

Salvage works two ways. In restoring or renovating a property the householder can become a supplier as well as a consumer of reclaimed goods. Most products can be reused but bricks, doors, tiles, slates and timber are the most actively traded.

The majority of materials from older houses which cannot be reused can at least be recycled. Problems occur mainly when dissimilar materials have been combined together – windows are a good example, containing putty, paint, glass, timber and ironmongery as a minimum. Working with reclaimed materials demands particular skills and almost always takes longer. Timber which contains nails or other fixings is time-consuming to prepare and considerable care must be taken to avoid damage to cutting tools in case they encounter hidden metal. Hardwoods can also be very difficult to work once they have aged. Reclaimed timber has the great advantage of being much less prone to deformation than new timber as it will have already done all its warping and twisting unless it is substantially re-milled, as this can release tensions within the wood.

For further information visit your local reclaim yard or see **www.salvo.co.uk.**

RECYCLED MATERIALS

Specifying products which have a high recycled materials content not only reduces the demand for raw materials but also helps to create a market for materials which are already recycled. WRAP – the Waste and Resources Action Programme – has produced a full survey of available construction products which are wholly or partially made from recycled material. The survey covers the following areas relevant to domestic property:

- Bricks and blocks
- Insulation (wall, floor and roof)
- Timber
- Timber boards and other timber products
- Roof coverings
- Floor coverings
- Kitchen furniture and work surfaces
- Doors and windows
- Drainage products
- Plaster and cement
- Plasterboard
- Hard landscaping products
- Substructure and external surfacing
- Waterproofing membranes
- Decking and fencing

For example, there is a damp-proof membrane available which is made entirely from post-use polyethylene waste, while meeting all relevant BRE and British Standards requirements.

Photo: Visqueen Building Products

In addition to the summary pages, detailed specifications and lists of suppliers are provided for all the products mentioned under these headings, together with the percentage of recycled materials used in each product.

For further information visit **www.wrap.org.uk** *and download the 'Construction Product Guide'.*

Deep green construction

No book on eco-building would be complete without at least mentioning some of the alternative construction methods that are available. Even though the primary subject of this manual is refurbishment, an extension or garden building sometimes affords the opportunity to experiment with different forms of construction.

TIMBER FRAME
There are two basic types of timber frame construction – primary frame and stud frame. Primary framing is based upon ancient techniques of post-and-beam construction and uses hardwoods such as oak or softwoods such as Douglas Fir. The primary frame accepts all the building loads and panels are usually infilled with insulated stud framing. The method gives a very fast build time and of course has the added attraction that the frame can be left visible on the interior.

Stud frames are more common and have even been used by some of the volume housebuilders – normally clad with brickwork on the outside although wooden cladding

works just as well. Vertical studs are placed at regular intervals to form the basic frame and accept all the structural loads of the building including the upper floors and roof. The resultant void can then be filled with insulating material. As a finishing board is used on the inside face, there may be little to distinguish visibly between a timber frame construction and a conventional masonry construction but there is the satisfaction of building with natural materials which have a low embodied energy.

Photo: Oak-Apple Frames

STRAW BALES

Straw is a waste product. It is inert, hard to ignite when compressed and of little interest to vermin as it contains negligible amounts of food. Foundations need to be raised to a sufficient level to avoid the bales becoming damp but as long as straw is kept relatively dry it has a life expectancy similar to conventional building materials. Rammed earth within old car tyres has been used as a low-impact foundation design for straw-bale buildings.

There are two principal types of straw-bale construction – load-bearing and non-load-bearing. In load-bearing straw-bale buildings the bales take the place of whatever normally holds up the upper floors and the roof. Essentially

Photo: Straw Bale Building Association

this is Lego on a giant scale, the bales being placed on top of each other in a stretcher bond pattern. Hazel pins are driven down through the bales to provide a positive connection between layers.

The other way to use straw bales is to build a primary frame out of timber which accepts all the structural loads. The bales are then used to infill the panel walls. This avoids the risk of compression of the bales but still takes advantage of the excellent insulating properties of straw.

In both cases the bales are then coated with lime render. The use of lime is important here as it is much more flexible than cement and can accommodate minor movements. Lime render will sometimes self-heal

Photo: ARCO2

when cracks occur. It also breathes, which is essential as vapour must be allowed to pass through the bales.

For further information visit
www.strawbalebuildingassociation.org.uk

HEMP

The fibres extracted from the hemp plant have a wide variety of uses including rope, paper and clothing. The residual material, including pith and sap, is known as hurds. The hurds can be processed and then combined with lime to make a type of lightweight concrete which is a highly effective building product.

Photo: Suffolk Housing Society

Photo: Suffolk Housing Society

Over 250 houses have been built of this material in France and there are a handful in England and Canada. A lightweight timber stud frame is built and shuttering panels are fixed temporarily to both sides. The resulting void is then infilled with a hurd/lime mix and compressed. The mix sets to give rigidity and strength and the panels are then

Photo: Suffolk Housing Society

removed. Hemp is an excellent insulator, is water resistant, and can be trowelled to a finish for the internal walls. One single building element can therefore replace the five or six elements that commonly make up walls in newly constructed houses in the UK, offering savings in time and material costs. Hemp is also much lighter than other aggregates, so it is possible that foundation widths can also be reduced.

The experimental hemp buildings in Suffolk shown in the photograph overleaf were part of a larger development where 'conventional' buildings were constructed alongside similarly designed hemp buildings to compare their performance. In summary, the hemp houses have proved very comfortable to live in and, once builders become familiar with

Photo: Suffolk Housing Society

Hemp homes.

the construction method, the costs should be equivalent to (or less than) the costs of 'conventional' construction.

For further information and results of the tests visit **www.suffolkhousing.org**

Photo: Lime Technology Limited

Blocks made from hemp and lime are now available and may soon offer a realistic alternative to conventional cementitious blocks.

CLAY BLOCKS

Clay-block construction is common in Europe but as yet few projects have made use of this technology in the UK. As with hemp construction, one building element can replace the complex series of materials used to make up the average wall. Some fired clay systems are designed so that the large blocks interlock and no mortar is required; others

only require a thin joint. Either system will deliver reduced build times and the structure of the blocks gives a superior thermal performance in comparison to conventional blocks. Unfired clay blocks are more commonly used for internal partitioning and to add thermal mass.

Left: Hemp block. Below: Clay block.

COB

Cob is an ancient building material and there are many cob houses still standing in the UK, mainly in the South-West. It generally consists of wet clay subsoil mixed with straw and laid in layers to form walls approximately 2ft thick, gaining strength as it dries. Cob is regaining popularity among eco-builders as it is a natural material which provides very good insulation and thermal mass. It also has negligible embodied energy as it is generally used at the site where the mud is dug. Cob is permeable to air and moisture so it needs protection from driving rain but any coatings must

Photo: Genesis Project

Cob in construction.

Photo: Chris Turner

allow the walls to breathe. It can also be pressed into blocks which are then laid with an earth or earth/lime mortar.

RAMMED EARTH

Rammed earth is similar to cob in that the principal component is subsoil. Subsoils vary widely so a small amount of cement is often added as a binder. A vertical channel 300–450mm wide is constructed, into which the earth mixture is poured. The earth is then compacted approximately every 150mm in depth before the formwork is removed. The resultant wall is extremely strong and decorative materials can be added to the mix or designs can be carved in the formwork to improve the appearance. Due to its density, rammed earth provides good thermal mass and excellent sound insulation.

Rammed earth wall finished with beeswax.

EARTH/CLAY PLASTERS

Earth and clay plasters have essentially the same ingredients as cob and rammed earth, with the addition of more sand, water or cow dung to increase workability and achieve a smooth finish. Lime can be added to increase strength, depending on the nature of the available soil. Earthen plasters can be applied over cob walls or over wooden lath structures – otherwise known as wattle and daub. In many parts of the world these are still the most common plastering materials.

For further information see: The Natural Plaster Book *by Cedar Rose Guelberth and Dan Chiras, New Society Publishers (2003).*

REFERENCES

[1] Lime Technology Ltd.
[2] Rainforest action network via www.savetherainforest.org
[3] www.seattle.gov
[4] IARC press release 2004.
[5] Wood Panel Industries Federation.
[6] AECB.
[7] West Sussex, North Somerset.
[8] Defra Market Transformation Programme BNPB2: 'Plasterboard – Waste Management 9/06'.
[9] Environment Agency Regulatory Note 11.
[10] Paul Hymers *Converting to an eco-friendly home*,
[11] National Green Specification (2006).

3 REDUCING HEAT LOSS

Why insulate?

The domestic sector accounts for over 30% of the UK's total energy use.

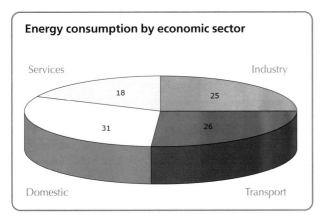

Energy consumption by economic sector

Services 18
Industry 25
Domestic 31
Transport 26

Source: DTI / National Statistics

Over 60% of domestic energy use is for space-heating. When most of our housing stock was built there was little understanding of how buildings perform thermally. Poorly-insulated older houses leak energy which is then dissipated and lost. Reducing energy consumption for space-heating by the effective use of insulation could make a significant difference to global warming and will certainly save money.

When renovating property it is more effective to spend

Above: Thermally uninsulated and insulated properties.
Below: Thermal image of city from above.

Photos: Horton Levi

effort and money retaining heat before considering any investment in renewable sources of heat generation. In crude financial terms, the cost of heating an uninsulated house is nearly three times that of heating a modern well-insulated property of the same living area.

SAP Rating	Semi-detached house with . . .	Typical annual heating and hot water costs
48	Basic gas central heating	£421
54	Basic gas central heating, windows double glazed and draughtstripped	£373
98	Basic gas central heating, full insulation and double glazed windows	£152
101	Full insulation, double glazed windows; heating to CHeSS HR6 (2005)	£145

Source: Energy Saving Trust

Insulation therefore not only reduces the environmental impact of housing, but also saves money in the medium term. Under the planned HIPS scheme, houses will be rated according to their environmental performance, so it is likely that a well-insulated house which is cheaper to run will command a higher price in the resale market. It may therefore be a false economy not to insulate on the grounds that the payback period appears to be longer than the planned stay in the property.

Private rented property is a much more difficult subject, as the person responsible for the structure of the building is not the person responsible for paying the heating bills. At present there is no legal requirement for landlords to install insulation, although this situation may change in the future. Enhanced capital allowances may be claimed in some circumstances and some local councils have introduced grant schemes specifically aimed at landlords. The 2005 budget announced discussions on the introduction of a 'Green Landlord Scheme' but at the time of writing these have not yet been concluded.

GRANTS

A number of grant schemes aimed at homeowners are in operation both nationally and locally, although at present these only cover cavity wall insulation and loft insulation and are limited in terms of the insulation materials that can be used. Some are linked to energy supply companies and some are aimed at people on low incomes. Independent schemes also operate nationally and cavity wall insulation schemes should offer a CIGA (Cavity Insulation Guarantee Agency) 25-year independent guarantee. Many installers are members of the National Insulation Association.

To find out up-to-date information on grant schemes contact the Energy Efficiency Advice Centre (calls are automatically routed to the local office) on 0800 512012.

PAYBACK PERIOD ON INSULATION

A payback period is the amount of time that it will take for an investment in insulation to repay the homeowner by means of reduced fuel bills. While payback periods for insulation of specific structural elements are quoted in some publications, insulation tends to be applied as part of a package of energy efficiency measures including draughtproofing, which is one of the most important. In practice the precise amount of money which can be saved by the application of insulation in specific cases is extremely difficult to quantify, so no attempt has been made to include such payback periods in the text. The minimum amount of insulation which is required for upgrading any thermal element will, in any case, be determined by the Building Regulations.

BUILDING REGULATIONS

Revisions to the Building Regulations in 2006 for England and Wales now mean that any replacement of a thermal element (for example a window, door, roof) must, by law, be carried out to the thermal standards set out in Approved Document L1B. This document requires that the element in question is insulated to specified U-values which are set out in the next section. However, the stipulation goes further than this. Wherever a new finished surface is created the regulations apply, so replacement of a floor deck or screed, re-roofing, or even replastering or rendering a wall, could all trigger the Building Regulations, depending on what proportion of the relevant area is being refurbished. If in doubt, consult your local authority 'Building Control' department. If the regulations are triggered, an application or notice to the local office must be made, along with the associated fees.[1] The practical effects of this legislation have yet to be determined.

There are certain exceptions to the values laid down in Document L1B and Building Control may be prepared to accept higher U-values where a calculation shows that the insulation will not pay back financially within 15 years, or that it is impractical to fit the required levels of insulation in certain locations, or that the floor area of a room would be decreased by more than 5%. Where it is impractical to meet the target values it is possible to 'trade off' reduced insulation for one element of a structure for enhanced insulation in another. This is subject to certain limits for individual elements.

Under self-certification schemes, work can be carried out by a 'competent person' who may issue a certificate to the local authority to demonstrate that the works have been carried out in accordance with the regulations. The replacement of doors and windows, for example, is covered by several self-certification schemes. It is worth noting that there are substantial fines for non-compliance and that the responsibility for compliance rests with the person who orders the work – in many cases this will be the householder.

It is also worth noting that while Building Regulations are stringent on levels of insulation and there are increasingly powerful means of enforcement, the regulations are silent on questions of embodied energy, resource depletion and the potential toxicity of some of the materials (or their manufacturing and disposal processes) which may be required to achieve compliance with the current standards. The Sustainable and Secure Buildings Act of 2004 goes some way to address these wider issues.

For further information see: 'The Effect of Building Regulations Part L1 (2006) on Existing Dwellings – Information for Builders and Installers in England and Wales' Energy Saving Trust CE53 (download).

For information on the application of regulations in Scotland see: 'The Domestic Technical Handbook' on possible ways of complying with the Building (Scotland) Regulations 2004. Visit **www.sbsa.gov.uk**

For information on the application of regulations in Northern Ireland see: Building Regulations Northern Ireland (2000), 'DFP Technical Booklet F1: 2006 – Conservation of fuel and power in dwellings'. Visit **www.dfpni.gov.uk/building-regulations**

Insulation values

It is possible to design and insulate a new house in such a way that no space-heating need be required at all. The heat generated from occupation – that is from lights, from cooking, from the occupants themselves and from passive solar gains – can be sufficient to maintain a comfortable internal temperature in all but the most extreme climates. This requires that the heat generated by occupation is retained within the building and that ventilation systems recover heat which would otherwise be lost with the exhausted air.

Older housing presents much more of a challenge when it comes to insulation as the structure already exists and floor heights are largely determined by staircases or by door and window lintels. In addition the doors and windows themselves may be an essential part of the character of the building. Insulating an existing building therefore requires a series of compromises and the measures necessary or possible will vary widely according to house type and date of construction.

Working out how much insulation to add to a house can be a complicated process because:

- The effectiveness of different types of insulation varies widely
- Certain types of insulation are not appropriate in some locations

Techie corner: U-values

Definition

A U-value is an indication of how much heat is conducted through a particular section of construction. The lower the U-value, the better insulated the structure is. For example, a wall with a U-value of 1.0 will lose heat twice as fast as a wall with a U-value of 0.5.

How to work out a u-value

All materials, however thin, have some thermal resistance. The higher the resistances, the less heat gets let through. The resistances of all the separate elements in a construction, together with their thicknesses, need to be considered. Added together, these give the total resistance or R. U-values are calculated by working out the reciprocal of R (U = 1/R). If R is large, U will be small. In other words, the greater the resistance, the lower the U-value.

In practice, the resistance of individual materials tends to be quoted whereas U-values are used to refer to the conductivity of a whole structure. For example, working from outside to inside, a typical 1970s cavity wall construction in the UK might consist of an outer layer of brickwork, a cavity, and inner skin of non-insulating blockwork, plaster and paint.

The total resistance for this type of wall construction is therefore 0.68. The U-value of this type of wall construction is therefore:

$$U = 1/0.68 = 1.47 \text{ W/m}^2\text{K.}[2]$$

Such a construction would conduct heat at a rate of 1.47 watts (W) per square metre (m²) for every degree of temperature difference (K) between the inner and the outer surfaces of the wall.

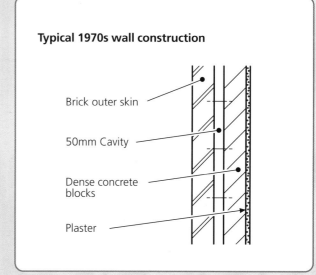

Typical 1970s wall construction

- Brick outer skin
- 50mm Cavity
- Dense concrete blocks
- Plaster

Element	Thickness	R-value
External Resistance (Rse)		0.04
Brick	100mm	0.14
Unventilated Cavity	50mm	0.18
Blockwork	100mm	0.16
Gypsum Plaster	15mm	0.03
Internal Resistance (Rsi)		0.13
Total		0.68

Source: Building Research Establishment

- Some houses already have some insulation present
- Different elements of a house require varying levels of insulation
- An integrated package of measures also needs to include allowances for ventilation and heating
- Building Regulations have specified certain minimum requirements

IMPROVING U-VALUES

2006 Building Regulations require the following U-values when elements of a property are upgraded or replaced: Best practice in refurbishment as recommended by the Energy Saving Trust (and others) is to go further than these U-values and to insulate to an even higher standard.

Element	Typical original U-value	Required U-value
Uninsulated floors	0.48	0.25
Solid 9in external brick walls	2.10	0.35
Roof (with 100mm flat loft insulation	0.44	0.16
Pitched roof (with insulation at rafters)	1.90	0.20
Flat roof	1.00	0.25
Windows (poor double glazing)	3.50	2.00

Source: Energy Saving Trust

WHAT TO USE WHERE

The table below shows which products are commonly used for particular applications.

| | Constructions | | | | | | | | | | | | |
| | Roofs | | | Walls | | | | | | | Floors | | |
Insulation materials	Insulation on pitch	Ceiling insulation	Flat roof	Internal insulation	External insulation	Cavity (full fill)	Cavity (partial fill)	Timber frame	Steel frame	Panel	Solid concrete	Suspended beam & block	Suspended timber
Expanded polystyrene (EPS)			■	■	■	■	■	■	■		■	■	
Extruded polystyrene (XPS) with CO_2	■		■	■	■		■	■	■	■	■	■	
Polyurethane (PU) with pentane	■		■	■	■		■	■	■	■	■	■	■
Foil-faced polyurethane (PU) with pentane	■		■	■	■		■	■	■	■	■	■	■
Polyurethane (PU) with CO_2	■		■	■	■	■	■	■	■	■	■	■	
Polyisocyanurate (PIR)	■		■	■	■	■	■	■	■	■	■	■	
Foil-faced polyisocyanurate (PIR)	■		■	■	■	■	■	■	■	■	■	■	■
Polyester fibre		■						■	■				■
Phenolic foam (PF)	■		■	■	■	■	■	■	■		■		
Foil-faced phenolic foam (PF)	■		■	■	■	■	■	■		■	■		
Mineral wool (glass) [≤ 160kg/m³]	■	■	■	■	■	■	■	■	■			■	
Mineral wool (glass) [> 160kg/m³]						■	■	■	■				
Mineral wool (glass) [≤ 150kg/m³]	■	■	■	■							■		■
Mineral wool (glass) [> 150kg/m³]	■		■	■				■	■				■
Sheep's wool	■	■	■					■					■
Cotton													
Cellulose fibre (recycled)		■							■				
Cork													
Vermiculite		■											
Perlite (expanded) board													
Wood fibre (WF)													
Cellular glass (CG)	■		■	■		■							
Straw bale													

Most common applications. The coloured cells indicate only the most common uses. So the fact that a cell is blank does not necessarily mean this type of insulation is not used for this application.

Source: Energy Saving Trust

THICKNESS OF INSULATION

The amount of insulation required will vary according to which element is to be insulated, which will then determine the target U-value to be achieved (see the 'Elemental U-values' table on page 45). Insulation materials also vary in their effectiveness, otherwise known as resistivity. A greater thickness of a material with a low resistivity will be needed in order to give the same resistance as that from a material with a high resistivity.

Resistance = Resistivity x Thickness.

Manufacturers often quote conductivity values (λ) rather than resistivity.

Conductivity = 1/Resistivity

A low conductivity value indicates an efficient insulant.

Insulation material	Conductivity value*
Expanded polystyrene (EPS)	0.038
Extruded polystyrene (XPS) with CO_2	0.033
Polyurethane (PU) with pentane	0.027
Foil-faced polyurethane (PU) with pentane	0.021
Polyurethane (PU) with CO_2	0.035
Polyisocyanurate (PIR)	0.021
Foil-faced polyisocyanurate (PIR)	0.017
Polyester fibre	0.040
Phenolic foam (PF)	0.025
Foil-faced phenolic foam (PF)	0.020
Mineral wool (glass) [$\leqslant$ 160kg/m³]	0.036
Mineral wool (glass) [> 160kg/m³]	0.036
Mineral wool (glass) [$\leqslant$ 150kg/m³]	0.036
Mineral wool (glass) [> 150kg/m³]	0.040
Sheep's wool	0.042
Cotton	0.038
Cellulose fibre (recycled)	0.040
Cork	0.048
Vermiculite	0.060
Perlite (expanded) board	0.051
Wood fibre (WF)	0.050
Cellular glass (CG)	0.046
Straw bale	0.055

*The thermal conductivity values are the mid range values obtained from the thermal conducvity values declared by UK manufacturers (or suppliers) and those given in the European Thermal Values publication.

Source: Energy Saving Trust

In practice, the calculation of required thicknesses to meet specific U-values is carried out by manufacturers. The calculations take into account the U-value of the existing wall and the thermal bridging through any stud fixing system which may be specified.

Improving roof insulation

The greatest heat loss from domestic property is generally through the roof because the roof is the part of the house most exposed to the elements and because warm air rises so heat tends to be concentrated on the top floor. Building Regulations therefore require a lower U-value for the roof structure than for any other element of a house. In summer months, attic rooms can easily overheat as a result of direct solar gains passing through the roof structure so the addition of insulation will also help to combat this problem.

When considering how best to insulate a roof, it is first necessary to work out how it is constructed and to ensure that ventilation is maintained, if the structure was originally designed to be ventilated. Failure to do this can lead to condensation or the trapping of leaked water, which can lead to outbreaks of dry rot, which can in turn cause structural failure, so it is important to get the detailing right.

PITCHED ROOFS WITHOUT A ROOM IN THE ATTIC

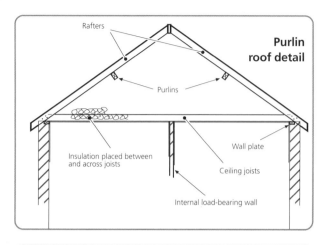

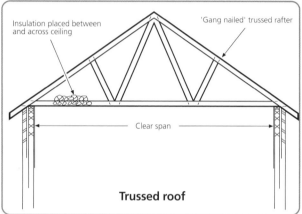

Warmcel loose insulation.

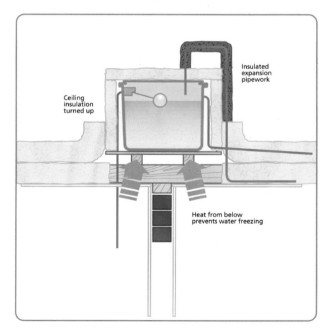

It is normally straightforward to install roof insulation to these types of buildings as insulation can be placed over the flat ceiling of the rooms on the top floor. Care must be taken to avoid damaging any electric cables which run over this ceiling structure and cables should not be covered by the insulation as they can overheat. Similarly, any recessed lights should have a sealed air space around them to prevent overheating. The ceiling structure itself will normally be capable of supporting the small additional load, but if there is any doubt the opinion of a suitably qualified professional should be sought.

Where insulation is already present and more is required to bring it up to the latest recommended level, current advice is to leave the existing insulation where it is and place the new insulation over the top, but laid at right angles to the existing. For example, 100mm of mineral wool has been already installed in many properties. To achieve the current recommended U-value of 0.16W/m²K using mineral wool, 275mm would be required. Subtracting the 100mm already present, this would require an additional 175mm to be laid, or slightly less if using a renewable product such as sheepswool, hemp or cellulose.

A boarded passage will be needed to access tanks and other essential services, as the thicker insulation will obscure the ceiling joists. When loft insulation is increased, the temperature in the attic will be reduced, so water tanks located above the insulation will need to be insulated. Omitting the insulation directly beneath the tank but returning it up the side and over the top of the tank will help to prevent freezing while maintaining the continuity of the loft insulation.

This kind of attic is normally ventilated at the eaves. If insulation is pushed into the eaves without making provision for ventilation the airflow through the roof will be interrupted and any water which finds its way in will be trapped and will not be able to evaporate easily. Eaves ventilators can be used to ensure that this does not occur.

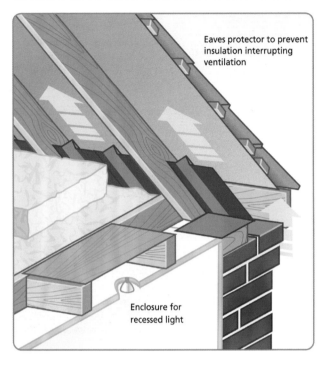

Eaves protector to prevent insulation interrupting ventilation

Enclosure for recessed light

Lastly, don't forget to insulate and draughtproof the loft hatch.

PITCHED ROOFS WITH A ROOM IN THE ATTIC

The insulation of houses with attic rooms is more complex because they do not have space available above the living accommodation, so the insulation must follow the line of the rafters for at least part of their length.

While re-roofing a property, insulation can be fitted on top of the rafters. This is known as a warm roof because the structure (rafters and ridge beam) is then encapsulated within the insulated envelope of the building. However, this is inappropriate for terraced streets – as the roofline will not be able to follow the rest of the terrace and any form of join in a roof is a potential source of future leaks – and any other location where ridge or eave height is a sensitive issue. Economically and environmentally, this is only worth considering at the same time as re-roofing a property.

In all other cases the choice comes down to fitting insulation between the rafters, under the rafters, or a combination of both. The decision must take into account the following factors:

- Insulation placed under rafters reduces headroom, which may be an important consideration in an attic room
- Rafters act as a thermal bridge – heat can pass through the timber, albeit at a reduced rate, even if there is insulation between the rafters
- Where insulation is being placed between the rafters it is important to leave a gap above the insulation to preserve the crossflow ventilation in the roof
- The risk of interstitial condensation

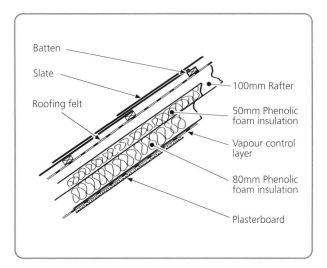

For example, where there are 100mm (4in) rafters, 50mm of phenolic foam insulation could be placed between the rafters, allowing 50mm for ventilation above the insulation. Next, the ceiling could be under-lined with 80mm of phenolic foam insulation. Finally a vapour control layer and plasterboard are normally added. This would reduce the U-value of the roof to 0.18, which would conform with the new regulations.[3]

Substitution by less efficient materials may have other environmental benefits but may not be thermally sufficient to comply with the Building Regulations that now apply to such a project where a new finished surface is to be provided. Similarly, reducing the thickness of under-lined insulation to preserve headroom would also reduce the insulative value and therefore would not comply with the Building Regulations, although it may be possible to argue successfully for reductions in some circumstances.

Where rafters are only 75mm deep, effective rafter depth can be increased by fixing battens to the undersides of the rafters. In some cases it may be possible to reduce the ventilation gap above the insulation to 25mm. The additional load of the insulation and finished surface on the rafters should in any case be checked by a suitably qualified professional.

Where the finished surface follows the rafters all the way to the apex of the roof, care must be taken to ensure that the ventilation is not compromised at the apex. This can easily happen if insulated plasterboard is placed hard up against the ridge beam.

This can be avoided either by installing ridge vents, which requires access to the roof and can be a significant expense, or by flattening the ceiling at the top to preserve the crossflow ventilation.

When installing insulation to the underside of rafters, the possibility of interstitial condensation must be addressed (see the technical note at the end of the next section). Manufacturers of insulation will normally carry out calculations and assess whether the addition of insulation to a pitched roof will give rise to any risk of interstitial condensation and may recommend the incorporation of a vapour control layer on the warm side of the insulation prior to applying the finished surface.

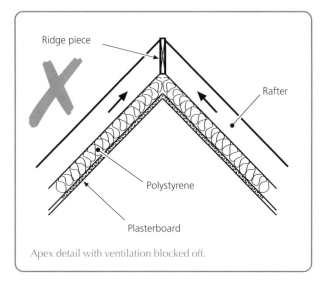

Apex detail with ventilation blocked off.

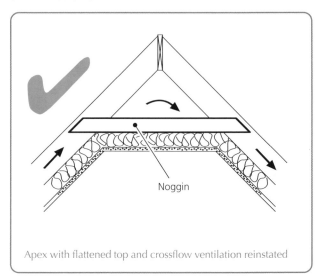

Apex with flattened top and crossflow ventilation reinstated

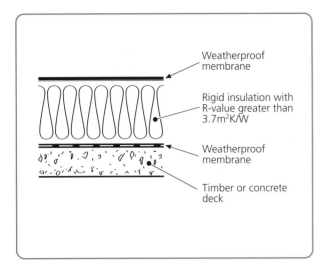

Weatherproof membrane

Rigid insulation with R-value greater than 3.7m²K/W

Weatherproof membrane

Timber or concrete deck

FLAT ROOFS

Flat roofs are normally designed to be walked on, so in general there will be no structural issues relating to added insulation. At 0.25 W/m²K the U-value required by the new regulations is also less exacting than for pitched roofs. Insulation can be added above, below or between the roof members (joists/rafters).

As with pitched roofs, if the insulation is added over the top of the structure this is known as a 'warm roof'. In some cases, as long as the structure and decking is sound, insulation can be added without having to remove the existing covering. Either a new weatherproof layer can be added over the top or ballast can be laid to hold down the insulation, which means that the weatherproof layer underneath must still be watertight to keep out any water which seeps through the joints in the insulation. Details are best agreed with the manufacturer of the insulation chosen, and with the installer. If ballast is used, the roof must be capable of supporting the additional load.

For further information see: 'Refurbishing dwellings: A summary of best practice' – Energy Saving Trust CE189 (download).

Improving wall insulation

TYPES OF WALL CONSTRUCTION

Before considering insulation to walls it is first necessary to work out how the walls of your house are constructed, in order to work out the U-value of the existing structure. Wall construction evolved considerably during the 20th century so it is helpful to know when your house was built. Note that these dates are only general guides and in all cases the exact nature of the construction should be ascertained by careful investigation on site.

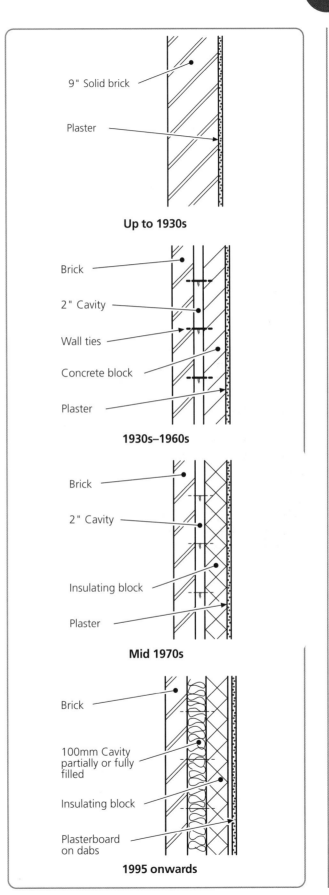

9" Solid brick

Plaster

Up to 1930s

Brick

2" Cavity

Wall ties

Concrete block

Plaster

1930s–1960s

Brick

2" Cavity

Insulating block

Plaster

Mid 1970s

Brick

100mm Cavity partially or fully filled

Insulating block

Plasterboard on dabs

1995 onwards

Cavity wall construction was introduced into the UK in the 1930s. If your house was constructed after 1930 it is likely that there is a cavity between the two layers of masonry which make up the external walls. A useful guide as to whether there is a cavity is to look at the pattern of bricks on the outside:

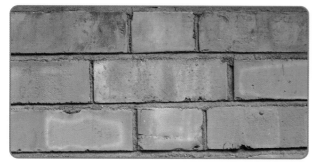

Solid wall, no cavity.

This wall has bricks at right angles to the face of the wall, known as 'headers', which act to tie the two skins of brickwork together. This is almost certainly a solid brick wall with no cavity, typical of Georgian, Victorian and Edwardian property.

Cavity wall, no 'headers'.

The bricks in this picture, on the other hand, are all running along the face of the wall. The bricks are called stretchers and the expanse of brickwork is referred to as stretcher bond. The absence of headers indicates that there is probably a cavity between the inner and outer skins of the wall.

Another useful way to find out whether there is a cavity is to measure the thickness of the walls by any entrance door or window. Cavity walls are normally at least 250mm (10in) thick, comprising two skins of 100mm masonry and a 50mm cavity (later cavity walls which include built-in

Below: Insulating block. Below right: Dense block.

insulation are even thicker). However, solid walls are sometimes as thick as 250mm, as internal plaster, careless bricklaying and external rendering will all have added to the thickness. Sometimes the ground floor of a larger solid wall construction is 1.5 bricks (13.5in) thick up to first floor level and reduces to 9in for the upper floors. Stone walls are much thicker; if the inside of the construction is also stone it is fairly safe to say that there is no cavity present (as opposed to stone-faced buildings which have a cavity and internal blockwork).

The requirement to insulate houses was only introduced in 1985. The insulation strategy used at that time was to introduce an insulated block in place of the inner skin of dense blockwork.

It is difficult to tell whether an insulated block has been used as it will be covered with plaster on the inside. A good tip is to take the cover off a penetration in the structure to check – for example where a vent or a cat flap has been inserted through a wall. Another way to tell is that insulated blocks are much easier to drill into than dense blocks or brickwork, as they are lightweight and contain plenty of voids/air. If you are unsure about the construction of your house and you have neighbours who live in similar houses, it is likely that one of them will already know the answer.

SUMMARY AND U-VALUES OF EXISTING MASONRY WALLS

Construction	U-value (W/m²k)
1. Solid masonry 225mm (9in)	2.10
2. Brick, 50mm cavity, block	1.60
3. Brick, 50mm cavity, insulated block	1.00
4. Brick, 50mm cavity, 50mm insulation, insulated block	0.45
5. Brick, 50mm cavity, 65mm insulation, insulated block	0.35

Where there is already insulation and a cavity (4 and 5 above) between the two skins of masonry, the potential for savings from adding further insulation to the wall is greatly reduced. The precise calculation is difficult to carry out, but it is important to be aware that, in certain cases, the energy saved over the lifetime of the building may not even exceed the energy required to manufacture, transport and install any additional insulation, given the materials currently available.

SOLID MASONRY WALLS

Where there is no cavity in the structure insulation can be added either on the inside or on the outside. It will be necessary to refer to the note on interstitial condensation at the end of this section.

External wall insulation

Insulating the outside of a property has the advantage that any masonry within the insulation acts as 'thermal mass' so the heat which is generated inside the property is stored within the masonry walls and acts as a reservoir or storage heater. The heat is retained by the insulated outer skin. In addition there is no loss of living space within the property.

There are a number of methods of covering or 'cladding' the insulation once installed, including timber rain screens, cement or lime renders and other bespoke systems including boards manufactured from wood fibre, which have the lowest environmental impact of all.

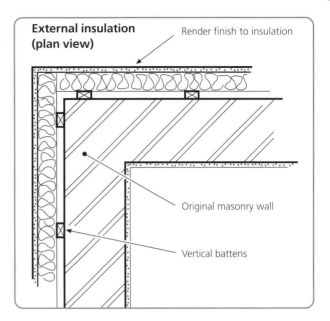

External insulation (plan view)

Render finish to insulation

Original masonry wall

Vertical battens

Above: External wall pre-insulation.

Above right and left: External wall during installation.

Right: External wall after insulation.

Photos: archipelago architects

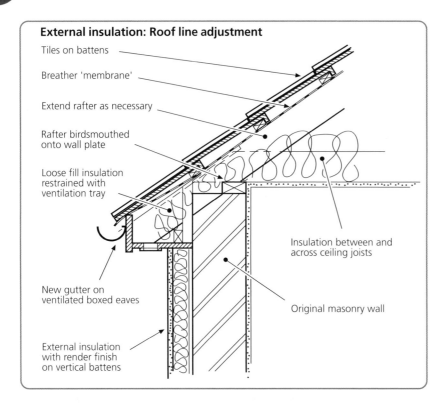

External insulation: Roof line adjustment

Tiles on battens

Breather 'membrane'

Extend rafter as necessary

Rafter birdsmouthed onto wall plate

Loose fill insulation restrained with ventilation tray

Insulation between and across ceiling joists

New gutter on ventilated boxed eaves

Original masonry wall

External insulation with render finish on vertical battens

For further information see: 'External Insulation for Dwellings' – Energy Saving Trust GPG293 (download).

Internal wall insulation

Where external insulation is not possible, or where the external appearance of the building is important, insulation can be added to the internal surface of the walls. It will be necessary to refer to the note on interstitial condensation at the end of this section. The main disadvantage to internal insulation of solid masonry walls is that space will be lost on the inner face of the external walls. There will be no thermal mass in the wall within the insulated shell of the building so the building will heat up more quickly but also cool down more quickly than an externally insulated dwelling.

After any electrical or plumbing services have been disconnected, and skirting boards and other projections have been removed and made good, rigid insulation boards faced with plasterboard can be glued directly to the internal face of the wall.

The roofline has to be extended to take account of the increased thickness of the walls, rainwater fittings have to be adjusted and external pathways may need to be widened, so the process can be very expensive.

External wall insulation is inappropriate for older buildings where the appearance of brickwork or stonework needs to be maintained. If the walls have already been rendered, the addition of external insulation makes little difference to the appearance of the building in cases where a rendered finish is applied afterwards.

Alternatively, vertical treated timber battens can be plugged and screwed to the wall, spaced to suit the insulation and the plasterboard. Rigid or semi-rigid insulation material can then be friction-fitted between the vertical studs. A vapour control layer may be required over the entire wall before a finishing board is fixed to the studs. The use of studs slightly reduces the effectiveness of the

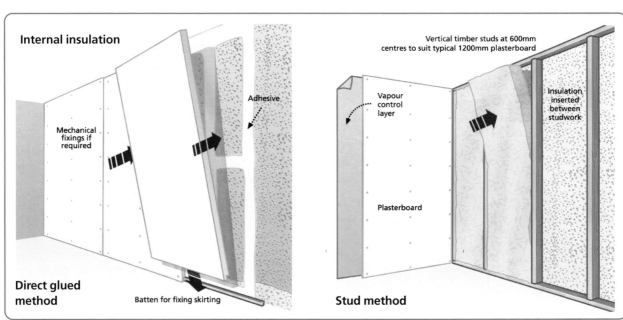

Internal insulation

Mechanical fixings if required

Adhesive

Direct glued method

Batten for fixing skirting

Vertical timber studs at 600mm centres to suit typical 1200mm plasterboard

Vapour control layer

Insulation inserted between studwork

Plasterboard

Stud method

insulation, so boards glued directly to the wall will minimise the amount of space lost within the room. However, it is necessary to check carefully the environmental issues relating not only to the insulation boards but also the glue, as some products may emit toxic fumes over a long period.

The addition of 100mm of mineral wool insulation fitted between studs on the inside of a 220mm solid brick wall would reduce the U-value from 2.10 to 0.35, which meets the current regulations.[4] In this case the loss of area within a room, including the plasterboard and skim, amounts to 115mm along the external walls.

When adding internal insulation, light switches, power outlets and wall lights will all need refitting in their new positions. This is relatively straightforward if there is excess cable which can be pulled through but is otherwise a more demanding task. Electricity cables heat up when carrying current, so hiding cables within internal insulation can lead to overheating or an increase in disconnection time. If in any doubt, seek advice from a qualified electrician. If there is a window in the wall to be insulated, the windowsill will need to be replaced with a deeper one.

Some insulating dry-lining manufacturers have bespoke metal framing systems that may reduce the thickness of insulation required. An air gap may be required between the insulation and the masonry wall.

For further information see: 'Practical refurbishment of solid walled houses' – Energy Saving Trust CE184 (download).

THERMAL BRIDGING

Thermal bridging occurs in an otherwise insulated structure where insulation has been missed out. Sometimes this occurs for technical reasons when refurbishing old buildings, as it can be impossible to 'break' the path from inside to outside where the structure is solid and there is no room to add insulation. Moist air will tend to condense on the coldest spots, so condensation or mould growth may form on internal walls for no apparent reason. In addition to ensuring that thermal bridges are avoided, good ventilation will help to prevent condensation from forming.

It is recommended that internal insulation should be returned at window and door reveals (*ie* fitted around the

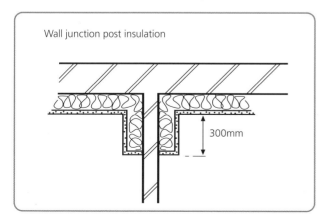

Wall junction post insulation

300mm

corner up to the frame) to avoid the risk of thermal bridging, where practicable. Where an internal partition wall interrupts an external wall, the insulation cannot be continuous unless the internal wall is partially rebuilt. The current prescription is to return the insulation 300mm along the internal wall to reduce the risk of condensation at that point.

For further information see: 'Internal wall insulation in existing housing' – Energy Saving Trust GPG 138 (download).

CAVITY WALLS

For cavity-wall masonry houses where there is no slab insulation product present on the inner side of the cavity (construction types 2 and 3 above and rendered blockwork with a cavity), the injection of insulation into the cavity will significantly improve the performance of the building without having to make any disruptive structural alterations. Normally holes are drilled in the outer skin of masonry and the insulation is blown in under pressure. The holes are then made good with mortar.

There are two main types of insulation used for injection into cavity walls: loose mineral wool or glass wool, and polystyrene beads.

As the installation of cavity-wall insulation requires specialist tools it must be carried out by professionals, and frequently they can install only one type. The environmental impact of insulation products is discussed in more detail in the section on 'Insulation products' in Chapter 2.

Photo: www.aranservices.co.uk

For further information see: 'Cavity Wall insulation in existing dwellings – a guide for specifiers and advisors' – Energy Saving Trust CE225 (download); 'Practical refurbishment of solid-walled houses' – Energy Saving Trust CE184 (download); and 'Advanced insulation in housing refurbishment' – Energy Saving Trust CE97 (download).

TIMBER-FRAME

Most people are aware if they live in a timber-frame house but it is impossible to tell whether there is a timber frame present simply by looking at the property, as it is common in the UK to clad the outside of timber-frame structures with a skin of brickwork.

Timber-frame buildings are often already insulated, as the void which is created during the construction of the frame will have been filled with insulation when the house was built. If you are unsure as to whether there is insulation in the walls, check any penetrations in the structure such as power points, making sure to turn off the relevant fuse first. Alternatively, remove the plasterboard

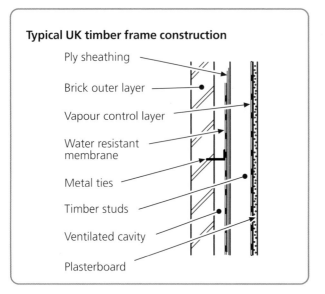

Typical UK timber frame construction

- Ply sheathing
- Brick outer layer
- Vapour control layer
- Water resistant membrane
- Metal ties
- Timber studs
- Ventilated cavity
- Plasterboard

and open up a small section of wall, taking care to avoid pipes and cables which may be running through the void.

Sometimes a small amount of insulation is present, for example 25mm may have been included when the frame was constructed. Frames are normally a minimum of 90mm deep so in this case a considerable amount of insulation can be added without having to increase the thickness of the wall. However, the requirements of the Building Regulations as explained at the beginning of this chapter should be noted.

If there is no insulation within the frame there are two methods by which it can be added. Either remove the inner skin of plasterboard and fit rigid or semi-rigid insulation between the studs, or drill holes in the plasterboard and blow loose fill insulation into the void. Blowing insulation into the frame requires specialist equipment but is less disruptive to the fabric of the building. It is possible that a vapour control layer will have to be added, which would necessitate the removal of the plasterboard in any case – see the note below on interstitial condensation. If there is a ventilated cavity

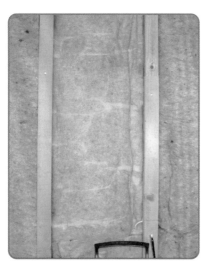

between the timber frame and a masonry outer skin, this should not be filled with insulation.

For further information see: 'Refurbishing dwellings: A summary of best practice' – Energy Saving Trust CE189 (download).

INTERSTITIAL CONDENSATION

Water vapour passes through walls in properties which are not built with integral vapour control layers. Many people assume that the main risk is that rainwater will penetrate from the outside but the problem is actually the converse. Water vapour generated by normal occupation of property passes from the inside to the outside of the wall and then evaporates. The temperature is normally higher inside than outside (at least in the UK) so the temperature within an external wall will fall, moving from inside to out.

Given the relative humidity, if the temperature falls below a critical level the 'dew point temperature' is reached and condensation will occur. If condensation occurs in a cavity, moisture can collect and cause problems. To avoid the risk of interstitial condensation a vapour control layer should be installed on the warm side of the internal insulation. The sheet must be carefully sealed at any penetrations and any joints lapped and taped.

A vapour control layer may not always be required. Once the insulation material has been selected, the manufacturers are normally prepared to carry out the calculations and advise accordingly. Some green builders are opposed to vapour control layers as they prevent walls from breathing.

There is at present only limited data available on how the addition of internal or external insulation will affect the movement of moisture within walls or within buildings generally, particularly in solid-walled old buildings which have hitherto always been able to breathe. It is also true that different elevations (north/south/east/west) perform differently in terms of their thermal characteristics and rates of absorbing and evaporating moisture, so considerable research is needed before arriving at definitive conclusions on this subject. The Building Regulations do not distinguish between elevations and currently determine the minimum levels of insulation which must be applied.

Reducing heat loss through windows and doors

More heat is lost through badly fitting doors and windows than is lost through the conduction of energy by thin glass. The first, and cheapest, place to start when looking at energy savings from doors and windows is therefore to draughtproof and seal wherever possible.

DRAUGHTPROOFING DOORS AND WINDOWS

The best time to check for draughts is during cold weather when there is some wind. If no draughts can be detected on one or more edges then there is evidently a good insulating fit and no point adding further material to that particular edge. If the fit is already very tight, the addition of some types of draught excluder can even cause problems with the operation of the door/window.

Once a draught has been detected, check the door/window in the closed position and see whether there is a uniform gap between the door and the frame. If the gap is consistent then strips of compressible foam tape can be used.

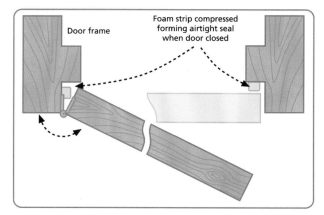

These strips are self-adhesive and are fitted to the door/window frame rather than to the door or window itself. On the opening side and at the top the tape is fitted around the inside of the closure. On the hinge side the tape should be fitted to the frame face. Once these have been fitted, a door tends to close slightly further out than before so the receiving plate on the latch and lock may need slight adjustment.

Where a door has warped slightly, adhesive strips will not have sufficient compression to form a seal all round the door so they are unlikely be effective. Aluminium (or pvc) door strips are designed to be fitted to the main body of the closure section of the frame, so they don't need to follow the exact line of the rebate.

With the door closed and locked, offer up the strip to the door and ensure that they are in contact. Apply light finger pressure only – do not attempt to compress the strip against the door or this may cause problems with the closing. Screw (or nail, if nails are supplied) the strip to the frame, through the middle of the oblong pre-drilled holes. Hardwood frames may require a pilot hole to be pre-drilled. In this case offer up the strip to the door and mark the holes with a pencil then remove and drill them all at the same time.

When the installation is complete, the strip can be moved in or out slightly by slackening off the screws and sliding the strip to the extent of the oblong pre-drilled holes.

Metal windows do not warp like wooden windows but they are prone to small gaps on the hinge side. Specialist draught strips are available, similar to those used for wooden windows. uPVC windows and doors are often specialist proprietary systems so if they need maintenance to correct draughts it is usually necessary to contact the manufacturer or installer.

Notch for corner joint.

DRAUGHTPROOFING FRAMES

Cracks often occur in buildings where dissimilar materials meet, due to differing rates of thermal expansion. Doors and windows are also subject to considerable wear and tear, especially if they have been binding or sticking and have been slammed, so cracks such as this are not uncommon. Sometimes it is possible to feel air passing through these cracks, so a good-quality decorators' filler should be used to fill any gaps. It is advisable to re-anchor the frame if it has worked loose and to correct any sticking doors or windows

in order to reduce the likelihood of the problem recurring.

When doors and windows have been effectively draughtproofed the available ventilation will be reduced. For information on ventilation and associated issues see the section on 'Ventilation and heat recovery systems' at the end of this chapter.

For further information on draughtproofing see: 'Improving air tightness in dwellings' – Energy Saving Trust CE137/GPG224 (download).

REPAIRING WINDOWS

It is a poor use of resources to replace windows which can easily be repaired and the embodied energy of producing, transporting and fitting new windows is considerable, in addition to the costs of disposing of the old ones.

People frequently fall into the trap of having windows replaced when there is rot damage only to the lower sill. Rot in this area is understandable, since all the rainwater which falls on the window will have to pass over the sill while draining away and, with the

Resin repairs.

Photos: Repair Care International

accumulation of debris and poor maintenance, water is more likely to collect and do damage there than anywhere else.

New timber can be spliced in where the rot is severe. Rot is also commonly found in the first few inches of the upright frame members above the sill. This type of rot can also be repaired effectively with the use of modern resins which bond to and expand and contract like the timber, thus preventing the cracking which is common after hard fillers have been used. Once a repair job like the one pictured above has been carried out the windows are quite literally as good as new. For older properties there is the added benefit that the character of the building is not compromised.

Draughtproofing strip inserted into frame.

Ventrolla sash repair system

There are also companies that specialise in the upgrading and draughtproofing of sash windows. A strip can be inserted into the casement which allows it to glide easily as the window slides open but which prevents the draughts associated with these windows.

It is even possible to replace the sliding casements themselves with double-glazed versions, but this is a specialist job as the counterweights in the sash boxes will need to be enlarged and space within the boxing is usually limited.

Modern sealants and mastics not only contain a variety of synthetic chemicals but may also appear incongruous when applied to older buildings. There are several DIY recipes for alternative mastics, the main ingredients being sand and linseed oil. This type of filler takes much longer to set than 'conventional' mastics.

REPLACING GLAZING

Original timber window with double glazing added.

Double glazing became – for a time at least in the UK – synonymous with uPVC replacement windows, although attitudes are again changing and estate agents are now beginning to mention original windows as a selling point, as inappropriate replacement windows can substantially reduce the value of a property. For substantially fixed glazing in timber structures such as bay windows it is normally possible to remove the original thin glass and to insert double-glazed panels without replacing the frame. Opening casements may require replacement but with minor adaptation the outer frames can often be retained.

Detail of window above from inside.

The insulation of glazing has evolved considerably during the 20th century. To assess the improvement in U-values that may be achieved through replacement glazing, the following table shows U-values for glazing specifications in common use during the past 100 years.

Glazing	Centre-pane u-value (W/m²K)
4mm single	5.8
4mm plus closed lined curtain and pelmet*	3.6
4mm plus secondary glazing	2.9–3.4
4–12mm gap – 4mm (standard double glazing)	2.8
4–12mm gap – 4mm low-emissivity	1.9
4–16mm gap – 4mm low-emissivity, air filled	1.7
4–16mm gap – 4mm low-emissivity, argon-filled	1.5
Triple Glazing, low e, argon-filled **	1.4

Figures have been quoted for hard coated low-emissivity glass. Soft coatings also exist which give even better u-values.

Sources – Pilkington, *English Heritage, **Herts Technical Forum

In England and Wales, changes to the Building Regulations in April 2006 require replacement windows to have a U-value of 2.0W/m²K, or a centre pane U-value of 1.2W/m²K. New windows in existing property, for example in extensions, are required to have a U-value of 1.8W/m²K or a centre pane U-value of 1.2W/m²K. (Also see the section on BFRC ratings below.)

SECONDARY GLAZING

Old glass has a look which cannot be replicated by modern production techniques. The imperfections and interesting reflections of old glass can be retained while the thermal performance is improved if secondary glazing is installed. It is important that sufficient sections of secondary glazing are able to be opened, both for the thermal comfort of occupants during hot weather and for reasons of fire safety.

Metal windows cannot accept thicker glazed panels so secondary glazing is a realistic and cost-effective measure to reduce heat loss while leaving the building's fabric and appearance essentially unchanged.

For further information on secondary glazing see: 'Advanced insulation in housing refurbishment' – Energy Saving Trust CE97 (download).

DOOR AND WINDOW REPLACEMENT

In some circumstances, replacing doors and windows is unavoidable. Natural materials such as wood generally have a much lower embodied energy and environmental impact than synthetic materials.[5] Synthetic materials can also be impossible to repair. If softwood joinery is well designed and made it should last a lifetime with minimal maintenance – paint technology has improved markedly in recent years. It is important to ensure that the timber comes from sustainable sources (see the section on 'Timber sourcing' in Chapter 2). By using timber, the existing windows and doors can be matched in order to avoid changing the appearance of the property.

Hardwoods are a scarce resource and the use of tropical hardwoods should be avoided. As window and door replacement is carried out very infrequently during the life of a building it would be worth specifying good-quality softwood joinery and well-insulated glazing.

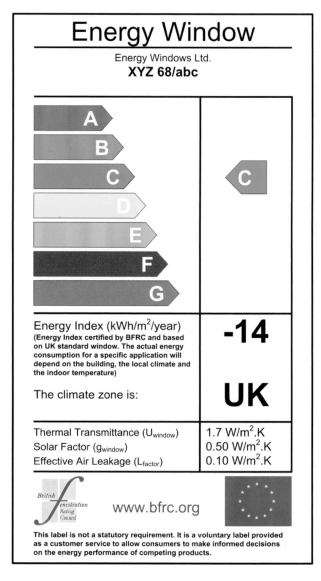

Energy Window

Energy Windows Ltd.
XYZ 68/abc

A
B
C
D
E
F
G

C

Energy Index (kWh/m²/year)
(Energy Index certified by BFRC and based on UK standard window. The actual energy consumption for a specific application will depend on the building, the local climate and the indoor temperature)

The climate zone is:

-14

UK

Thermal Transmittance (U_{window})   1.7 W/m².K
Solar Factor (g_{window})   0.50 W/m².K
Effective Air Leakage (L_{factor})   0.10 W/m².K

www.bfrc.org

This label is not a statutory requirement. It is a voluntary label provided as a customer service to allow consumers to make informed decisions on the energy performance of competing products.

According to the 2006 amendments to the Building Regulations, the local Building Control office must be notified whenever a thermal element such as a door or window is replaced. If the person carrying out the work is registered with approved organisations such as FENSA, CERTASS or the BSI in respect of that type of work then the work can be self-certified by the contractor. In all other cases an application must be made to Building Control, together with the associated fees; the work will then have to be inspected to ensure that it conforms with the new regulations. It is worth noting that these institutions (and most contractors) are unlikely to advocate repair or upgrading rather than replacement (see 'Replacing glazing' on page 59).

BFRC RATINGS

While doors are still rated according to U-values, window performance may now be rated according to a new European window energy rating system. In the UK this scheme is known as the British Fenestration Rating Council (BFRC) and takes into account the energy performance of the whole window. While U-values can be difficult to compare, as the U-value of the frame must be taken into account in addition to the U-value of the glass and thermal bridging which occurs through the spacers between sheets of glass, the BFRC rating takes all these factors into account. The BFRC rating also allows for the calculation of heat gain through glass and arrives at a net figure over a year. Through good design and the use of low-energy glass, some windows can now result in annual thermal gains rather than losses. Some changes to glazing specification can increase the U-value (making it appear to lose heat more quickly) while improving the BFRC rating, which illustrates the contrast between the two systems.

As an alternative to the U-values quoted earlier, the 2006 changes to the Building Regulations in England and Wales allow replacement windows which have a BFRC rating in band E or above. New windows in existing buildings (for example in extensions) must have a BFRC rating in band D or above.

For further information see: 'Windows for new and existing housing' – Energy Saving Trust CE66 (download).

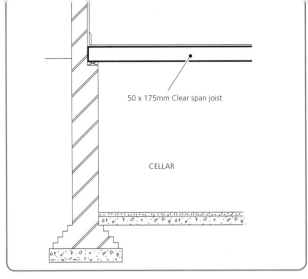

50 x 175mm Clear span joist

CELLAR

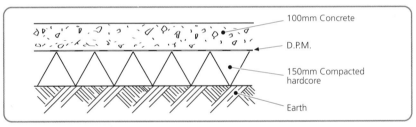

50 x 100mm Joist

Honeycombed
sleeper wall

Reducing heat loss through ground floors

Firstly, it is necessary to work out how the ground floor has been constructed. There are four common forms:
Many older properties have a combination of suspended and solid floor types, especially if they were built on a slope. Solid uninsulated concrete ground floors conduct heat directly away into the ground upon which they are laid. The primary heat loss through suspended wooden floors is caused by draughts as the cold air which intentionally circulates below the floor is drawn up into the living areas through gaps in butt-jointed floor timbers. Later timber floors were constructed with tongued-and-grooved boards that reduce or eliminate the draughts from below.

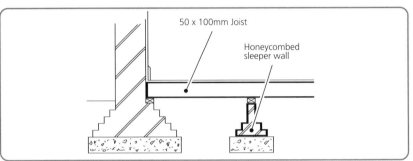

100mm Concrete

D.P.M.

150mm Compacted hardcore

Earth

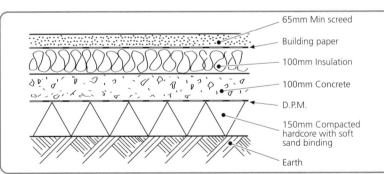

65mm Min screed

Building paper

100mm Insulation

100mm Concrete

D.P.M.

150mm Compacted hardcore with soft sand binding

Earth

Above: T&G floor.
Below: Butt-jointed floor.

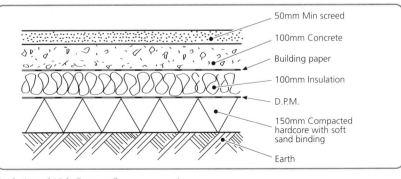

50mm Min screed

100mm Concrete

Building paper

100mm Insulation

D.P.M.

150mm Compacted hardcore with soft sand binding

Earth

Evolution of 20th Century floor construction

SUSPENDED TIMBER FLOOR WITH CELLAR

Insulating this type of floor is relatively straightforward as access to the underside of the floor is clear. Batt (semi-rigid) insulation can be friction-fitted between the joists and they can be under-lined with netting, hardboard, plasterboard or recycled timber to retain the insulation in position.

Photo: Patrick Stevenson

SUSPENDED TIMBER FLOOR CRAWLSPACE/ SLEEPER WALL CONSTRUCTION

Where access to the sub-floor space is restricted it is more difficult to retro-fit insulation and there are basically two methods by which it can be achieved. Either open up a small section of the floor and persuade a small agile person with no fear of spiders or vermin to crawl in and friction-fit insulation while lying on his/her back, or else completely remove the floor and install the insulation from above.

Where the floor surface is completely removed, netting can be laid over the joists to retain the insulation and avoid having to fix anything to the underside of the joists. The original floor surface can then be fitted back down. It would be a waste of resources to replace good-quality timber floorboards with a sheet material at this point, as the draughts will have been eliminated by the insulation. There are also health concerns about the chemical binders used in some panel products (see section on 'Composite/particle boards' in Chapter 2). If a small number of boards are

damaged, cut out the bad sections and replace with new. Most builders' yards carry planed timber which can easily be machined down to the correct width and, after some staining down, it will make a good match.

Alternatively, where the original floor surface is of poor quality and there is no prospect of ever reusing it, draughts can be reduced by fixing hardboard to the surface of the floor. If there is movement in the underlying floor, screwing the hardboard down rather than nailing will prevent the problem of nails lifting after repeated use. Glues are best avoided as some emit a variety of toxic fumes and combining materials with glue makes them difficult to recycle. Draughts also arise from gaps under the skirting boards and from penetrations through the floor to allow for radiator pipes so it is important to seal these gaps at the same time as laying sheet material. Technically this might trigger the requirements of Part L1B but in practice Building Control are unlikely to object to this kind of measure.

Note: The undersides of floors in these types of houses are designed to be ventilated. While insulation is being installed, check to make sure that vents are open and unobstructed – they often get covered by 'improvements' to front or rear gardens and it is only the gaps in the floorboards that draw through adequate ventilation to prevent rot and mould growth.

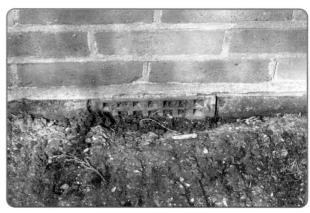

Above: Sub-floor vent obstructed.
Below: Sub-floor vents protected.

Photo: Patrick Stevenson

UNINSULATED CONCRETE SLAB

This is the most difficult type of floor to insulate, and concrete slabs are very cold surfaces. It is sometimes the case in this type of construction that the load-bearing walls have been built on top of the concrete slab (it will have been thickened under the walls), so even if a homeowner is

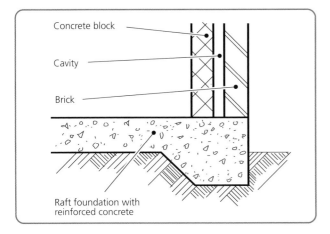

Concrete block

Cavity

Brick

Raft foundation with reinforced concrete

brave enough to want to break out the floor and insulate underneath it before relaying concrete, it may not be technically possible to accomplish. Also see the section on radon in Chapter 9 if considering breaking out a solid floor.

Instead, the only practical way to address this problem is to insulate above the floor. Head-height then becomes the critical issue, particularly at door openings, so it is worth remembering that a little insulation is better than no insulation at all and that insulation generally has a graph of diminishing returns – adding more and more insulation will keep improving the thermal performance of a building, but by progressively smaller amounts.

Even though Building Regulations require upgrading insulation to modern standards whenever a new surface is added, as a guide, 25mm of polystyrene will improve the U-value to 0.45W/m²K, while 40mm of polyisocyanurate foam will improve the value to 0.31W/m²K. The U-values achieved will vary according to the size and shape of the room and the build-up of the existing solid floor slab.[6]

Insulation over existing slab

65mm Floating screed

Building paper

Insulation

New D.P.M.

Existing concrete

OR

Boarding fixed to battens

Insulation

D.P.M.

Existing concrete

A new floor surface must of course be laid over the insulation. This must be secured down, so bearers can be fixed to the concrete sub-floor and insulation placed between them. The finished surface can then be fixed to the bearers. Some floating floor installations may be sufficiently stable to be laid directly over this type of insulation without the use of bearers but specialist advice should be sought from the manufacturer.

Note: Care must also be taken at the junction of the floor and the wall, as there is a possibility that a thermal bridge at this point will cause condensation, damp and mould if not correctly detailed. It may also be necessary to install a damp-proof membrane whilst carrying out this type of insulation if this was not built into the floor when the slab was cast.

Where a staircase rises from an area which is to be insulated, the increase in ground floor level would effectively reduce the height of the first step. Building Regulations require that risers (the amount each step goes up) are consistent throughout the staircase to avoid trip hazards. To address this problem, the first step needs to be

Alteration to staircases after insulation of floor

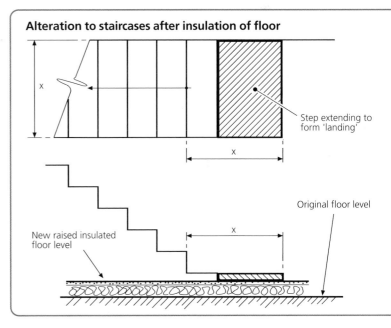

x

Step extending to form 'landing'

x

New raised insulated floor level

x

Original floor level

extended and effectively become a landing. The landing must be at least as deep as the width of the staircase.

This alteration is not always possible, especially, for example, where the entrance to the staircase is restricted in a hallway. It is advisable in all cases to check with the local Building Control officer before making alterations to a staircase. Door handles and door heights may also become an issue if floor levels are raised. Where it is impossible to fit any insulation to a solid concrete ground floor, a great deal of heat can still be retained by fitting a carpet or even a wooden floor using a thermal underlay.

For further information see: 'Practical refurbishment of solid walled houses' – Energy Saving Trust CE184 (download).

Ventilation and heat recovery systems

As insulation levels are increased, air leaks become a more significant source of heat loss. Improving air tightness to reduce this loss can, in turn, result in poor indoor air quality, so controlled ventilation becomes more important. The ventilation system itself then becomes a more significant source of heat loss, so it may be necessary to introduce a heat recovery system.

Ventilation can be organised on a single-room basis or by means of a whole-house system, with or without heat recovery. The flow of air can be mechanically driven or operate passively as a result of wind or temperature and pressure differential.

THE NEED FOR VENTILATION

In most modern houses, indoor air is substantially more polluted than the outside air, even in cities. As people spend up to 90% of their time indoors, indoor air quality is

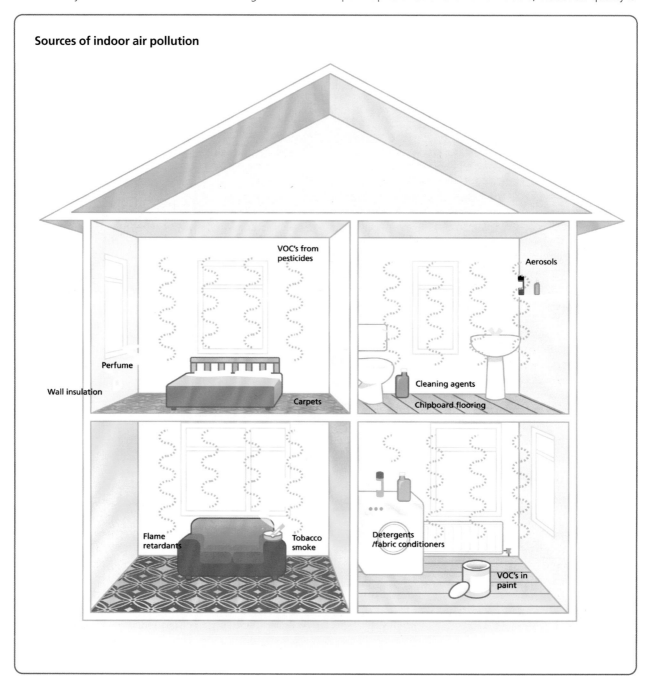

Sources of indoor air pollution

VOC's from pesticides

Aerosols

Perfume

Cleaning agents

Wall insulation

Chipboard flooring

Carpets

Flame retardants

Tobacco smoke

Detergents /fabric conditioners

VOC's in paint

Common air leakage paths

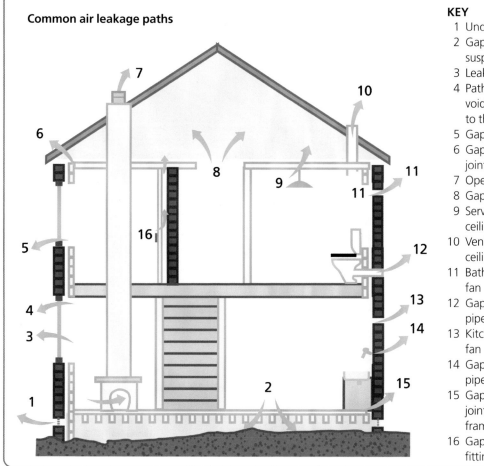

KEY
1. Underfloor ventilator grilles
2. Gaps in and around suspended timber floors
3. Leaky windows or doors
4. Pathways through floor/ceiling void into cavity walls and then to the outside
5. Gaps around windows
6. Gaps at the ceiling-to-wall joints at the eaves
7. Open chimneys
8. Gaps around loft hatches
9. Service penetrations through ceilings
10. Vents penetrating the ceiling/roof
11. Bathroom wall vent or extract fan
12. Gaps around bathroom waste pipes
13. Kitchen wall vent or extractor fan
14. Gaps around kitchen waste pipes
15. Gaps around floor-to-wall joints (particularly with timber frames)
16. Gaps in and around electrical fittings in hollow walls

Source: Energy Saving Trust

a serious health issue. A wide variety of airborne toxins are introduced into dwellings by carpets, furnishings, cleaning products and several modern building materials (see chapters 2, 8 and 9).

For further information see: Residential Ventilation Association (RVA), Indoor Air Quality Statement (July 06).

Moisture generated by bathing and cooking needs to be expelled, as condensation and mould growth result from excessive humidity. Boilers are always ventilated to the outside but gas cookers release the products of combustion, including moisture, into the indoor environment unless an extractor has been fitted. Cooker extractors that simply filter rather than expel stale air to the outside do nothing to reduce condensation. Tobacco smoke is also a significant pollutant where there is no direct ventilation.

Fires and stoves require an adequate supply of oxygen and the amount of air required for this purpose is laid down in the relevant Building Regulations, although a higher level of ventilation will in any case be required in order to expel pollutants and humidity.

The inadequate ventilation and associated problems of condensation which have been experienced in many modern buildings have led to the requirement to provide specified levels of ventilation as set out in the 2006 edition of the Building Regulations – Approved Document F.

AIR LEAKAGE

In older properties, it was understood that air leaks through windows and doors (and even through the main body of the structure itself) would be sufficient to provide the necessary amount of background ventilation. As warm air tends to rise, fresh air will be drawn in through the lower parts of the house and ultimately exit through the upper floors. This is known as the 'stack' effect.

Uncontrolled ventilation of this type results in substantial heat loss, which increases significantly with wind speed. Measures to reduce such leakage will have energy-saving benefits, but it is pointless to seal a building completely and then to have to reintroduce ventilation by drilling holes in windows and walls. Building Regulations, however, require that new constructions perform within specific maximum standards for air leakage.

MECHANICAL VENTILATION VS PASSIVE VENTILATION

In most houses air is expelled by means of fan vents in the 'wet' rooms – bathrooms and kitchens. Replacement air is admitted by means of trickle vents and air leakage. When fans are not operating in these rooms, in modern 'sealed' houses, the ventilation is unlikely to be sufficient, particularly in rooms which do not lie on the ventilation pathway unless there is a substantial gap under the door.[7] When fans are working, they consume energy, in addition to the energy which is lost with the warm expelled air.

These fans are likely to have been installed in accordance with earlier Building Regulations or during previous renovations and are unlikely to provide a balanced whole-house system of ventilation. Previous regulatory requirements on wiring fans to light switches in bathrooms with an added time overrun have also resulted in the operation of fans for up to 20 minutes when the bathroom light may only have been switched on for a minute or two; this is not only a waste of energy but can also be a nuisance to the occupants.

Mechanical extract ventilation simply combines the ducts from wet rooms and expels the air through a common vent. As the fan works continuously at low speed, the system can deliver a more consistent flow of air than intermittent extractor fans; the fan can be set to a higher speed manually or automatically when greater ventilation is required. A well designed and built installation can minimise the energy required to run the system.

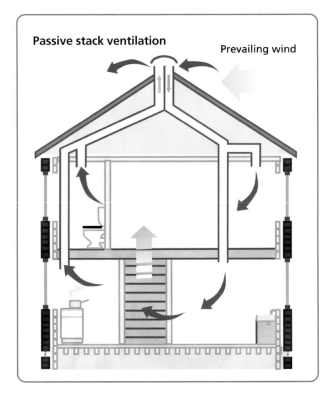

Passive stack ventilation

Prevailing wind

Passive ventilation is based upon a combination of wind pressure and the stack effect. Warm (moist) air is drawn from the wet rooms and expelled at ridge height, as the vent design uses the available wind to pull the air through the system. Fresh air can be supplied from background ventilation or admitted at roof level through different channels in the same system and then ducted to the rooms below.

Passive stack ventilation has the advantage that it is silent and energy-free in operation, but the disadvantage that its operation is dependent upon available wind, so it may not deliver sufficient ventilation when most needed unless it is mechanically assisted. As with simple mechanical ventilation, the heat in the expelled air is lost.

HEAT RECOVERY

For much of the year in the UK, the temperature of outside air is below what most people regard as a comfortable internal temperature, so the arrival of fresh air is commonly perceived as an uncomfortable draught. However, ventilation does not necessarily mean the loss of warm air and the introduction of cold air. The heat which is present in the stale air can be partially recovered (up to 75%) and used to preheat the incoming fresh air by means of a simple heat exchanger. This is known as heat recovery.

Heat recovery ventilation systems in theory deliver the best of both worlds – plenty of fresh air and minimal heat loss. They are most effective when designed for a whole house, so that warm air can be drawn from rooms where

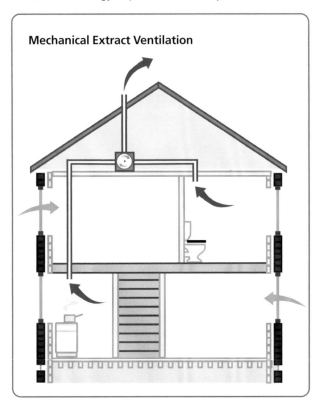

Mechanical Extract Ventilation

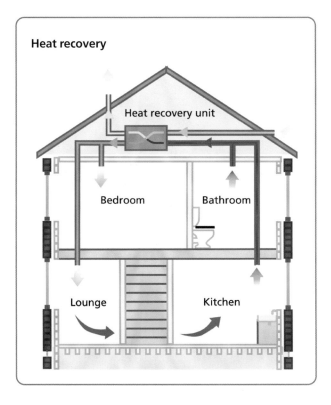

Heat recovery

Heat recovery unit

Bedroom

Bathroom

Lounge

Kitchen

the moisture level is high, such as kitchens and bathrooms, and used to heat the incoming air which is ducted and fed into other rooms. Compared to single-room heat recovery ventilators, whole-house systems also have the advantage that the source of the incoming air can be kept at a distance from the exit point for stale air to avoid used/moist air being drawn back in.

However, as with other system-based ventilation strategies, the required ductwork may be highly visible or otherwise difficult to fit to downstairs rooms in existing properties. It is also worth noting that heat recovery systems only deliver an energy-saving benefit in properties which are airtight, so that all the warm air is forced to pass through the heat exchanger.[8]

POSITIVE INPUT VENTILATION

In most ventilation strategies, the system is designed to expel stale air and to allow fresh air to filter in through trickle vents and leakage pathways. By reversing this principle, ventilation can be achieved by pushing fresh air into the building by means of a fan, which is normally located in the attic space if available. The air is supplied to a central communal space such as a landing and then finds its way out through the air leakage pathways described above. This type of system is not so effective at removing the moist air generated in kitchens and bathrooms but is particularly useful for areas where radon is a significant risk.

For further information see: 'Energy efficient ventilation in dwellings – a guide for specifiers' – Energy Saving Trust GPG 268 (download).

CLEANING INDOOR AIR

In addition to the ventilation strategies outlined in this section, it is worth noting that indoor plants can significantly enhance indoor air quality. Spider plants in particular are thought to be effective at reducing formaldehyde levels indoors.[9] Household plants, in varying degrees, can also reduce concentrations of carbon monoxide, benzene and trichlorethylene among other chemicals.

Ionisers are also thought to improve indoor air quality by attracting pollutants to the negatively charged ions which they produce and causing them to fall to the floor, where they are gathered in the normal cleaning process.

REFERENCES

[1] Table A1: Approved Document L1B: 'Conservation of Fuel and Power in Existing Dwellings'.
[2] Energy Saving Trust GPG 155.
[3] Energy Saving Trust CE184.
[4] Energy Saving Trust GPG155 and CE184.
[5] *Window of opportunity: The environmental and economic benefits of specifying timber window frames* by Christian Thompson, WWF-UK (2005).
[6] Energy Saving Trust CE184.
[7] Energy Saving Trust GPG268.
[8] Energy Saving Trust GPG268.
[9] 'Detoxification of Formaldehyde by the spider plant and by soybean suspension cultures' M. Giese, U. Bauer-Doranth, C. Langebartels, and H. Sandermann, Jr, April 1994, GSF-Forschungszentrum fur Umwelt und Gesundheit GmbH, Institut fur Biochemische Pflanzenpathologie, D-85764 Oberschleissheim, Germany.

4 HEATING

All the heating systems discussed in this chapter are subject to Building Regulations. Approved Document L1B states that where the work involves the provision or extension of a heating or hot water system or part thereof, reasonable provision would be the minimum recommendations of the *'Domestic Heating Compliance Guide'*. Some minor work will be exempt, but where Building Regulations approval is required, a Building Notice or Full Plans must be submitted to the local authority unless an approved contractor is used.

Comparison of available fuels

With the exception of nuclear, geothermal and solar power, all fuels are based upon carbon in one form or another. Burning carbon gives rise to carbon dioxide emissions. The carbon dioxide emitted from burning fossil fuels such as gas, oil or coal simply adds to the carbon dioxide already present in the atmosphere. The burning of carbon from renewable fuels such as wood or biomass has the advantage that CO_2 has been captured in the growing of the fuel by the process of photosynthesis. If growing plants or trees for fuel simply displaces other crops then there is no net gain to the environment but, where land is under-utilised, the switch to renewable sources of fuel will reduce the CO_2 burden if it displaces fossil fuel consumption.

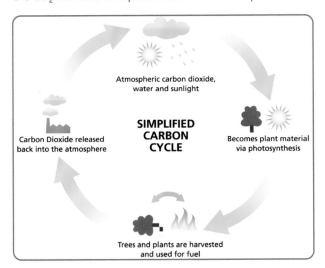

SIMPLIFIED CARBON CYCLE

Atmospheric carbon dioxide, water and sunlight

Becomes plant material via photosynthesis

Trees and plants are harvested and used for fuel

Carbon Dioxide released back into the atmosphere

Almost all domestic properties in the UK are served by mains electricity and most are served by mains gas. Where gas is unavailable, the choice of primary fuel for heating rests on a trade-off between price, convenience, the local supply chain and environmental impact. Alternative and renewable sources of heat are discussed later in this chapter.

The following table ranks fossil fuels in terms of their CO_2 emissions for a given heat output. The prices quoted are for comparative purposes only and will need to be updated for an accurate picture of the situation.

Comparative price and CO₂ emissions of fuels

Fuel	Price (p/kWh)	CO₂ emissions (kg/kWh)
Wood logs	2.20	0.03
Wood pellets (bulk)	3.00	0.03
Wood pellets (bagged)	5.00	0.03
Natural gas	1.63	0.19
LPG (bulk)	3.71	0.23
LPG (bottled)	4.32	0.23
Heating oil	2.17	0.27
Coal	1.91	0.29
Electricity (7-hour off-peak)	2.94	0.42
Electricity	7.12	0.42

Source: SAP 2005 (3-year averages)

The CO_2 emissions from electric heating are more than double those from gas for a given heat output. Of all the available fuels, electricity is one of the most expensive and least efficient for space heating or water heating. This is largely due to the energy losses associated with the generation and distribution of electricity. 40% of the UK's electricity is currently generated in power stations fuelled by natural gas,[1] so it is clear that it should be cheaper and more efficient to burn gas for heat rather than convert it into electricity first and then into heat.

The environmental impact of heating by oil can be reduced if it is possible to fuel the boiler with biodiesel derived from vegetable oil rather than fossil-fuel diesel. Pure biodiesel which is used for heating is currently not subject to the duty which applies to ordinary diesel, although most biodiesels used for heating are blended with fossil-fuel diesel. It is ironic that Rudolf Diesel, inventor of the engine which bears his name, originally intended to run it on biodiesel.

When the opportunity to change primary fuel arises, the final point to consider is the cost of installation and servicing of the system. New flue regulations mean that solid fuel boilers can be expensive to install and oil-fired systems are significantly more expensive than gas or LPG. Electric heating is cheaper to install, but the high running costs rapidly offset the apparent savings.

BIOMASS, BIOGAS AND COMMUNITY HEATING
Biomass is a generic term which covers any material which is grown to provide fuel. Two of the most common plants grown for this purpose are miscanthus grass and short rotation coppice willow, although it is common for forestry waste to be used in biomass schemes. There are plenty of examples of small groups of houses or even whole communities which have a shared heating (or combined heat and power) system, including several household waste incineration schemes where the heat produced is used to provide hot water to the surrounding community, or to generate electricity. Biomass can also be fermented to make ethanol which can be blended with gasoline. Biogas is most often produced from processing farm

waste via anaerobic digestion and this can be a very efficient way to produce heating fuel if the transportation distances are kept to a minimum.

Although this book is aimed at the individual householder, there are many situations in which it may be beneficial for people to club together to set up biomass-fuelled community heating (or CHP) schemes, particularly in the countryside where mains gas is unavailable. Although the available land area in the UK for biomass production is limited and there are ecological issues to be addressed, judicious use of renewable fuels may yet hold the key to heating older properties in a sustainable manner where insulating to modern standards is impractical.

Space heating systems

Once a house has been thoroughly draughtproofed and insulated the demand for space-heating will be greatly reduced, but there are several other ways to reduce heat demand before making costly alterations to heating systems.

TURNING DOWN THE THERMOSTAT

Centrally-heated houses are often kept well above generally accepted comfort temperature levels, so a considerable amount of energy can be saved by turning down the thermostat (if fitted) by a degree or two, without noticing the effect.

The old advice to put on a sweater rather than turn up the heating saves money and reduces CO_2 emissions. Comfort levels do, of course, vary according to how active you are, according to age and to state of health, so it would be dangerous to suggest absolute levels, but the following table

Room	Design Temp (°C)
Lounge/sitting room	21
Dining room	21
Kitchen	18
Kitchen/Breakfast	21
Hall	18
Cloakroom	18
Utility room	18
Study	21
Bedroom	18
Landing	19
Bathroom	22

is useful as it illustrates the typical contrast between rooms.

Guide temperature for the living room is higher than for the bedrooms – many people prefer a slightly cooler temperature for sleeping and believe it to be healthier – and lower for the kitchen, where people tend to be more active. A higher temperature in the bathroom is generally preferred.

THERMOSTATIC RADIATOR VALVES

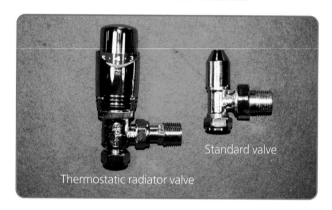

Standard valve

Thermostatic radiator valve

The best way to set different temperatures for each room is to fit thermostatic radiator valves (TRVs) to radiators. This is now standard practice for new central-heating systems and it is not an expensive job to fit them to an existing system. The TRVs can then be adjusted to sense and deliver the correct temperature for each room.

After draughtproofing and introducing good levels of insulation, heat demand will be much lower so existing radiators may now be oversized. Fitting TRVs will also help to solve this problem without having to replace radiators. Modern slim-line radiators may be more efficient than the existing radiators but TRVs are less costly and disruptive to fit. There is also an embodied energy cost in replacement radiators which needs to be offset against any energy savings obtained by replacement.

If a TRV is fitted to *every* radiator (or every radiator within a zone) then it will also be necessary to fit an automatic bypass valve at the boiler. This is a specialist job for a plumber and no alterations to heating systems should be made without consulting a qualified professional.

If the system already has a room thermostat, TRVs should not be installed in the same room as the thermostat.

HEATING CONTROLS

The aim of any heating control system is to provide heat when there is a demand for it and to avoid wasting money and energy when there is not. Occupancy patterns vary so it is difficult to generalise. For a household which is unoccupied during the day, a simple timer or programmer which sets the heating system to come on in the morning and again in the evening will save a considerable amount of energy. More sophisticated is the programmable room thermostat which allows for different temperatures to be set depending on the activity level of the occupants over the course of a 24-hour period.

Weather compensators not only measure the temperature outside but also 'learn' how the heating system functions and adjust accordingly to make it run more efficiently. Primarily they do this by predicting when the external temperature will rise sufficiently to warm the building so they can shut off the boiler earlier, saving money and energy. Opinions vary as to their effectiveness but they are certainly more sensitive than a simple room thermostat.

UNDERFLOOR HEATING

Warm air rises, so the most efficient means of delivering heat to a room is by means of underfloor heating. Radiators need to be at a high temperature to radiate and convect heat to all corners of a room but underfloor heating can be run at a lower temperature to deliver the same degree of thermal comfort. This in turn means that the boiler can operate more efficiently, so saving money and greenhouse gas emissions.

Underfloor heating is not practicable for most refurbishment projects as it involves raising the floor level. If you are considering an extension, it may be possible to add an underfloor heating system to the existing boiler and radiator circuit without having to install a new boiler. It is also possible to connect solar water heaters to underfloor heating systems (see the section on Solar water heating in this chapter).

Underfloor heating is normally arranged by laying pipes in formwork or clips and then pouring a cementitious screed over the top to form a slab, which then stores and dissipates the heat. There are other systems available which do not require a screed, as a finished floor surface can be laid directly over the pipes if they are laid in channels within load-bearing insulation.

Photo: Jupiter Heating Systems

Electric underfloor heating can be expensive to run, like other systems which use electricity as their primary fuel.[2]

AIR-BASED SYSTEMS

Air requires much less energy to heat than water, so air-based heating systems produce a much faster response time. Air-based systems are common in the USA and Canada, partly because they can also provide cooling as well as heating, which cannot be achieved via radiators. Generally, air-based systems are more expensive to install than water-based systems due to the large duct sizes

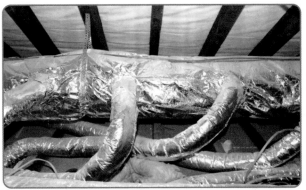

Photo: Unico System International

Photo: Unico System International

required, but they typically use 25–30% less energy in operation.

Warm-air systems can be combined with air conditioning and ventilation systems to provide an integrated atmospheric control system. Air can be heated in the same way as water – usually by a gas- or oil-fuelled boiler, but warm-air systems are often connected to heat pumps in addition to, or instead of, a fossil-fuel source (see the section on 'Ground-source heat pumps').

ELECTRIC STORAGE HEATERS

In highly insulated homes, where gas is not available and electricity is purchased via a green tariff, modern electric storage heating can be a relatively environmentally efficient means of space heating.

Electric storage heating systems are designed to take advantage of the fact that electricity is cheaper to purchase at night than in the daytime under an Economy 7 pricing tariff. Heat generated at night is stored in bricks or other dense material and released during the daytime and evening. Modern electric storage heaters may be fitted with

automatic charge controls which detect the rate of temperature fall during the night and adjust the amount of heat input accordingly, making them even more efficient.

Storage heaters give out heat by radiation and by convection. Heat radiated from electric storage heaters is difficult to control, but the rate of convected heat can be varied according to demand. Modern heaters may be fitted with thermostats to control heat output and may be fan-assisted to improve the warm-up time in rooms that are intermittently occupied. As with most other heating systems, temperature and time controls are essential to the economy of the system.

For further information on electric heating see: 'Domestic Heating by Electricity' – Energy Saving Trust CE185 (download).

INDIVIDUAL ROOM HEATERS

Individual electric fires (direct acting heaters) are one of the most expensive forms of heating. If a property is heated primarily by means of direct acting electric heaters, it is strongly recommended that another form of heating system is installed. Unlike storage heaters, electric fires cannot take advantage of the relatively lower cost of electricity during the off-peak period.

Individual gas-fuelled room heaters (wall heaters and fires) are becoming less common. However, in contrast to some decorative-flame gas fires they are a relatively cost-effective form of heating, as they warm up rooms quickly and allow heat to be delivered when and where needed. Once insulation has been installed, depending on layout, it may not be necessary to fit gas heaters in all rooms in order to heat the whole property.

AIR-CONDITIONING SYSTEMS

One of the effects of climate change is thought to be the increasing incidence of heat waves. New buildings are required to be designed to prevent summer overheating and therefore reduce the demand for air conditioning. Air conditioning can consume a surprising amount of energy. During the heat wave of 2006, electricity supply companies became seriously concerned about their ability to meet the high demand for power resulting from the surge in the use of air-conditioning plant. However, energy demand for air conditioning can be reduced by a number of methods.

Heat pumps can be operated in reverse during hot weather to provide cooling. The most energy-efficient system during hot weather would be ground- or water-based, as the source temperature is lower than the air temperature (see the section below on Ground-source heat pumps).

Ventilation systems can be operated at low energy to provide summer cooling. Passive stack ventilation (see 'Ventilation and heat recovery systems' in Chapter 3) uses no energy at all, although fan-assisted systems are likely to be more effective during a heat wave.

Good design and summer shading will both reduce overheating. Planting a tree on the southern side of the property will provide shade and projecting awnings will prevent the sun from shining directly into the house when at its highest, while allowing plenty of natural light to penetrate the interior. Overheating is also exacerbated by a lack of thermal mass in modern buildings – the heat has nowhere to go, so the interior heats up rapidly in warm weather (see the section on 'Passive solar design' at the end of this chapter).

Water heating systems

Water can either be heated and stored in a cylinder or heated 'on demand' and delivered directly from the heating unit to the tap.

STORED WATER – IMMERSION HEATER ONLY

It is increasingly rare for an immersion heater to be the only method of water heating in a home and an immersion heater is now more often used as a backup. An immersion heater is simply an electric element which is fitted into the hot water cylinder. Temperature is controlled by means of a thermostat.

The 'Economy 7' tariff encourages users to heat their water at night when electricity prices are lowest. The hot water can then be stored and used throughout the day. A timer and a large well-insulated cylinder are required for this process to be energy-efficient. Transferring electricity demand from daytime to night-time makes more effective use of the capacity of the electricity generation and distribution system, which is why rates are cheaper at night.

Even if the cylinder is well-insulated, an alternative means of water heating would provide savings, as electricity is an expensive method of heating water and generates a high level of CO_2 emissions per kW of useful heat.

STORAGE CYLINDER WITH DIRECT BOILER SYSTEM (VENTED)

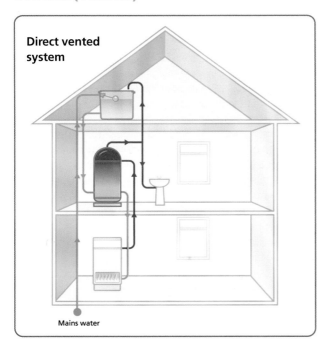

Direct vented system

Mains water

Cold water is fed from the cylinder to the boiler, which heats it and returns it to the cylinder higher up. When a tap is opened, hot water is drawn from the top of the cylinder and is replaced by cold water lower down. Water is heated directly, either by the boiler or by an immersion heater, and is then used. The cylinder simply stores the hot water before use. Direct hot water systems are increasingly rare and no longer installed.

STORAGE CYLINDER WITH INDIRECT BOILER SYSTEM (VENTED)

With an indirect water system, the water which is heated by the boiler circulates in a loop through a heat exchanger (coil) in the cylinder and then back to the boiler. The water which is actually used at the hot taps is fed into the cylinder, heated by means of the heat exchanger and fed out again without passing through the boiler.

Both the direct and the indirect systems described above are known as 'vented' systems. Vented systems operate at

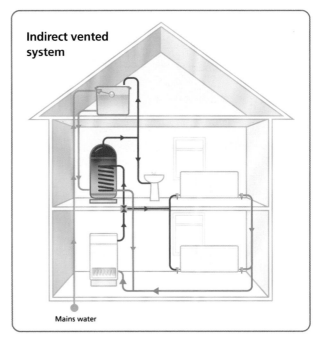

Indirect vented system

Mains water

atmospheric pressure, so flow rates tend to be low. They also require feeding from a separate cold water cistern which takes up space, generally in the loft.

STORAGE CYLINDER WITH INDIRECT BOILER SYSTEM (UNVENTED)

In an unvented system, the cold water inlet comes directly from the mains water supply rather than via a cold water cistern, so flow rates are normally much higher than vented systems are able to deliver. Otherwise, the principles are similar to vented systems although a stronger cylinder is required to deal with mains pressure.

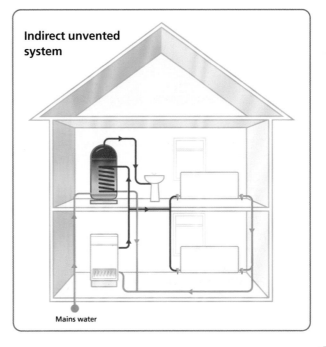

Indirect unvented system

Mains water

RENOVATION RECOMMENDATIONS FOR STORED WATER SYSTEMS

The recommendations for upgrading the three types of system described previously are as follows:

- Insulate the hot water cylinder or replace with a high-performance cylinder
- Ensure that timer controls are fitted to the boiler
- Ensure that a cylinder thermostat is fitted

Boiler efficiency is discussed in the next section. If you are considering replacing the cylinder, note that a dual-coil cylinder will allow a renewable source of energy such as solar to be added in the future at substantially reduced cost (see the sections on 'Wood-pellet heating' and 'Solar water heating'). Building Regulations require that replacement hot water storage vessels meet the same requirements as in new buildings and have an adequate control system in place.

COMBINATION BOILERS

Combination boilers combine the functions of a central-heating boiler and an instantaneous multi-point water heater. Priority is given to the supply of domestic hot water, so heating will not operate while a hot tap is open.

As there is no wastage of heat from stored water, combination boilers were originally more cost-effective than conventional boilers. However, advances in insulation and boiler technology have narrowed the gap. Hot water cylinders may also enable the connection of renewable heat sources such as solar water heaters, woodburners or heat pumps, whereas it is difficult or impossible to do this with a combination boiler.

SINGLE-POINT WATER HEATERS

Single-point gas heaters provide hot water on demand. They operate by sensing the arrival of cold water in the internal reservoir when a tap is opened. This triggers the ignition of the burners which heat the water. The hot water rises to the top and is available almost immediately. Generally they are sited near to the point of use, so the 'dead leg' is very short.

Single-point gas heaters are becoming increasingly more rare as they have largely been replaced by gas combination boilers which can serve more water outlets and can also provide central heating. Single-point electric heaters are more common – an electric shower is a good example. As with any electric device that requires rapid heating (for example a toaster or a kettle) the demand for power is high and these are the energy guzzlers of the water heating world.

THERMAL STORE SYSTEM

A recent British development, the thermal store system uses the principle of indirect water heating in reverse. The water heated by the boiler is stored in a highly insulated cylinder – the thermal store – from where it is taken to the central heating radiators. Mains water is fed through the cylinder via a heat exchanger (coil) and on to the hot water outlets.

Thermal store capacities range from 170–500 litres and systems can deliver flow rates of between 18–30L/min. Thermal store systems are ideal for the future connection of alternative heat sources – woodburners, heat pumps and solar – which are discussed later in this chapter.

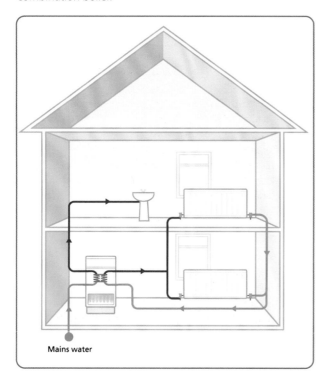

Mains water

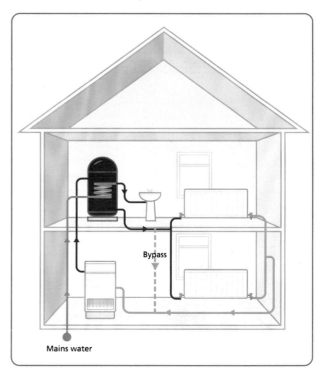

Bypass

Mains water

Boiler efficiency

BOILER SIZING

It is important to size the boiler correctly for each particular house, taking into account any improvements that have been made in the insulation of the property. If the boiler is oversized, it will run less efficiently, resulting in higher heating bills and higher CO_2 emissions.

For further information see: 'Whole House Boiler Sizing Method for Houses and Flats' – Energy Saving Trust CE54 (download).

BOILER EFFICIENCY

To look up how efficient your existing gas or oil boiler is, visit the SEDBUK (Seasonal Efficiency of Domestic Boilers in the UK) website (**www.sedbuk.com**). The SEDBUK rating represents the average annual efficiency achieved in typical domestic conditions and the website lists most current and obsolete boilers.

With rare exceptions, newly installed gas boilers are now required to be condensing boilers, which means that they achieve efficiencies of around 90%. Condensing boilers are so named because they recover and use some of the heat present in the hot flue gases. At this point water vapour in the combustion gases will condense and then be drained away. (This water is very slightly acidic.)

For further information see: 'Domestic Condensing Boilers – the benefits and the myths' – Energy Saving Trust GIL74 (download).

Central heating systems as a whole run less efficiently if they are not maintained – that is, if sludge builds up from lime-scale and/or corrosion deposits. The system can be flushed out with chemical additives to break up this sludge, but treating the water with inhibitors will help to prevent this problem from occurring in the first place.

TYPICAL ANNUAL FUEL COSTS

The table below shows the effect of variation in boiler efficiency on annual running costs for typical domestic properties in the UK with central heating and a gas boiler. Although the costs in the table are typical for the type of property, there will be wide variations in individual cases due to climate, exposure, occupancy patterns, heating controls, insulation and other factors.

Annual fuel costs

	Boiler			
	Old (heavyweight)	**Old** (lightweight)	**New** (non-condensing)	**New** (condensing)
Seasonal efficiency	55%	65%	78%	88%
Flat	£267	£231	£197	£178
Bungalow	£341	£293	£249	£224
Terrace	£354	£304	£258	£232
Semi-detached	£397	£340	£289	£259
Detached	£550	£470	£396	£355

Source: SEDBUK

SYSTEM REPLACEMENT

When a complete heating system is being replaced, significant efficiency improvements may be achieved. It is also an opportunity to reassess the choice of primary fuel used for heating. The standards to which any new system should conform in order to meet Building Regulations are set out in 'CHeSS, Basic and Best Practice Specifications for the components of domestic wet central-heating systems that are critical to energy efficiency'.

For further information see: 'Central Heating System Specifications' (CHeSS) – Energy Saving Trust GIL 59 (download); 'Domestic heating by oil: boiler systems' – Energy Saving Trust CE29 (download); and 'Domestic heating by gas: boiler systems' – Energy Saving Trust CE30 (download).

RANGE COOKERS

Range cookers (such as Rayburns) are designed primarily for cooking but many can also provide hot water and some provide central heating. They can be fuelled by oil, gas or coal (a few stoves can use wood). Although they may be a useful source of heat in winter they are an inefficient and expensive means of cooking in summer, when there is no demand for heat. A secondary cooker is therefore needed and in many instances there is also a secondary heating system.

Woodburning stoves

WOOD AS FUEL

Wood is considered a carbon-neutral fuel as the CO_2 emitted from burning wood is the same as (or slightly less than) the CO_2 which is absorbed as the tree grows. Even allowing for emissions of fossil carbon dioxide in planting, harvesting, processing and transporting the fuel, replacing fossil fuel with wood fuel will typically reduce net CO_2 emissions by over 90%. Wood produces negligible amounts of sulphur dioxide or nitrous oxides, unlike fossil fuels, so burning wood does not contribute significantly towards the problem of acid rain.

Logs must be dry and well seasoned, so if you are planning to install a woodburner you must make provision for storage of the fuel – a well-ventilated dry space is ideal, as it is the air which does the work in drying timber. Depending on the time of year when it is cut and the species of timber, it can take up to three years to season wood before it is ready for burning. Burning wet or unseasoned wood is not only less efficient but can also cause harmful deposits to build up in the chimney. When wood is fully dry, the bark should come off easily and splits should be visible in the end-grain. Another tip is to bang the ends of two logs together: unseasoned wood gives out a dull thud whereas good, dry, seasoned wood rings like a bell.

Wood varies by species in terms of its calorific (heat) value. Hardwoods are denser than softwoods so they will burn for longer and give off more heat, but it is important to ensure that the wood is split to no more than 4in (100mm) diameter in order to burn efficiently.

In order to remain carbon-neutral as a fuel, it is important that the wood is grown close to where it is used and that the local distribution system is efficient. Timber which is harvested for fuel must also be replaced in order that the CO_2 emitted during combustion is re-absorbed by new trees as they grow.

Waste wood often ends up in landfill, so burning waste wood for heating is a good use of a sometimes free resource, although painted or treated timber should not be burned, as this would release a number of toxic chemicals. Pallets have often been treated so burning these should also be avoided, although treated pallets can be reused for many other purposes.

STOVES

A woodburning stove is much more efficient than an open fire – *ie* it produces more heat than an open fire from a given amount of fuel, primarily because an open fire loses a great deal of its heat straight up the chimney, especially if it consists simply of a dog grate in an inglenook. Woodburning stoves are not to be confused with cooking stoves.

Many woodburners have built-in secondary and

Photo: Stovax Ltd

Photo: Stovax Ltd

WOOD COMPARISON CHART

Wood (fully air dried)	Weight (per m³ in kg)	Gross heat value kW/kg (Btu/lb)	% Moisture when green	Seasoning time in summers
Ash	674	4.1 (6,350)	35	1
Beech	690	4.3 (6,700)	45	1–2
Birch	662	4.1 (6,350)	45	1
Elm	540	4.6 (5,600)	60	2–3
Oak	770	4.5 (7,000)	50	2–3
Poplar	465	2.6 (4,100)	65	1
Pine/Fir	410	2.6 (4,100)	60	1

Source: Solid Fuel Association

tertiary burn systems which ensure that very little smoke is produced (smoke contains particles of unburned fuel). Clean-burn systems have the added advantage that they produce very little tar. The build-up of tar deposits is a common cause of problems with chimneys.

INSTALLATION AND MAINTENANCE

Any installation of a heating appliance, or modification to a chimney, such as relining, has to be carried out in accordance with Building Regulations (Part J in England and Wales and Section 3 in Scotland). In England and Wales there is also a requirement that Building Control consent is obtained for such work unless the work is carried out by a Competent Person. For solid fuel and woodburning appliances a Competent Person is defined as someone who is registered with HETAS. Where there is a radiator from a fossil fuel boiler in the same room as the woodburner, it should be fitted with a TRV. Any solid fuel appliance requires an adequate supply of air. The requirements for ventilation are set out in Approved Document J of the Building Regulations (Technical Handbook in Scotland).

When burning wood, it is important to have the chimney swept regularly: twice a year is the current recommendation. Failure to sweep regularly can lead to build-ups of material within the chimney which may later ignite and cause chimney fires, leading to structural damage and the production of toxic fumes. Slow burning (or banking up to keep the fire 'in' overnight) can also lead to the build-up of harmful deposits.

For further information see: British Flue and Chimney Manufacturers Association, **www.feta.co.uk/bfcma***; The National Association of Chimney Engineers,* **www.nace.org.uk***; The National Association of Chimney Sweeps,* **www.chimneyworks.co.uk***; The Guild of Master Sweeps,* **www.guild-of-master-sweeps.co.uk***; The Solid Fuel Association,* **www.solidfuel.co.uk***; and HETAS (Heating Equipment Testing and Approval Scheme),* **www.hetas.co.uk***.*

Wood actually produces very little ash – less than 1% is common. This is high in potash and therefore a useful garden fertiliser; the ash can be mixed with other composted material in order to disperse it evenly.

SMOKE CONTROL AREAS

Many parts of the UK are designated as Smoke Control Areas, which means that emissions of smoke from domestic properties are banned.

If you do live in a smoke controlled area, this need not prevent you from using a woodburning stove. Some stoves burn wood so efficiently that they are designated as 'Exempt Appliances'.

To find out whether you live in a smoke controlled area and for a full list of 'Exempted Appliances' (by region), visit **www.uksmokecontrolareas.co.uk**

CONNECTING TO WATER-HEATING SYSTEMS

Woodburners may include an integral back boiler which is used to provide hot water. As with indirect fossil fuel boiler systems, the back boiler on a woodburner is generally linked to a coil in the cylinder. A pump is normally used to circulate the water, although 'gravity' (hot water rising) may be sufficient to induce movement around the loop. For advice on pumps visit the British Pump Manufacturing Association website at **www.bpma.org.uk**

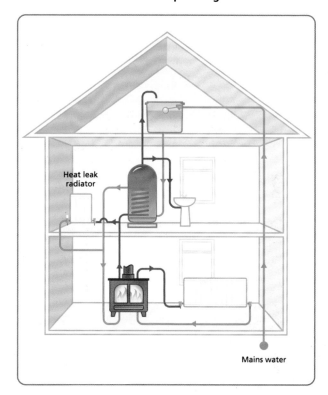

Radiators can also be connected to woodburners which have back boilers, though this may require the addition of an accumulator. An accumulator simply stores the heat produced by a wood-fuelled boiler and delivers it to the radiator system in a controlled manner. The introduction of an accumulator into the system means that the woodburner may only need to be fired up twice a day, eliminating the need to feed it constantly. Where no accumulator is fitted there is the danger that excessive heat will build up in the back boiler, so at least one radiator (known as a 'heat leak') connected to the back boiler must be left without a TRV to ensure that the heat is dissipated when the burner is operating while the rest of the radiator system is switched off.

If a stove used primarily for space heating also provides the hot water, in warm weather it would be an inefficient use of fuel to fire the stove simply to heat water, so it may be useful to have a backup water-heating system.

It is also possible to combine woodburning stoves with fossil fuel boilers and solar water heaters to create a highly efficient multi-fuel system which takes best advantage of

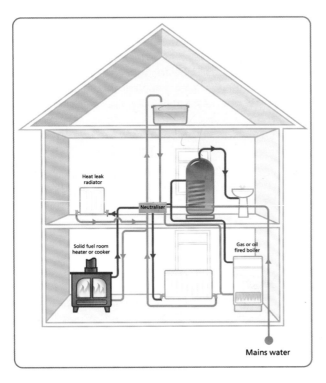

Photo: Rural Energy

the natural and renewable sources of heat and minimises fossil fuel use. This will mean the addition of a neutraliser and a considerable amount of additional plumbing and control equipment will be needed. A neutraliser prevents a pumped circuit from a fossil fuel boiler setting up an induced circuit through an alternative heat source (such as a solid fuel boiler) when it is not in operation.

This is a specialist area, and if you are making alterations to an existing heating system the services of a heating engineer will be required. It is impossible to make general recommendations as even standardised systems may have been altered.

For further information see: 'Domestic heating: solid fuel systems' – Energy Saving Trust CE47 (download); The National Energy Foundation, **www.nef.org.uk***; and The Solid Fuel Association,* **www.solidfuel.co.uk***.*

Wood pellet heating

PELLETS

Wood pellets are manufactured from waste wood products such as ground wood chips, sawdust and bark, all of which are created by the wood processing industry. No chemical additives are needed as the natural lignin in the wood serves as a binder when the pellets are compressed. They have a low moisture content and a relatively high energy content for their volume. Typically they are about 20mm long and 8mm wide.

As pellets have a higher energy density, they require fewer deliveries and less space to store than wood in its natural state. Effectively, they can be made to flow like a liquid, so the consistency of their size and moisture content mean that automatic feed systems can deliver controlled heating on demand.

PELLET STOVES

Stoves have been designed specifically to burn wood pellets. They can be fed from a hopper that will hold enough fuel for up to three days and the ash pan only needs to be emptied monthly or even less often, depending on usage. Many people consider them to be more convenient than a conventional woodburning stove.

Photo: Rural Energy

While pellet stoves look similar to modern woodburners, they use built-in microprocessors to achieve efficiency and a clean burn. Thermostatic controls and fans distribute warm air around the room where they are situated, whereas conventional woodburners rely on radiated heat, resulting in uneven temperatures.

PELLET BOILERS

Pellet boilers have mostly been used to heat larger systems such as those to be found in schools and factories. Recently,

Firefox pellet boiler.

however, domestic-scale boilers have been successfully developed which are an excellent substitute for fossil fuel boilers, although they are still significantly more expensive. The small size of pellets means that the boiler response time is fast and the heat output is easily controlled. It also allows them to be fed into a boiler automatically. As with pellet stoves, microprocessor technology controls the air and fuel intake rates to achieve efficiencies up to 90%. Several makes of pellet boilers from Europe and North America are available and a few models are now manufactured in the UK.

Heating with pellet boilers is almost as convenient as using oil. A simple push-button ignition starts the boiler and no supervision of the equipment is required, although the pellet burner will need cleaning about once a month. The ash must be removed at the same time although, like stoves, the quantity is small as the pellets burn very thoroughly. As with oil or LPG, storage space is required for the pellets. Depending on demand and the size of the storage facility, delivery might be required approximately once a month.

Wood chips (as opposed to wood pellets) are only used for larger installations which fuel district-heating systems for a groups of houses or for commercial property.

PELLET SUPPLY

The decision to use a pellet boiler must in part be based upon the security of supply of the pellets. To find a supplier in your area call 01908 665555.

For further information on all kinds of wood heating visit
www.nef.org.uk/logpile

GRANTS

In England and Wales, under the Low Carbon Buildings Programme, the grant available for pellet stove installation is a maximum of £600, regardless of the size of the installation and subject to an overall 20% limit of the cost of the stove, exclusive of VAT (to be reviewed April 2009). For wood-fuelled boiler systems the grant is a maximum of £1,500 regardless of size, subject to an overall 30% limit, exclusive of VAT.

In Northern Ireland grants may be obtained from Reconnect, administered by Action Renewables. The grant for a pellet stove is £1,500 regardless of size and subject to an overall 50% limit, inclusive of VAT (to be reviewed March 2008). The grant for a wood-fuelled boiler system is £3,250 regardless of size, subject to an overall 50% limit, inclusive of VAT.

In Scotland, under the Scottish Community and Householder Renewables Initiative (SCHRI) the grant is set at 30% of the installed cost of a renewable measure up to £4,000 (to be reviewed March 2008).

Solar water heating

Solar water heaters collect energy from the sun and use this to heat water. (People often refer to 'solar panels' when they mean photovoltaic panels, which generate electricity. These are discussed in Chapter 6.)

Solar collectors are commonly mounted on a south-facing slope of the roof but they can operate just as effectively on the face of a building or even on the ground as long as they have an unobstructed view of the sun during the warm parts of the day.

Even in the UK's temperate climate, solar water heaters work remarkably well, generating heat even on sunny winter days. On average, domestic systems will provide around 50% of the energy required to deliver hot water, allowing for heat losses from stored water. (This is known as the solar fraction.)

Much of the energy required to heat water is used to take it from cold to lukewarm temperature. A smaller additional amount of energy is then required to raise the temperature to that which is comfortable for a bath or a shower. On hot or even warm days, solar panels can collect sufficient energy to heat water from cold to normal bath/shower temperature, while on duller days they can still do most of the work by heating the water to a lukewarm temperature. Solar water heaters are therefore normally used in conjunction with another heat source, such as a woodburner or a fossil fuel boiler, which can bring the warm water up to the required temperature using very little additional energy.

In the system illustrated below, both heat sources work indirectly via heat exchangers in the cylinder. The lower coil is connected to the solar water heater on the roof or face of the building and the upper coil is connected to the boiler. Water is circulated through the boiler circuit coil via the normal pump, and liquid is circulated through the solar panel by a second pump which is switched on automatically by a controller. The controller works by means of sensors which measure the temperature in the cylinder and in the panel. The controller switches on the solar circuit pump when the water in the solar collector is warmer than the cylinder.

As with conventional indirect water heating systems, the water which goes to the taps is heated as it passes through the cylinder. The boiler loop and the solar loop are independent and sealed. In the case of the solar loop, antifreeze is normally added as the panels are exposed in all temperatures although some systems automatically drain back the water from the solar collector to avoid frost damage and to prevent summer overheating. It is also possible to power the pump which runs the solar loop by means of a photovoltaic panel, making the whole system carbon-neutral in operation. Although it is not as sophisticated as other systems, there is added advantage that the collector loop can only circulate when there is sufficient sunshine and can reduce the need for control equipment.

Photo: Imagination Solar

TYPES OF COLLECTOR

There are two main types of solar collector – flat plate and evacuated tube. Evacuated tubes are slightly more efficient than flat plate collectors, so smaller panels can be used for the same heat output if space is at a premium. Evacuated tube systems tend to be more expensive than flat plate collectors as the technology is more complex. For a three-person household, a solar water heater with an area of 2–4m^2 should be sufficient.

Diagram labels:
Automatic air vent
Solar loop
Twin coil cylinder
Boiler loop
Pump
Mains water

Photo: www.aranservices.co.uk

Flat plate collector.

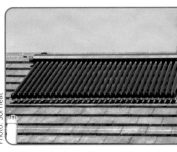

Photo: Sol Heat

Evacuated tube collector.

ORIENTATION

South-facing roofs are ideal but solar collectors can work efficiently up to 45° either side of due south.

PLANNING PERMISSION

Planning permission is not normally required for solar water heaters, although there may be restrictions in Conservation Areas or in other architecturally sensitive locations. Some flat plate collectors look very similar to a conservation roof light, so they will not necessarily look obvious when mounted on an old building. Listed buildings are special cases and consent would be required for any visible alterations.

SPACE AND SYSTEM REQUIREMENTS

Where there is a hot water storage cylinder and water is presently heated indirectly (see 'water heating systems' earlier in this chapter) it is simpler, less disruptive and less costly to install a solar water heating system.

For many types of installation, single-coil cylinders will need to be replaced but the existing pipework to the boiler can be re-used. It is important to note that the coils within the cylinder must be sized correctly for the boiler and panels to be attached to them, so make sure that this is discussed with your solar panel/cylinder supplier and heating engineer.

Combination boilers heat mains-pressure cold water directly, which makes it difficult or in some cases impossible to combine them with a solar water heating system. If a solar water heater is used to pre-heat water before it passes through a combi, the boiler would need to be fully modulating – that is to say, it would need to sense the temperature of the incoming water and adjust the burn rate accordingly, otherwise the boiler would overheat with potentially serious consequences. If a heat store is introduced into the system it is possible that some combi boilers can be converted and retained. All systems vary, so it is essential to consult an experienced heating engineer who is familiar with solar water heating and thermal storage.

GRANTS

In England and Wales, under the Low Carbon Buildings Programme, the grant available for a solar thermal hot water installation is £400, regardless of size, subject to an overall 30% limit, exclusive of VAT (to be reviewed April 2009). DIY installations are not eligible and grants may only be claimed for accredited products or systems. VAT is set at 5% for accredited professional installations and 17.5% for DIY products. For details of accredited products see the Low Carbon Buildings Programme website at **www.lowcarbonbuildings.org.uk/home**

In Scotland, under the Scottish Community and Householder Renewables Initiative (SCHRI), the grant is set at 30% of the installed cost of a renewable measure up to £4,000 (to be reviewed March 2008).

In Northern Ireland grants may be obtained from Reconnect, administered by Action Renewables. The grant is £1,125 regardless of size subject to an overall 50% limit, including VAT (to be reviewed March 2008).

PAYBACK PERIOD

The payback period is the amount of time it takes for the cost of the installation to be repaid through savings in fuel bills. This payback period has been worked out purely as an example and you will need to insert up-to-date figures in order to work out the actual payback period.

If interest rates and fossil fuel price escalation are unequal over the long term this significantly affects the calculation. If fuel prices rise more quickly than the absolute level of long-term interest rates, the payback period for solar water heating

	Example	Actual
Discount rate p.a.	5%	
Fossil fuel	Gas	
Fuel price escalation p.a.	5%	
Installed cost incl. new cylinder	£2,500	
Grant	£400	
Net cost	£2,100	
Gas price*	2.5p/kWh	
Annual water heating cost (based on *)	£100	
Solar fraction	50%	
Annual fuel saving: 50% x £100 =	£50	
Full payback period: 2,100 ÷ 50 =	42 years	

will be shorter. If the primary heating fuel is not gas, the payback period will again be shorter. The financial payback period may not be the only consideration in deciding upon a solar water heating system. Solar water heating also reduces CO_2 emissions and fossil fuel consumption.

The payback period can be dramatically reduced if you build and install your own solar water heater. For further information see: *Solar Water Heating: A DIY guide* - Paul Trimby, published by the Centre for Alternative Technology.

SOLAR WATER HEATERS AND UNDERFLOOR HEATING

It is also possible to provide an element of space heating by linking up solar water heaters to underfloor heating systems. Underfloor heating runs at a lower temperature than radiator-based systems so it is well-suited to the lower temperatures obtainable from solar water heaters at times when there is a demand for space-heating. However, another energy source will still be required. If you already have underfloor heating (or are thinking of installing such a system), a specialist contractor would be needed in order to link it up to a solar water heater.

Heat pumps

GROUND-SOURCE HEAT PUMPS

Ground-source heat pumps take low-grade energy from the ground and convert it into usable energy at a higher temperature for space and water heating. They work on the same principle as a refrigerator but operating in reverse. The ground is heated to a temperature of approximately 12°C by the sun, so ground-source heat pumps are actually making use of solar energy.

Open-loop systems take groundwater and pump it to the surface, extract the useful heat energy and return the water to the ground. These systems tend to be used on large commercial applications where the initial exploratory costs, environmental concessions and long-term maintenance issues can be justified.

In a closed-loop system the heat exchanger in the ground consists of a sealed loop of polyethylene pipe which is buried approximately 1.5m deep in horizontal trenches or vertically in a borehole. Typically, boreholes are between 50 and 90m deep.

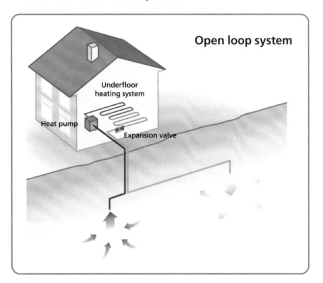

Photo: EarthEnergy Ltd

Heat pumps

The great majority of heat pumps work on the principle of the vapour compression cycle. The main components in such a system are the compressor, the expansion valve, and two heat exchangers referred to as the evaporator and the condenser. The components are connected to form a closed circuit, through which a volatile liquid, known as the working fluid or refrigerant, is driven by the pump.

When the fluid is forced through the compressor it increases in temperature. This heat is then given off by the heating circuit (the 'condenser') as it travels around the house. When the fluid passes through the expansion valve, the

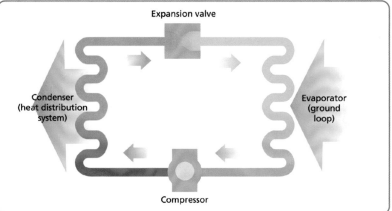

rapid drop in pressure results in a cooling of the fluid. The fluid then absorbs heat from the ground collection loop (the 'evaporator') before being re-compressed.

Heat pumps require energy to run the pump. The ratio of the kW of heat energy produced by the system to the kW of electrical energy needed to power the pump is known as the coefficient of performance (CoP). Most systems have a CoP of between 2.5 and 4, which means that up to four times the amount of energy is produced than it takes to run the system. In other words, for 1 unit of electrical energy input, you might get 3 units of heat energy output. The cost of the electrical energy required means that ground-source heat pumps can be slightly more expensive than natural gas but still a cheaper form of

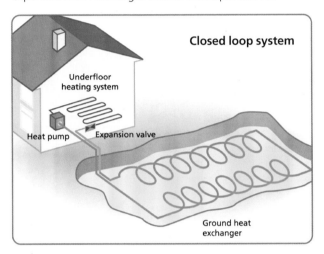

Closed loop system

Underfloor heating system

Heat pump

Expansion valve

Ground heat exchanger

heating in operation than oil, LPG, solid fuel or electricity. If there is a consistent and reliable source of renewable electrical energy available then the system could be completely carbon-neutral in operation but, in practice, electricity from the grid will normally be required.

Ground-source heat pumps are normally only appropriate for new buildings because they require either a substantial area of ground (approximately 10m of trench per 1kW of heat energy produced) or the drilling of a deep hole. The sizing of the ground loop will be determined by the following variable factors:

■ Annual heat demand for the building, including hot water if required
■ Mean ground temperature at the location
■ Local ground conditions/geology
■ The selected heat pump

The cost of installation is relatively high, particularly where a vertical ground loop is necessary but, for detached houses with no mains gas supply, ground-source heat pumps can be an economically viable option. As they contain very few moving parts they may be expected to last for many years and require only minimal maintenance.

Ground source heat pumps work best when combined with an underfloor heating system, as they start off by capturing low-grade heat. Since underfloor heating runs at a lower water temperature than conventional radiator

systems, less energy is required via the pump to concentrate the heat to a useful level.

In the summer the ground temperature is lower than the required internal temperature. Some systems can be reversed to supply cooling and air conditioning by taking heat out of the building and depositing it into the ground via the ground loop. If the climate in the UK continues to become warmer, ground-source heat pumps will become increasingly efficient in comparison to conventional fossil-fuelled systems.

AIR-SOURCE HEAT PUMPS

Air-source heat pumps work on the same principle as ground-source heat pumps, taking low-grade energy and converting it to useful energy by means of the vapour compression cycle. Compared with ground-source heat pumps they have the advantage of being cheaper to install, but the disadvantage that in cold weather the air will be at a much lower temperature when heat is needed most. The pump thus has to work harder to supply the heat required, so the efficiency of the system drops

rapidly. However, if an air source heat pump is combined with another source of heating, the system can be programmed so that the air-source heat pump only works when it is efficient and the overall efficiency of the heating system will have been improved.

There are currently no grants available in England and Wales for the installation of air-source heat pumps, but grants are available at present under the Scottish Community and Householder Renewables Initiative and, in Northern Ireland, from Reconnect, administered by Action Renewables.

WATER-SOURCE HEAT PUMPS

Water-source heat pumps harvest their low-grade energy from nearby bodies of water. The heat can be collected, as in ground-source systems, either by an open loop or a closed loop. Water abstraction for open-loop pumps which use rivers or other public bodies of water will require permission from the Environment Agency.

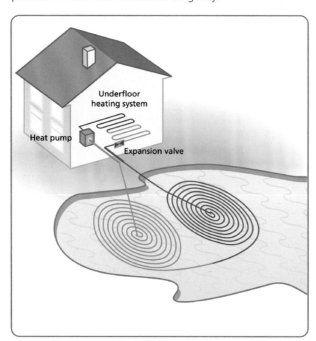

GRANTS

In England and Wales, under the Low Carbon Buildings Programme, grants of £1,200 are available for the installation of ground or water heat pumps, regardless of size, subject to an overall 30% limit, exclusive of VAT (to be reviewed April 2009).

In Scotland, under the Scottish Community and Householder Renewables Initiative (SCHRI), the grant is set at 30% of the installed cost up to £4,000, including ground works (to be reviewed March 2008).

In Northern Ireland, grants may be obtained from Reconnect, administered by Action Renewables. The grant is £3,000 regardless of size, subject to an overall 40% limit, inclusive of VAT (to be reviewed March 2008).

For detailed information on heat pumps see: The National Energy Foundation, **www.nef.org.uk/gshp**; *The Heat Pump Association,* **www.feta.co.uk**; *The UK Heat Pump Network,* **www.heatpumpnet.org.uk**; *'Heat pumps in the UK – a monitoring report' – Energy Saving Trust GIR72 (download); and 'Domestic ground source heat pumps: design and installation of closed-loop systems' (2004 edition) – Energy Saving Trust CE82/GPG339 (download).*

GEOTHERMAL ENERGY

Ground-source heat pumps should not be confused with geothermal heating. Geothermal heating is rare as it relies on heat generated from within the earth, rather than solar energy stored near the surface of the earth. The temperature of the earth rises approximately 2.5°C with every 100m of increasing depth. Where geological conditions lead to hot springs arising, this energy can be harnessed cheaply for heating and power systems, but normally it is necessary to drill very deep wells and pump in water under high pressure to take advantage of this resource. Rare examples in the UK include Southampton city centre and the Roman baths at Bath.

Passive solar design

Newly-built houses can be designed to admit and collect the heat of the sun during the day and radiate it back into the living environment during the evening and night. Glass is a particularly useful material for generating solar gain, as it allows short-wave infrared frequencies through, but not the low-frequency heat waves which are radiated back out from the building fabric.[3]

The house pictured below and illustrated on the next page require very little space-heating as the large glazed southern facade allows the energy of the sun to flow directly into the building. Heat received in this way is known as 'solar gain'. The internal walls are built of dense

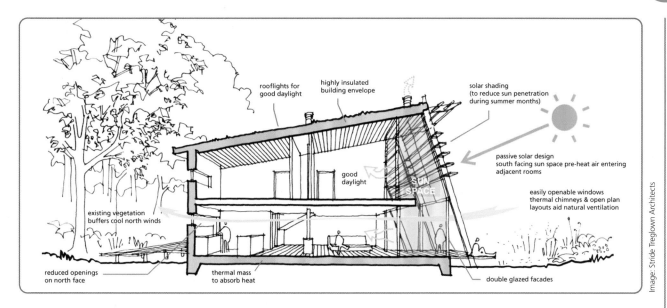

Image: Stride Treglown Architects

Labels on diagram:

rooflights for good daylight

highly insulated building envelope

solar shading (to reduce sun penetration during summer months)

passive solar design south facing sun space pre-heat air entering adjacent rooms

good daylight

SUN SPACE

easily openable windows thermal chimneys & open plan layouts aid natural ventilation

existing vegetation buffers cool north winds

reduced openings on north face

thermal mass to absorb heat

double glazed facades

masonry in order to absorb the heat – a technique known as 'thermal mass' construction.

Where a complete renovation is planned, locating the rooms to be lived in on the warmer (southern) side of the house will reduce heat demand by taking best advantage of solar gain. Cooler rooms such as kitchens are best located on the northern side of the house. Reducing glazing on the northern side or improving the insulation of the glazing will reduce heat loss. By contrast, increasing glazed areas on the southern side will increase heat gain. However, this also accelerates the rate of heat loss, as walls are better thermal insulators than glass, so a balance must be struck depending on the building's heat (and light) demand and its orientation. An absence of thermal mass can lead to problems of overheating in buildings designed for solar gain so it is essential to include plenty of heavyweight fabric within the insulated shell in order to soak up the available heat during the day.

Existing housing, however, can do nothing to alter its

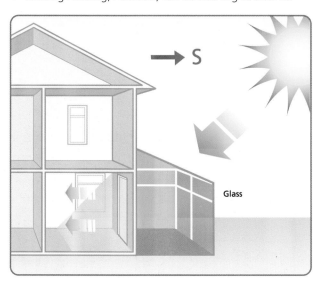

Glass

aspect and little to alter the size and shape of the windows. Where houses overlook each other, people also tend to use net curtains for privacy, which further reduces the solar gain. Passive solar heat gain can be increased without making alterations to the windows by adding a conservatory or other heavily-glazed structure on the southern side of the property.

The internal wall then becomes a heat store which can radiate the heat back out after the sun has set. The extra room can also act as a heat store and as a buffer between the internal and external space, in effect providing additional insulation. A

considerable amount of heat can be collected in a conservatory even on a winter day if the sun shines.

Conservatories cost nothing to heat but can reduce heating bills. This is negated, of course, if a radiator is situated in a conservatory, although modern building regulations require any heat source in a conservatory to be independently controlled.

For further information see: 'Passive Solar House Designs' – Energy Saving Trust GIL25 (download).

REFERENCES
[1] Association of Electricity Producers.
[2] National Energy Foundation website.
[3] *The Good House Book* by Clarke Snell, Lark Books (2004).

5 ELECTRICITY DEMAND

Terms and measurements

It is useful to understand the basic units and terminology of domestic electricity in order to put into context the various savings that can be achieved. This is also helpful when considering the installation of any kind of electricity-generating equipment.

At the domestic level, the *rate* of electricity consumed is measured in watts or kilowatts (thousands of watts). A 60W light bulb uses 60W per hour; a single-bar electric fire uses 1,000W (1kW) per hour.

The *amount* of electricity used is the rate multiplied by the time. The amount of electricity used by a single-bar fire switched on for an hour is therefore 1kW x one hour, or one kilowatt-hour (1kWh). The amount of electricity used over days, months or years is based on this measure and is always quoted in kWh.

AVERAGE UK DOMESTIC ELECTRICITY CONSUMPTION FIGURES IN KWH (where heating and hot water are not fuelled by electricity)

Type of property/occupation	Quarterly	Yearly
1-bedroom flat, single person	730	2,920
2-bedroom house, two people	1,003	4,012
3-bedroom house, family of four	1,277	5,108

Note that these are only average figures and actual consumption will vary widely depending upon lifestyle and the efficiency of electrical goods in the house.

To get a better idea of your own electricity consumption, take a look at some recent electricity bills. Bills that correct an underestimation or overestimation on previous bills will not give an accurate picture and ideally the bills should cover a period of a year as consumption will probably be higher during the winter months. Normally 1 unit equals 1 kWh.

Electricity

Tariff C - Customer reading E - Estimated reading No code - Company reading	Units	Price of each unit in pence	Amount £ p	
Domestic Standard				
-Standard energy	919	9.21	84.64	–
Monthly Direct Debit Discount			5.07 CR	
Service charge at 10.060p for 87 day(s)			8.75	–
VAT at 5.00% on charges of £88.32			4.41	
Total this invoice			**92.73**	
Balance from previous bill			13.18	
Payment received 28 September 2006			39.00 CR	
Payment received 28 October 2006			39.00 CR	
Payment received 28 November 2006			39.00 CR	–
Credit budget account balance carried forward			**11.09 CR**	

For dwellings where neither cooling nor space-heating is supplied by electricity, the breakdown of consumption is as follows:

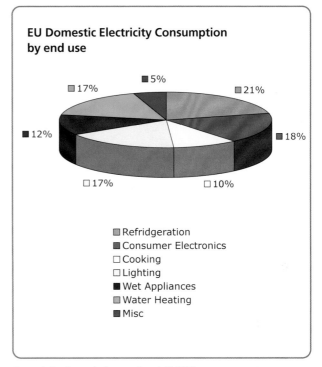

EU Domestic Electricity Consumption by end use

- ■ 5%
- ■ 17%
- ■ 21%
- ■ 12%
- ■ 18%
- □ 17%
- □ 10%

- ■ Refridgeration
- ■ Consumer Electronics
- □ Cooking
- □ Lighting
- ■ Wet Appliances
- ■ Water Heating
- ■ Misc

Source: Carbon Futures for European Households/DETR

It is clear that appliances are responsible for a significant proportion of electricity consumption and this has been growing in recent years as the number of appliances in the average home has been increasing rapidly.

Appliances

Electricity is one the most expensive domestic fuels and (at the power plant) it generates a high level of CO_2 emissions, so it is worthwhile taking a few simple steps to reduce consumption. Much can be done to reduce costs and consumption by changing the way we use our homes and our electrical equipment and need not require any significant expenditure.

STAND-BY

Many appliances such as televisions and DVD machines are operated by remote control and switched off by remote as well. This leaves the appliance on 'stand-by', ready for the next time the remote button is pressed. Leaving appliances on stand-by uses a surprising amount of energy – a television consumes 7% of the energy on standby that it consumes when in use and a video recorder uses 85% of its total energy requirements while on stand-by.[1] In general, although the amount of energy consumed on stand-by is small, the cumulative effect is significant.

Appliance category	Standby time (Hours/day)	UK energy consumption (GWh)
Microwaves	23.8	451
Electric ovens	24.0	225
Gas ovens*	24.0	145
Domestic laptops, desktop PCs & servers	4.6	134
TVs	19.9	2,099
Video recorders	22.7	1,591
External power supplies (eg transformers)	23.0	2,354
Broadband	17.5	268
Mobile phone chargers	4	102
Gas boiler*	11.7	383
Clock radio	24	218

* Electricity standby consumption only

Source: Market Transformation Programme

Photo: Product Creation Ltd

The hassle of turning off several appliances can be reduced by using a multiple-gang extension lead and switching off the extension lead at the wall socket. Take care not to overload the extension lead but televisions and stereos do not demand a high current. Some extension leads incorporate switches, as it may be easier to reach the head of the extension lead than the wall socket. A few appliances reset the memory when switched off completely, although internal batteries are increasingly used to maintain the memory and settings.

For further information see: 'The Rise of the Machines' Market Transformation Programme/Energy Saving Trust.

OTHER ENERGY-SAVING TIPS
Washing machines can be run at 40° rather than 60° as most modern detergents work just as well at the lower temperature. It is also more efficient to wash full loads rather than part loads, even if the machine has a reduced load programme.

Fridges lose cold air when the door is open, replaced by warm air that then has to be cooled again, so keep the door open for the minimum amount of time. Allow leftover food to cool before placing it in the fridge. Defrost regularly (self-defrosting machines are energy-efficient in this respect).

Kettles consume large amounts of energy for short periods of time, so significant amounts of energy can be saved by using them efficiently. Build-up of lime-scale on the element slows down the rate of heat transfer from the element to the water. Only boil the water which is needed for immediate use, otherwise the energy used to heat the remaining water simply dissipates as the kettle cools. Some kettles have a gauge so that the amount of water to be boiled is clearly visible; in the most sophisticated versions, a simple push-button transfers water from an integral reservoir to the boiling chamber.

The tumble dryer is a good example of an energy-consuming device that it is possible to do without altogether in many circumstances. If a garden or other outside space is available, drying clothes outside saves energy and money. Where tumble dryers are not vented directly to the outside, they can be a significant source of unwanted moisture indoors, leading to condensation and encouraging mould growth. Even the most efficient dryers available still use up to 3kWh to dry a 6kg load.[2]

EU ENERGY RATINGS SYSTEM
The EU energy label rates products from A (the most efficient) down to G (the least efficient). Refrigeration equipment labelling also extends to A+ and A++ ratings, A++ being the most efficient appliance available. By law the label must be shown on all refrigeration and laundry appliances, dishwashers, electric ovens and light-bulb packaging.

For refrigeration appliances, the energy consumption is shown in kilowatt hours per year. For washing machines and dishwashers, the energy consumption is shown in kilowatt hours per cycle. To work out the expected annual running cost of a

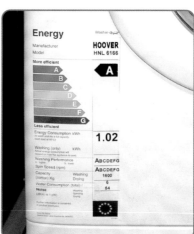

particular machine, simply multiply the kWh consumption figure by the average unit price of electricity. For example, an A+ fridge-freezer using 267 kWh per year would cost £26.70 per annum to run at 10p per kWh.

Washing machines and dishwashers also have ratings for washing, spinning and/or drying performance. The A–G indicators are similar to the main efficiency ratings and labels for some models also include information on noise levels – the lower the number, the less noise is emitted. Advanced machines which employ fuzzy logic can monitor conditions during the wash and adjust various inputs such as water intake, wash time, temperature settings, rinse performance and spin speed to deliver optimum cleaning performance while consuming the minimum amount of water and energy.

Replacing appliances purchased new in 1995 with equivalent new efficient models would save the following approximate amounts, based on a family of four and an electricity cost of 10p/kWh (2006 figures):

ENERGY SAVINGS FROM NEW APPLIANCES

Appliance	EU energy rating	Saving/year
Fridge freezer	A+	£45
Upright/chest freezer	A+	£35
Refrigerator	A+	£20
Washing machine	A	£10
Dishwasher	A	£20

Savings for A++ refrigeration appliances are, on average, £6 per year greater.(3)

'ENERGY SAVING RECOMMENDED' LOGO

The 'energy saving recommended' logo is a UK scheme managed by the Energy Saving Trust. It only endorses the most energy-efficient products available. The logo acts in conjunction with the EU label and means that the product is guaranteed to save energy, cost less and help to protect the environment.

THE EUROPEAN ECOLABEL

Some products are also awarded the Ecolabel. It may appear on the packaging, for example on the EU energy ratings label. This means that the product has been independently assessed to meet strict environmental criteria from production through to packaging, use and eventual disposal. The Ecolabel is a voluntary European scheme which has been in existence since 1992 and is used for a wide variety of products (paint, floor coverings, cleaning products and so forth) in addition to electrical appliances.

SAVAPLUG

Fridges and freezers are among the most expensive domestic appliances to run per annum. The motor which pumps the coolant around the system is switched on and off by the thermostat. The motor needs more power to start the coolant moving around the system than it uses to keep the coolant circulating.

In response to this the Department of Energy has helped to develop the Savaplug, a device that senses the reduced need for current and adjusts the power sent to the motor accordingly. Typically it can save 20% on the annual running cost of a fridge or freezer. The plug simply replaces the existing plug on the appliance. However, the Savaplug is incompatible with a range of appliances – for further information visit **www.savawatt.com**

POWER MONITORING

There are several devices now available which enable the consumer to monitor the energy use of appliances in order to work out their efficiency and even CO_2 emissions. The exercise of monitoring power use has been shown to make consumers more aware of their energy consumption and to make reductions accordingly.

Electrisave.

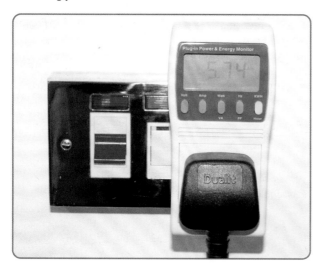

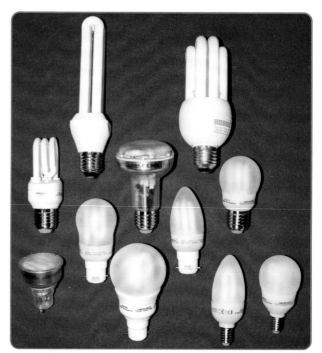

HEAT REPLACEMENT EFFECT

All electrical appliances and lights give off heat and this heat contributes toward the warming of a dwelling. As appliances become more efficient, this heat output is reduced. In summer the heat output from electrical appliances is unwanted, so more efficient products represent an absolute saving in energy and CO_2 emissions. In winter, however, there is a small but significant addition to the heating requirements in a house. This is known as the 'Heat Replacement Effect' and has been studied in some detail.

For further information see the briefing note 'BNXS29: The Heat Replacement Effect – thermal simulation of domestic lighting and appliances', published by the Market Transformation Programme (updated 2006).

Lighting

LOW-ENERGY LIGHTING

Conventional light bulbs generate more heat than light. Low-energy light bulbs are designed so that most of the energy produces light rather than heat, so they are a more efficient way of lighting your home, although the quality of

light which they produce is not to everyone's taste. An improved range of 'colour temperatures' is now available in some energy-saving lamp designs – the lower the colour temperature the 'warmer' the light.

Most compact fluorescent lamps (CFLs) take a second or two to light and can take up to a minute to attain their full brightness, so they may not be suitable for all locations – such as staircases, where immediate full illumination is required. They are best suited to areas where lights are left on for long periods – for example in living rooms or in hallways that need to be lit constantly. Outside security lighting which needs to be left on and is not sensor-controlled is a good candidate for low-energy bulbs. Typically, energy-saving bulbs use a quarter of the energy required by conventional bulbs.[4]

COMPARISON OF CONVENTIONAL AND ENERGY-SAVING BULBS

Ordinary bulb	Energy-saving equivalent
40W	7–10W
60W	15–18W
100W	20–25W
150W	32W

Note that low-energy bulbs may not be suitable for use with some sensors, timers and dimmers.

PAYBACK

Of all the improvements that can be made to domestic property, energy-saving bulbs have one of the fastest payback times:

	Example	Actual
Original bulb	60W	
Replacement bulb	15W CFL	
Cost of CFL	£4.00	
Hours per day	6	
Price per kWh	£0.10	
Cost of use of original bulb per day	60/1,000 x 6 x £0.10 = 3.6p	
Cost of use of CFL bulb per day	15/1,000 x 6 x £0.10 = 0.9p	
Saving per day	3.6p – 0.9p = 2.7p	
Payback period	400 ÷ 2.7 = 148 days	

Conventional bulbs generate heat as well as light so they contribute towards the heating of the house. Allowing for the loss of this 'useful heat' the payback period for switching to a compact fluorescent lamp on these assumptions is approximately seven months.

CFLs cost approximately ten times the amount of conventional bulbs but on average they last ten times longer. The net result is that over a sufficient period of time the cost of the bulbs themselves (rather than their energy use) is about equal at current prices.

Look for the 'Energy Efficiency Recommended' logo on the bulb packaging, as there are cheaper 'economy' bulbs around which may not last as long or save so much energy. Also check for the EU Energy label, which should be 'A' for all energy-saving bulbs. Alternatively, the Ecolabel has a wider set of criteria regarding manufacture, packaging and disposal rather than just energy use.

CFLs draw more current when starting up than in operation so in some cases, where there is more than one fluorescent lamp on the same switched circuit, cables and switch gear may need to be uprated. If in any doubt, consult a qualified electrician.

It should be pointed out, however, that CFLs contain at least 5mg of mercury, which is a toxic chemical and one of the main substances targeted by the RoHS 2006 legislation (see the section on 'Electronic equipment' in Chapter 9). This mercury is released into the domestic environment if the bulbs are broken and the number of lamps which can safely be disposed of via normal household waste is unclear.[5] The recycling of fluorescent lamps is only now (somewhat belatedly) being developed so it is possible that most of the mercury might eventually be recovered in this way.

See also the comments on 'Building Regulations' at the end of this section.

FITTINGS

When changing over light bulbs to more efficient versions (retrofitting), it is essential that lamps and lamp-holders (caps and bases) match up correctly.

Some types of lamp-holder can only accept low-energy bulbs, so people are then obliged to use low-energy lighting. However, most fittings in domestic property are of the 'bayonet cap' type and the most common energy-saving bulbs have been designed to suit this type of fitting. Energy-saving bulbs are now available to suit the smaller bayonet base and both sizes of screw fittings, although at present these are slightly harder to obtain.

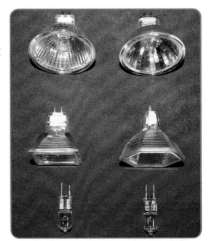

HALOGEN LAMPS

Halogen or dichroic lamps are popular as they give out an attractive light which is normally concentrated in a beam. They are available in either standard (240V) or low-voltage (usually 12V) versions and, while they give off slightly more light than conventional bulbs, they tend to be used in multiples so they do not necessarily deliver any saving to the householder or to the environment.

LEDS

Light-emitting diodes (LEDs) are relatively new to the domestic lighting market but many people believe them to be the future of lighting design. They are well known in the electronics industry and are used widely in panel indication applications. There are relatively few LED lights available for use in homes at present but the market is growing rapidly.

LEDs are available in a wide variety of colours including a range of different white 'temperatures'. Although the control gear can generate some heat, the lamps themselves produce very little (and have no fragile filament) so LEDs can be installed in certain locations where fitting other kinds of lights would be impossible.

Photos: Landing Light Company

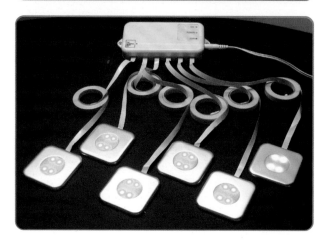

LEDs also last much longer than other types of light emitters – a typical high-power LED will be emitting 70% of its initial lumen output after 100,000 hours and it will be millions of hours to total electrical failure. As they produce a negligible amount of heat they are highly energy-efficient and comparable at present to the best CFLs.

LED version of Halogen GU 10.

COLD CATHODE BULBS

Like LEDs, cold cathode bulbs are only just being developed for the domestic market. They are currently used in torches, lightboxes and in electronic goods such as scanners and monitors. Essentially they are discharge lamps and are similar in many ways to fluorescent bulbs. In addition to consuming very little energy, they are known to have a long life in comparison to most energy-saving bulbs, so it is possible that cold cathode bulbs will become more widely available.

EXTERIOR LIGHTING

Security lights are sometimes used more for outdoor space lighting than for security. It is often possible to replace a 500W lamp in a security light with a 150W lamp and find that it does the required job just as efficiently. If not angled carefully, security lights can cause nuisance as they are bright and have a wide beam, even if they are only on for a short period of time. Reducing the wattage of bulbs in security lights will reduce this problem in addition to saving energy and, as less heat is generated, the luminaire units will also tend to last longer, since they can become brittle through extended use. Also see the comments on 'Building Regulations' at the end of this section.

Several garden light ranges are now available which use low-wattage halogen or LED bulbs. Solar-powered garden lights do not increase electricity consumption, although the cheaper models may not last, so some will turn out to be simply a waste of money and resources.

LOW-VOLTAGE LIGHTING

There is sometimes confusion over low-voltage lighting, as some people believe that low-voltage systems are automatically low energy consumers. This is not necessarily true, as it is the type of bulb which matters most, not the voltage at which it is operating. In general, low-voltage lamps (for example 12V or 24V) require more current (amps) to deliver the same wattage as the equivalent lamp running at 240V. Put simply, volts x amps = watts.

However, it is worth bearing in mind that battery systems powered by PV or wind are usually running at 12V, so it would be efficient to use 12V CFLs in conjunction with alternative power sources to avoid the need for a separate inverter. (See the next chapter for more information on low-voltage alternative energy sources)

Note that as low-voltage lighting draws more current on the load side of the transformer (if present), cables and switch gear need to be sized accordingly.

CONTROL SYSTEMS

We have become accustomed to good levels of lighting throughout our houses, but lights are often left on in places where we are not, illuminating unoccupied space and burning energy needlessly. This most commonly occurs in what is known as the 'communication areas' of dwellings – *ie* halls, stairs, landings and corridors. Lights

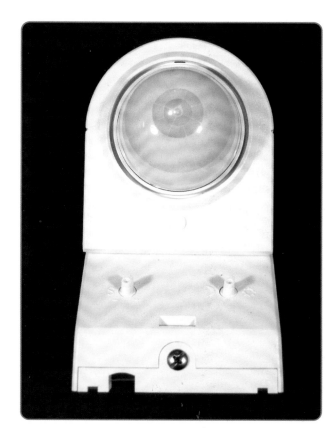

also tend to be left switched on in rooms which we visit briefly but regularly.

Most lights in homes are controlled by simple on/off switches. It can make sense to install sensors in halls or landings so that the lights switch on automatically when you enter the area and switch off automatically after a pre-set time. Most people are familiar with this technology as Passive Infra Red (PIR) switching is widely used for security lighting and burglar alarm systems. PIRs are activated by movement in their field of detection.

PIRs can be adjusted to suit three different variables – time overrun, sensitivity and light levels. Time overrun is simply the time that the light remains on once the switch has been activated by the PIR. Of course a pre-set timer may mean that the light stays on after you have left the area, consuming further energy, so people who habitually turn off the lights as they leave rooms, corridors or stairs would not benefit from installing PIRs.

Sensitivity controls allow the user to set the approximate size of signal which is required to trigger the switch. This avoids the light switching on whenever pets, for example, enter the detection field. It has been known for insects to trip PIRs in burglar alarm systems and cause considerable inconvenience!

Light levels vary throughout the day so once the PIR has detected movement in its field it must then 'decide' whether to switch on the light. If there is already sufficient daylight present it will detect this via a photocell and avoid switching on the light unnecessarily. It is possible to fit photocells to dim or turn off lights, depending on daylight levels, without the use of a PIR. Note that some PIRs are not suited to work with low-energy bulbs.

CABLE

Most cable sold in the UK is sheathed with a protective layer made from PVC. In the event of a fire, this emits toxic smoke containing hydrochloric acid, among other chemicals. An alternative product, low smoke and fume (LSF) cable, gives off greatly reduced amounts of smoke but still emits halogens, whereas low smoke zero halogen (LS0H) cable is the safest of all in a house fire. Of course, if the LSF cable is distributed through PVC trunking then the additional effort and expense has been wasted, as the PVC content of the trunking would probably exceed that of the cable.

BUILDING REGULATIONS

The Approved Document L1B which came into force in 2006 requires that whenever an existing lighting system is being replaced as part of rewiring works, 'reasonable provision' must be made for occupiers to obtain the benefits of efficient lighting. This is defined as the provision of at least one energy efficient light-fitting per 25m^2 of floor area or one per four fixed light fittings, whichever is the greater. This requirement also covers extensions or changes of use.

Furthermore, whenever fixed external lighting is newly fitted, the lamp capacity may not exceed 150W and must switch off automatically when there is sufficient daylight, or the fittings must have sockets which are only capable of receiving a low-energy lamp. For both internal and external lighting, a low energy lamp is defined as having an efficacy greater than 40W/lumen.

For further information see: 'Cost Benefit of Lighting' – Energy Saving Trust CE56 (download); 'Low energy domestic lighting' – Energy Saving Trust GIL20 (download); and 'Low energy domestic lighting – looking good for less': case studies – Energy Saving Trust CE81 (download).

Daylighting

Homes which have plenty of natural daylight are generally regarded as being healthier and easier to live in. As with so many aspects of eco-renovation, when faced with dimly-lit rooms overshadowed by other buildings or suffering from absurdly small windows, the homeowner is entitled to say with hindsight 'I wouldn't have built it this way'. However, there are some steps that can be taken to improve daylighting in existing buildings and reduce the demand for artificial light.

WINDOW CLEANING

Dirty windows can reduce the amount of light entering a room by up to 20%. Dirt on the windowpanes also affects the quality of the light.

CURTAINS AND BLINDS

When fixing curtain track, allow for an area either side of the window so that the curtains can be drawn back without covering any part of the glazed area itself.

Blinds vary in size and fixing design but often they are fixed within reveals rather than above them. If fitted above the reveal they can be rolled or pulled up without obstructing the window.

Above: Blind above window reveal.
Below: Blind within window reveal.

Many old buildings have splayed window reveals to admit more light. Some eco-builders have started to reintroduce this detail into housing – a good example of green building techniques mirroring those which were common before the 20th century. Splayed reveals allow a smaller (thus cheaper) window to admit more light, with a corresponding reduction in heat loss.

Splayed reveal – above, old; below, new.

ROOF LIGHTS

Roof lights are excellent at admitting daylight because the view of the sky is usually unobstructed from the roof. Technically, it is usually easier to add a roof light than to add a window, and much less likely to require planning permission. Roof lights are particularly useful over landings – landing lights being the ones most commonly left on when not needed – avoiding the need for electric light altogether for most of the day.

LIGHT PIPES

Some parts of a house are difficult to get daylight into by conventional means. A light pipe takes light from outside (usually the roof) and then transfers it down a reflective tube to where it's needed. The tubes are sized to fit through rafters and floor joists.

Inside the house, a light pipe looks similar to a fluorescent panel light. An electric light can even be located within the tube for night-time use. At roof level the pipe protrudes only slightly through the roof covering; flashing kits are available to suit most kinds of roof.

Light pipes generally need no maintenance as the roof glass should be self-cleaning. In terms of saving money or CO_2 emissions a light pipe would have a very long payback period but it is an excellent way of delivering natural light to dark corners. Light pipes can also be combined with ventilation systems, so they are particularly useful for bathrooms and kitchens.

Where major building work is planned, light wells can be introduced (in place of light pipes), which admit considerably greater amounts of light. Light wells are much more common in commercial buildings than in domestic property.

REFERENCES
[1] Powergen plc
[2] Market Transformation Programme BNW18: EC Energy Labelling of Domestic Tumble Driers.
[3] Energy Saving Trust.
[4] National Energy Foundation/Energy Label (Light Sources) Monitoring Programme, Market Transformation Programme of Defra, June 2003.
[5] European Commission Directorate – General environment study on hazardous household waste (HHW) with a main emphasis on hazardous household chemicals (HHC). Final report WRc Ref: CO 5089-2 July 2002.

Photos: Solalighting Ltd

Installing a Tubular Daylight System

Tubular daylight systems vary in design so it will be necessary to check the installation instructions provided with any particular system. The following example is based upon the installation of a 'Solatube 250mm Daylight System', courtesy of Solalighting Ltd.

The Solatube system comprises:

- Dome and Reflector
- Roof flashing kit
- Pre-assembled adjustable angle top tube
- Pre-assembled adjustable angle bottom tube
- Diffuser
- Sealants, fixings and installation instructions

Tools Required

- Hole Saw
- Hammer
- Tile saw (or angle grinder)/slate cutter
- Drill
- Screwdriver
- Roof Access System

Note: *Access to the roof is required to fit the flashing kit and the dome. Ensure that the enclosed health & safety recommendations for roof access are followed. Please visit* **http://www.hse.gov.uk/falls/roof.htm** *and take note of the relevant suggestions before commencing work.*

1 Identify the desired location on the ceiling for the diffuser, ensuring that the path from the diffuser to the roof will be free of obstacles such as joists, pipes or wires. Check also that the roof flashing fits in the desired location. Ideally, the tubing should run as straight as possible between the roof and the ceiling, but pitched roofs, attic obstructions and diffuser location can make this difficult. Adjustable angle adapters allow you to adjust the top and bottom tubes to the degree necessary to allow easy connection between the roof and the ceiling.

2 Mark up the hole to be cut for the diffuser on the ceiling, using the template provided. Carefully cut a hole in the ceiling with a hole saw.

3 Turn the angle adjuster so that the bottom tube points towards the roof flashing. Insert the bottom tube components into the ceiling hole and twist the locking arms to secure the bottom tube to the ceiling.

6 If a light reflector is provided, clip this into the dome and orientate the dome so that the reflector faces south. Ensure that the dome seals are securely placed and fix the dome to the flashing.

7 Within the loft space, join the top and bottom tubes using the extension tubes. Ensure the protective film on the inside of the top and bottom tube and any extension tubes  is removed before final assembly. Seal the tubes carefully using the aluminium tape provided to prevent insects and dust from entering the tubes. Self tapping screws may be required to join longer tube lengths securely and support wires should be used if the tubing is travelling any significant distance across the loft space.

4 Establish safe access to the roof. Remove tiles or slates from the location identified for the dome. Fix the roof flashing to the battens. Replace any tiles or slates, cutting as necessary and seal to ensure water-tightness as directed in the instructions for the particular roof type on your property.

5 Now take the pre-assembled top tube components and drop them into the turret of the roof flashing. Check in the loft space that the top tube is pointing towards the bottom tube. Turn the angle adjuster to achieve this if necessary.

8 Finally, attach the ceiling diffuser to the bottom tube assembly to complete the installation.

6 MICRO-GENERATION

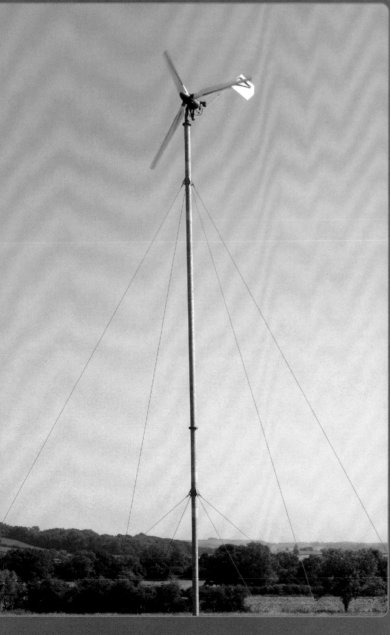

Photo: Carymoor Environmental Centre

The great advantage of micro-generation is that the energy is generated at the point where it is consumed, so avoiding the transmission losses associated with the distribution system for electricity generated in power stations. It has the added advantage that people who have micro-generation systems installed become much more aware of their consumption of electricity and tend to use it more efficiently as a result.

Micro-generation can be independent of the mains supply or linked to it. Where the system is independent, storage facilities such as batteries will be required. The most effective way to use the energy generated is at the same voltage, avoiding the cost of an inverter and the efficiency losses associated with transforming to higher voltages.

The examples of payback periods given in this chapter are based on assumptions that are likely to change. When calculating payback periods it is therefore important to make sure that current information is used. Financial considerations may not be the only important factor in arriving at a decision on micro renewables. Other factors might include:

- Environmental benefits
- Appearance
- Planning permission
- Perceived risk
- Anticipated disruption
- Availability of installers
- Added value upon sale of the property

The energy used to manufacture, transport and install any equipment used to generate electricity constitutes the 'embodied energy' of that equipment. This has not been taken into account in the examples given in this chapter, as it is difficult at present to calculate this accurately. Where a decision to invest in renewable energy technology is taken primarily on the basis of energy balance, allowance should be made for embodied energy, given the expected life of the product. In other words, just as there is a financial payback period for micro-generation, there is also an energy payback period, after which it will have generated more energy than was needed to put the technology in place.

ROCS

The Renewables Obligation was introduced in April 2002 and obliges electricity suppliers in the UK to prove that a certain share of their electricity is generated from renewable energy sources. The share is increasing annually from 3% in 2002/3 to 16.4% in 2015/16.

Renewables Obligation Certificates (ROCs) are available for electricity generated from micro renewable energy sources but not for electricity from micro-CHP. The minimum electricity generation necessary to qualify for a ROC is 500kWh per year. The amount generated is then rounded up or down to the next full MWh (1,000kWh) and payments are made per MWh.

Domestic small-scale producers of electricity can still take advantage of this system even though it was not designed for them. A system generating approximately 750kWh per annum will qualify for one ROC. This ROC can be sold – the value changes from year to year as supply and demand vary on a national scale. In recent years the price of ROCs has varied between £40 and £50 so, if consumers manage to sell their ROCs successfully, the additional income reduces the payback period for micro-generation equipment significantly.

However, the bureaucracy involved is so time-consuming and complicated at present that many domestic producers do not bother to claim this credit. This situation is changing and progress is being made towards a simplified system and other incentives for renewables are also being considered. The ROC system is expected to remain in place until at least 2027.[2]

For case studies on renewable energy in UK housing see: 'Renewable energy in housing case studies' – Energy Saving Trust CE28 (download); 'The Hockerton housing project case study' – Energy Saving Trust CE15 (download); and 'Integrating renewable energy into existing housing – case studies' Energy Saving Trust CE191 (download).

Photovoltaic cells

Photovoltaic cells convert the energy in light (photons) into electrical energy (volts), hence the name. Individual photovoltaic cells produce very small amounts of electricity so they are grouped together into modules. A panel consists of several modules linked together. Where several panels are grouped together this is known as an array.

Photo: solarcentury.com

Installation in progress.

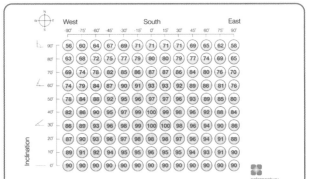

Cell   Module   Panel   Array

The power generated by photovoltaic cells is direct current at low voltage. Unless the power is being used solely to run low-voltage d/c appliances, it needs to be converted to 240V a/c by means of an inverter. Apart from the inverter, photovoltaic generation systems do not take up any internal space. A cable connects the panels to the inverter and the system is then connected into the mains.

Inverter.

Generation of electricity by means of photovoltaic panels is silent and they do not require direct sunlight to operate, which means that they are still effective at generating power even in the UK's frequently cloudy conditions. Once panels have been installed, the electricity which is produced is free. Panels may be expected to last 20–30 years and require little or no maintenance. The electricity is non-polluting and generates no CO_2 or other emissions while the system is in use.

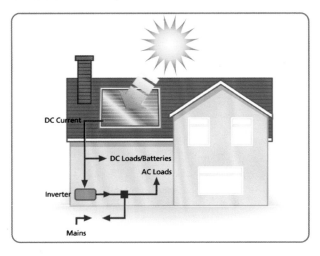

MOUNTING AND ORIENTATION

Panels are normally mounted on south-facing roofs, although any roof facing south-east to south-west will perform relatively well. Any overshading from trees or surrounding buildings will reduce the power output. The ideal slope for mounting panels is 30° to 40° which works well with roof pitches commonly used in the UK.

Illustration: solarcentury.com

Flat roofs are also suitable for PV installation. Suitably angled mounting brackets will be needed to compensate for the fact that the sun is not high enough in the sky for a long enough period in the UK for the panels to be laid flat.

For installations on pitched or flat roofs, it is necessary to check that the roof can support the additional weight of the panels. Installers should address this question but, if there is any doubt, the opinion of a structural engineer should be sought.

Photo: solarcentury.com

Photovoltaic cells

A photovoltaic cell consists of a junction between two thin layers of dissimilar semiconducting materials. These materials are usually based on silicon, although photovoltaic cells can also be made from other materials.

The first layer, known as the 'p' type layer, is created by doping the silicon with tiny amounts of boron. This effectively causes a shortage of electrons and hence a positive charge. The second layer, known as the 'n' type layer, is doped with small amounts of phosphorus, which creates a surplus of electrons and hence a negative charge. The barrier between these two layers is known as the p-n junction. When energy in the form of light is applied at this point, the electrons are given enough energy to move across the junction. This in turn creates a 'potential difference' or 'voltage'. If the circuit is completed, this potential difference drives the flow of electrons around the circuit and an electrical current is produced.

There are four main types of PV cell:

Monocrystalline cells are the most expensive and efficient cells presently in mass production. A single silicon seed crystal is drawn into a cylinder and cut into thin wafers which are then doped to create the 'n' and 'p' type layers described above. Monocrystalline cells are considered to be the most durable of currently available PV cells.

Polycrystalline cells are cut from a mass of silicon which has been melted and recrystalised. The rest of the process is similar to that used to create monocrystalline cells. Polycrystalline cells are slightly cheaper to produce but approximately 20% less efficient.

Thick film silicon is formed by depositing a layer of polycrystalline silicon onto a prepared base material by means of a continuous process. The result is a cheaper but much less efficient system.

Amorphous silicon is not based upon crystalline structure. Instead a thin homogenous layer of silicon is used to absorb the light, so these type of cells can be spread on a range of substrates. Although they're much less efficient than crystalline cells, they perform well in diffuse light and have the added advantage that they can be used on curved surfaces.

Photo: solarcentury.com

ROOF TILES

PV cells can also be made into roof tiles. These are more expensive than panels so it is really only worth considering this option if you are building an extension or carrying out a major refurbishment which includes re-roofing, as the cost of the omitted roof covering can be offset against the cost of the tiles. PV tiles can be fully integrated into a roof covering, so they may be preferable to panels for both technical and aesthetic reasons.

OUTPUT

The output from PV panels varies significantly over the

Photo: solarcentury.com

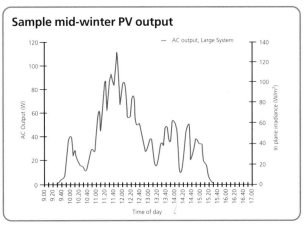

Sample mid-winter PV output

Source: DTI: Domestic Photovoltaic Field Trials

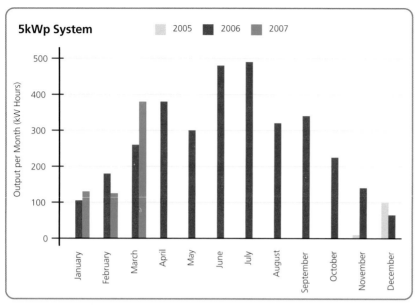

5kWp System   2005   2006   2007

Source: St. James's Church, Piccadilly.

course of the day, peaking at around 1:00pm if the sun is out. Output from PV panels is measured at the peak rate of production, shown as kWp – kilowatts produced at peak.

A 1kWp system may be expected to produce at least 750kWh of usable electricity per year.[1] This is equivalent to approximately 20% of the average (non-heating) annual consumption of electricity per household in the UK. To meet a total household demand of 4,000kWh, a 5kWp system would therefore be required, although measures to reduce electricity consumption will reduce this figure significantly.

GRID CONNECTION

PV panels generate most of their electricity during the daytime when domestic demand is generally low, which is the opposite of what is needed, so mains electricity will still be required. Unless the property is off-grid or the system is designed to be independent and used primarily to run low-voltage applications, it makes sense to connect the PV panels to the grid. Surplus electricity which is not used in the household can then be sold back to the electricity supplier. During the time when the panels are not generating, electricity will have to be imported and paid for as normal. Generally this requires two-way metering. Not all suppliers offer this and charges and prices vary. In some cases the charges may have a significant impact on the payback period – see below.

It is the installer's responsibility to inform the local distribution network operator (DNO) that a new PV system has been connected to the grid and this is usually carried out as part of the standard service.

GRANTS

In England and Wales, under the Low Carbon Buildings Programme, grants are available to cover up to 50% of the cost of installed PV systems, exclusive of VAT (to be reviewed April 2009). There is a maximum of £3,000 per kWp installed and an overall maximum grant of £15,000. VAT on domestic photovoltaic panels currently stands at the reduced rate of 5%. Grants may only be claimed for accredited products or systems. For details of accredited products visit **www.lowcarbon buildings.org.uk/home**

In Scotland there are currently no grants available for PV installation.

In Northern Ireland, grants may be obtained from Reconnect administered by Action Renewables. The grant is £3,000 per kWp installed, up to a maximum of £15,000 and subject to an overall 50% limit of installed cost, inclusive of VAT (to be reviewed March 2008)

PAYBACK PERIOD

The payback period is the amount of time it takes for the cost of the installation to be repaid through savings in fuel bills. The details given here have been worked out purely as an example and you will need to insert up-to-date figures in order to work out the actual payback period.

For the sake of convenience it is assumed that the discount rate and the rate of fuel price escalation are equal. To calculate the simple payback period for a 1kWp system:

	Example	Actual
Interest rate p.a.	5%	
Fuel price escalation p.a.	5%	
Installed cost net of VAT	£6,000	
Grant	£3,000	
VAT at 5% on £6,000	£300	
Net cost including VAT therefore =	£3,300	
Peak system output	1kWp	
Amount of electricity produced p.a.	750kWh	
Price of electricity	10p/kWh	
Annual saving	£75	
Payback period = £3,300 ÷ £75 =	44 years	

Charges imposed for two-way metering by a network operator (if applicable) must also be taken into account. The calculation also takes no account of ROCs (see above). Using the example figures in the payback calculated above, based on a consistent ROC price of £40, the payback period would fall from 44 to 29 years: £3,300 ÷ (£75 + £40) = 29.

Interest rates are important because the value of future payments (or savings) needs to be discounted to arrive at a present value. The value of £1 now is not the same as £1 promised to you in a year's time, as you would rather have the £1 now and earn interest for a year. If interest rates and fossil fuel price escalation are unequal over the long term this affects the calculation. For example, if fuel prices rise more quickly than the absolute level of long-term interest rates, the payback period for PV generation will be significantly shorter.

In order to justify the expense of installation, the payback period must be less than the expected life of the system. However, the financial payback period may not be the only consideration when deciding upon a PV system. PV generation also displaces consumption of fossil fuels and reduces CO_2 emissions (325kg/year per kWp installed) and other pollution associated with fossil fuel generation.

PLANNING PERMISSION

Planning permission is not normally required to fit PV panels or tiles to a roof. However, it is always best to check with your Local Authority. Permission would probably be required for houses in conservation areas and conservation consent would be needed in order to fix PV panels to a listed building, although adjacent unlisted outbuildings might be suitable locations for panels in such situations.

Wind turbines

Wind has been used to generate power in the UK for centuries. Like photovoltaic systems, wind turbines generate electricity from a clean and renewable source of energy, in contrast to fossil fuels.

BUILDING-MOUNTED MINI WIND TURBINES

Many people associate mini wind turbines with their much larger cousins which have been the source of much controversy, as older models are noisy and they all have a very significant visual impact on the landscape. In fact, mini wind turbines produce comparatively little noise and are not much larger than a satellite dish.

Not all buildings are structurally suitable for mounting mini wind turbines. The manufacturers have obviously gone to great lengths to ensure their mechanical and electrical safety but a weak or defective

building should be checked carefully. In some circumstances a bespoke support structure will be required.

At present, in Northern Ireland an application to Building Control is required for building-mounted wind turbines. However, approval from Building Control is not currently required for free-standing wind turbines unless structural changes are made to the building which benefits from the output of the turbine. The situation in the rest of the UK is far from clear at present and the turbine installer should clarify the updated position on Building Control requirements.

SMALL WIND TURBINES

Small wind turbines (for example 2.5kW to 25kW) are the next size up from mini wind turbines. They are usually independently pole-mounted as they need to be sited sufficiently high and far away from obstacles to avoid turbulence. They are therefore only suitable for houses with sufficient land but are very useful in rural areas. Some turbines require guy ropes to provide stability and therefore have quite a significant 'footprint'. Larger turbines (5kW or more) can also be used for shared power schemes, as they can generate more power than is needed for the average UK domestic property. Shared schemes normally involve setting up an ESCO (Energy Services Company) through which the shared source of energy can be purchased and managed and costs can be allocated. Any independent pole-mounted turbine will probably require planning permission.

Photo: Carymoor Environmental Centre

OUTPUT

The power of a wind turbine is proportional to the square of the diameter of the rotor blades and to the cube of the wind speed:

Where :   D = air density
          A = area swept by the blades
          V = wind speed
          C = capacity factor
          $P = C \times D^2 \times A \times V^3$

So, for a given wind speed a turbine with a diameter of 2m will be producing four times as much power as a turbine with a diameter of 1m. Similarly, a turbine will produce almost double the amount of power at a wind speed of 6m/s compared with a wind speed of 5m/s. Not all the energy available in the airstream can be harvested by the turbine or the air would have no energy left to blow away downstream; the theoretical maximum is 0.59, known as the Betz limit but for the purposes of calculation it is realistic to assume a capacity factor of 0.5.

Wind turbines are rated by comparing their output at a given wind speed of 12m/s (27mph). This does not mean that average wind speeds are expected to be at this level; it is purely a means of rating the turbines. Given a wind speed of 12m/s, a 1kW wind turbine will be generating at 1kW. Typical wind speeds in the UK are much lower than this, so the turbine will normally be operating at a greatly reduced rate, producing no power at all at wind speeds below 3m/s. At very high wind speeds, wind turbines have safety cut-outs to prevent damage to the system.

The actual output of any particular wind turbine is therefore sensitive to three factors: geographical location, obstructions and turbulence, and height of mounting. The last two are similar – at greater height there are, of course, fewer obstructions, but average wind speed also increases significantly with increasing height, quite independently of obstructions. Annual output figures quoted by manufacturers in terms of kilowatt hours are very sensitive to local wind speed and conditions, so many sites can be expected to produce much less than the quoted figures. If it appears that your home is unsuitable for a mini-wind turbine, a similar reduction in environmental impact might be achieved by investing the equivalent sum in a wind farm. Local co-operatives can also be formed to invest in medium-sized turbines on sites nearby which have a better wind resource.

WIND SPEEDS

Wind speed varies widely across Britain. Data on wind speeds for every part of the country is available from the NOABL database. This can presently be accessed via the British Wind Energy Association at
www.bwea.com/noabl/index.html

Average wind speeds are also available from the Met Office website at **www.metoffice.gov.uk/climate/uk/averages/19712000/index.html**

The available wind speed data takes no account of turbulence which will be thrown up by neighbouring buildings, trees and other obstructions. Speeds are also quoted for heights that are greater than those at which an average building-mounted turbine will be operating, so the figures must be treated with some caution.

Where average wind speeds are less than 5m/s, the economic viability of a wind turbine should be calculated carefully and will be very dependent on the site and the height of the mounting. Other areas with higher wind speeds may still be unviable if there is significant turbulence in the location selected. There are programmes available to assist with the calculation of the effect of turbulence – for example see: **www.windpower.org/en/tour/wres/shelter/index.htm**

GRID CONNECTION

In grid-connected systems, the output from the turbine is converted to 240V a/c by means of an inverter and the power generated is used primarily to serve the domestic electricity demand by means of a direct connection to the distribution system within the house. However, wind turbines generate power at rates which are completely independent of consumption patterns, so during the time when the turbine is not generating (in excess of consumption), power will have to be imported and paid for as normal.

Surplus electricity which is not used in the household can be sold back to the electricity supplier. Generally this requires two-way metering. Not all suppliers offer this service and charges and prices vary. In some cases the charges may have an impact on the payback period – see below.

As with a PV system, it is the installer's responsibility to inform the local distribution network operator that a mini wind turbine has been connected to the grid and this should be carried out as part of the standard service.

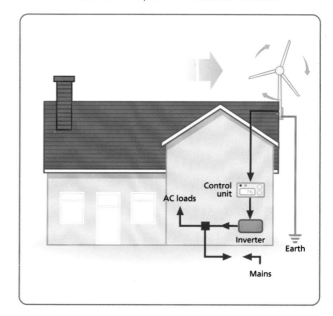

GRANTS

In England and Wales, under the Low Carbon Buildings Programme, grants are available to cover up to 30% of the cost of installed systems, exclusive of VAT (to be reviewed April 2009). There is a maximum of £1,000 per kWp installed and an overall maximum of £5,000. VAT on domestic wind turbines currently stands at the reduced rate of 5%. Grants may only be claimed for accredited products or systems. For details of accredited products see the Low Carbon Buildings Programme website at **www.lowcarbonbuildings.org.uk/home**

In Scotland, under the Scottish Community and Householder Renewables Initiative (SCHRI), the grant is set at 30% of the installed cost of a renewable measure up to £4,000 (to be reviewed March 2008).

In Northern Ireland grants may be obtained from Reconnect, administered by Action Renewables. The grant is £2,000 per kW installed, up to a maximum of £8,000 and subject to an overall 50% limit of installed cost, inclusive of VAT (to be reviewed March 2008).

COSTS AND PAYBACK

This payback period has been worked out purely as an example and you will need to insert up-to-date figures in order to work out the actual payback period. For the sake of convenience it is assumed that the interest rate and the rate of fuel price escalation are equal.

	Example	Actual
Interest rate p.a.	5%	
Fuel price escalation p.a.	5%	
Installed cost net of VAT	£1,600	
Grant	£480	
Vat at 5% on £1,600	£80	
Net cost including VAT	£1,200	
System output at 12 m/s	1kW	
Amount of electricity produced p.a.	1,000kWh*	
Price of electricity	10p/kWh	
Annual saving	£100	
Payback period = £1,200 ÷ £100 =	12 years	

*Annual output is subject to testing and to local wind conditions. Actual output may be less than the quoted figure, which will extend the payback period accordingly.

Charges imposed for two-way metering by a network operator (if applicable) must also be taken into account.

Interest rates are important because the value of future payments (or savings) needs to be discounted to arrive at a present value. If interest rates and fossil fuel price escalation are unequal over the long term this affects the calculation. For example, if fuel prices rise more quickly than the absolute level of long-term interest rates, the payback

period for a mini wind turbine will be significantly shorter. The payback period may be further reduced by taking into account the value of any ROCs which may be claimed – refer to the section on ROCs at the beginning of this chapter.

In order to justify the expense of installation, the payback period must be less than the expected life of the system. However, the financial payback period may not be the only consideration when deciding upon a mini wind turbine. Wind-turbine generation also displaces consumption of fossil fuels and reduces CO_2 emissions (400kg/year per kW installed) and other pollution associated with fossil fuel generation.

PLANNING PERMISSION

Planning permission is currently (2007) required for mini wind turbines. Parliament is considering removing this restriction in order to encourage the take-up of micro-renewables and to allow turbines to be installed under 'permitted development' rules. Planning permission will probably be needed in any case for installations where the rotor diameter exceeds 2m. Permission will also almost certainly continue to be needed for conservation areas or for listed buildings.

For further information see: 'Installing small wind-powered electricity generating systems' – Energy Saving Trust CE72 (download).

Micro-CHP

Combined heat and power (CHP) systems take advantage of the fact that heat is produced during generation of electricity by means of burning fuel. The excess heat generated by CHP systems has so far been used primarily for district-heating and commercial applications, as the pooling of demand leads to greater efficiencies. Shared schemes also allow for CHP to be run from renewable power sources such as biomass or wood-chip, with the result that both the power and the heat generated are close to being CO_2 neutral and the consumption of fossil fuels is avoided. Even given the energy used in harvesting and transportation, biomass schemes deliver net carbon reductions of up to 90% in comparison to burning fossil fuels.[3]

More recently, CHP technology has been adapted to operate on a domestic scale, so every house with a gas supply has the potential to become a mini power station, generating its own electricity and heat simultaneously. Micro-CHP engines are based on the Stirling external combustion engine, patented in 1816. They are quite unlike internal combustion engines and produce little more noise than a conventional boiler. From the householder's point of view, a micro-CHP engine is simply a boiler which also generates electricity. Electricity is only generated when

Photo: Whispergen

CHP engine.

there is a demand for heat, so a mains electricity supply will still be required.

The micro-CHP engine converts gas into electricity very efficiently and any electricity produced is used at the point of generation, avoiding the transmission losses associated with electricity provision through the national grid.

When operating, a domestic CHP unit will generate approximately 1,000W (1kW) of electrical power. While this will be sufficient to power lights and some small appliances, when kettles and similar appliances are running additional input from the mains will be needed. As with other micro-generation technologies, an import/export meter will be fitted to allow the householder to take advantage of times when supply exceeds demand and surplus electricity is exported to the grid.

It is expected that micro-CHP units will be purchased when replacing boilers, as the cost of installation will then be offset by the cost of a new boiler. CHP engines are more expensive than boilers but, based on an electricity saving of £150 per annum, they can repay the additional investment within a few years.[4] They will, however, require additional maintenance as they are more complicated than a boiler, which only generates heat. The basic design of the heating side of a micro-CHP system is similar to a conventional vented system with a hot water cylinder (see 'water heating systems' in Chapter 4).

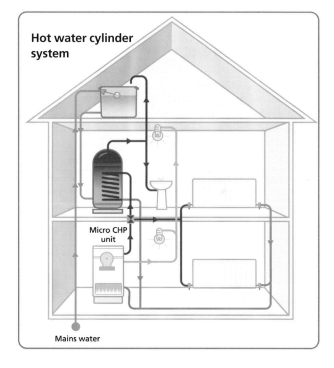

CHP system

Heat >78%

Micro CHP unit

Exhaust 10%

Gas 100%

Electricity 12%

In contrast to gas boilers, which are designed to heat water quickly and then to shut down, CHP engines are designed to run for long periods to maximise the amount of electricity generated. A micro-CHP engine has a relatively low heat output and the heating system will take longer to reach full temperature than a system fuelled by a conventional boiler. A micro-CHP engine will therefore need to run for longer periods – for example, starting earlier in the morning – to deliver the same level of thermal comfort. They are designed to be free-standing or wall-hung in the same way as a conventional boiler but due to the length of time for which they run and produce noise they may not be suitable for installation in living areas such as open-plan kitchens or directly below bedrooms.

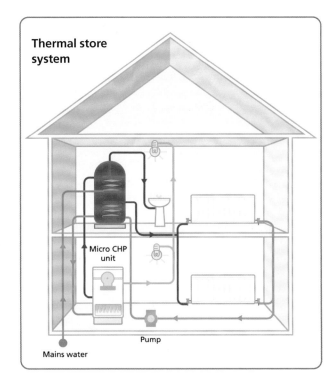

Thermal store system

Micro CHP unit

Pump

Mains water

a fossil fuel (gas). Micro-CHP may well become a step in the direction of reducing CO_2 emissions while other technology continues to reduce our dependency on fossil fuels still further.

Grants have not yet been finalised for micro (or district/renewable) CHP – for updated information on grants contact the Energy Saving Trust.

For further information see: The Combined Heat & Power Association, **www.chpa.co.uk***; and 'Renewable energy sources in rural environments' Energy Saving Trust CE70 (download).*

Micro-hydro

Water wheels were once widely used across the UK and streams can now be harnessed as a reliable and consistent means of generating electricity. Unlike wind turbines and photovoltaic panels, micro-hydro generators can operate constantly throughout the day and night. Even if the flow-rate of a stream is reduced in the summer months, these are the times when energy demand is likely to be lowest. In the winter months, when demand is higher, flow rates and energy generation are also likely to be at their maximum.

Electricity is produced from water flowing from a high level to a lower level, making use of the potential energy of water that falls on high ground. This change in elevation is called 'head' and supplies the pressure that drives the turbine. 'Flow rate' is the other factor contributing to power production and is limited by the size of the stream and variations in rainfall. The amount of electricity produced is directly proportional to the head and the flow.

Additional plumbing work may therefore be required if the unit is located in an outhouse or a purpose-built exterior shelter.

From a system designer's point of view it is best to think of a CHP engine as an electricity generator which happens to produce useful heat. As micro-CHP engines are designed to run for long periods, the heat output is ideally suited to running a thermal store system (see 'water heating systems' in Chapter 4). Thermal store systems require a lower-rated source of heat supply than a conventional boiler but the thermal store allows the central-heating system to provide a much faster response time than a conventional heating system which is connected to a CHP engine.

Micro-CHP technology is still under development but the government has a commitment to encourage micro-CHP as it delivers undoubted benefits in efficiency and therefore reductions in CO_2 output, even though it is still consuming

Photo: Whispergen

CHP engine housed outdoors.

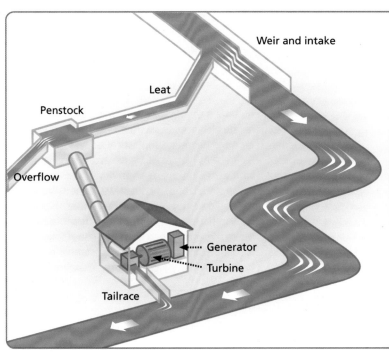

Weir and intake

Leat

Penstock

Overflow

Generator

Turbine

Tailrace

If the head or flow is increased the power output increases proportionally. The hydro power in a stream or river can be calculated as follows:

Hydro power (kW) = head (m) x flow (m³/s) x acceleration due to gravity

For example, if the head is 3.0m and the available flow is 0.12m³ per second, the hydro power is:

3.00 x 0.12 x 9.81 = 3.5kW

At 50% equipment efficiency, in this example the turbine would generate electricity at the rate of 1.75kW. Depending on the degree of sophistication, water turbine efficiencies can be as high as 90%. No abstraction is required – the water which is used to drive the turbine is returned to the stream and, if correctly designed and installed, the equipment should have negligible environmental impact. Distance from the stream to the property where the energy is to be used need not be a problem as voltage drop over moderate distances is not excessive. Various different types of turbine are available:

Turbine type	Head range
Propeller, Water Wheel	1.5–5m (ultra low)
Crossflow, Propeller, Kaplan	5–20m (low)

GRANTS

In England and Wales, under the Low Carbon Buildings Programme, there is a maximum grant available of £1,000 per kW installed, up to a maximum of £5,000 subject to an overall 30% limit of the installed cost, exclusive of VAT (to be reviewed April 2009).

In Northern Ireland grants may be obtained from Reconnect, administered by Action Renewables. The grant is £2,000 per kW installed, up to a maximum of £8,000 and subject to an overall 50% limit of installed cost inclusive of VAT (to be reviewed March 2008).

In Scotland, under the Scottish Community and Householder Renewables Initiative (SCHRI), the grant is set at 30% of the installed cost of a renewable measure up to £4,000 (to be reviewed March 2008).

Grants are also available for community or heritage groups to set up shared hydro schemes or to restore old waterwheels.

Tariff comparison for buyback

Where micro-generation equipment has been installed, not all supply companies offer to buy back electricity which is surplus to immediate demand from the house. Where they do offer to purchase the surplus at the same price at which electricity is sold to the consumer, the result is known as 'net metering'.

In other cases, companies may offer to buy the electricity at a lower price – say 50% of that which they charge for their supply. This reflects the fact that suppliers can buy electricity more cheaply on the wholesale market at what is known as the 'system buy price.'

However, transmission losses are negligible for locally-generated power so the value of that power to the supply company is greater than the system buy price as they have not had to pay to shift the electricity from the power station to the consumer. There is therefore a good argument for companies to purchase micro-generated electricity at a price pitched between the system buy price and the price normally paid by the consumer.

In order to measure the amount of electricity which is generated by micro-renewables a replacement meter will usually be required. The supply and fitting of these meters is expensive and the amounts of surplus electricity generated by most domestic installations will be small if not insignificant, so presently there are considerable economic barriers to putting net metering arrangements into place.

The situation with buyback is changing continually. It is best to check with a range of suppliers to see who is offering the best deal, taking into account the green credentials of the supply company when making the decision. Some companies have a standing charge for the incoming supply and, as they own the meter, make a second standing charge for the export meter. This can tip the scales and make net metering unviable from a particular supplier for a given size of installation, so it is always necessary to get up-to-date information.

Summary of grants for renewable energy

ENGLAND AND WALES
In England and Wales, grants are available to support the use of small-scale renewables under the DTI's Low Carbon Buildings Programme, which runs from 1 April 2006 for three years. There are several preconditions that must be met before any of the following grants will be made available:

■ Loft insulation – a minimum of 270mm must be installed
■ Cavity wall insulation – must be installed if you have cavity walls
■ Low-energy light-bulbs must be fitted in all appropriate light fittings
■ Basic controls for central heating including a room thermostat and a programmer or timer must be fitted

Electricity generation

Type of generation	Max per kWp	Max as % of cost	Overall maximum (per property)
Photovoltaics	£3,000	50%	£15,000
Wind turbines	£1,000	30%	£5,000
Micro-hydro	£1,000	30%	£5,000

Alternative heating sources

Type	Max grant	Max as % of cost
Solar water heaters	£400	30%
Heat pumps	£1,200	30%
Wood-pellet heaters	£600	20%
Wood-fuelled boilers	£1,500	30%
Renewable CHP	TBA	TBA
Micro-CHP	TBA	TBA

Notes
Percentages are expressed of costs exclusive of VAT.
Costs mean installed costs.
Grants for up to three different renewable technologies may be claimed for one building.

Grants are administered by the Energy Saving Trust. The guidance notes and an application form can be downloaded from **www.lowcarbonbuildings.org.uk**, or telephone 0800 915 0990.

To obtain a grant you must first obtain a quote for the installation chosen from an accredited installer. A list can be found at **www.lowcarbonbuildings.org.uk/info/installers**.

Read the guidance notes carefully before filling out the application form. Grants are paid *after* the installation is complete, the installer has been paid, and the installation has been certified. Among the conditions it is important to note that grants will not be paid if the installation has been commenced before a grant offer letter has been received.

SCOTLAND
In Scotland, grants may be obtained under the Scottish Community and Householder Renewables Initiative (SCHRI) for the following technologies:

■ Wind turbines
■ Solar water heating
■ Solar space heating
■ Micro-hydroelectric
■ Automated wood fuel heating systems (boilers and room heaters/stoves)
■ Heat pumps (ground, air or water)

Funding for householders is set at 30% of the installed cost of a renewable measure up to £4,000. Householders can also apply for separate grants for two different technologies. The following criteria must be met:

- The applicant must own the property where the renewable energy system is to be installed
- The renewable energy system must be for a permanently-sited building or mobile home
- One quote from an accredited installer must be provided
- The system must be designed, installed and commissioned by an approved installer using approved system components

For further information visit **www.est.org.uk/schri**, *or call 0800 138 8858. The scheme will run until March 2008 at which point it will be reviewed.*

It is also possible for householders in Scotland to apply for grants from the Low Carbon Building Programme but only one grant can be received for any particular installation.

NORTHERN IRELAND
In Northern Ireland grants may be obtained from Reconnect (formerly the Environment and Renewable Energy Fund Household Programme), administered by Action Renewables, 0800 023 4077

Electricity generation

Type of generation	Max per kWp	Max as % of cost	Overall maximum (per property)
Photovoltaics	£3,000	50% inc VAT	£15,000
Wind turbines	£2,000	50% inc VAT	£8,000
Micro-hydro	£2,000	50% inc VAT	£8,000

For a list of accredited installers in Northern Ireland visit the Household Programme website at **www.energy.detini.gov.uk/householdprogramme**.

Alternative heating sources

Type	Max grant	Max as % of cost
Solar water heaters	£1,125	50% inc VAT
Ground/water-source heat pumps	£3,000	40% inc VAT
Air-source heat pumps	£2,400	40% inc VAT
Pellet stoves	£1,500	50% inc VAT
Wood-fuelled boiler	£3,250	50% inc VAT

The scheme will run until March 2008 at which point it will be reviewed.

It is also possible for householders in Northern Ireland to apply for grants from the Low Carbon Building Programme but only one grant can be received for any particular installation.

Green electricity suppliers

One simple way for householders to make a contribution towards improving the environment and reducing their CO_2 emissions is to switch to an electricity supplier which generates some or all of its power from renewable sources such as wind or hydro. The three main companies that provide this service at present are Ecotricity, Good Energy and Green Energy.

Photo: Ari Liddell

ECOTRICITY
Ecotricity is the trading name of the Renewable Power Company (**www.ecotricity.co.uk** or 08000 326 100). This company has a programme of investment into new sources of renewable electricity, so it is constantly adding to its clean generating capacity. Presently about 25% of its power is generated by renewables, but the company expects this to rise quickly as new generating schemes come online. The 'New Energy Tariff' is available in England, Scotland and Wales.

GOOD ENERGY
In contrast to Ecotricity, Good Energy (**www.good-energy.co.uk** or 0845 456 1640) purchases its energy from renewable energy sources and does not have an active investment programme of its own. However, by providing a marketplace for small renewable energy producers it encourages the production of clean energy. 100% of energy supplied by Good Energy has been purchased from renewables suppliers checked by the company.

GREEN ENERGY
Green Energy (**www.greenenergy.uk.com** or 0845 456 9550) is similar to Good Energy in that it is also a small

independent company which purchases electricity from renewable sources. It has two available tariffs – Green Energy 100 is supplied 100% by renewables, while Green Energy +10 aims to beat by 10% the statutory minimum (currently 5%) set by the government for power companies to source their supply from renewables. The company plans to invest 50% of its profits in new renewable energy generation.

OTHER GREEN TARIFFS

Several power companies offer 'green' tariffs but these need to be treated with some caution. Their welcome investment in renewable energy is frequently negligible in comparison to their power derived from fossil fuel sources, or they may compete for finite existing renewable sources which are then 'sold on' via these tariffs, adding nothing to the supply of green energy.

In some cases the companies (or their parent companies) offering the tariffs have a highly questionable environmental record, so it pays to do your research if you really want to make a difference by switching your electricity supplier.

TRADING IN ROCS AND LECS

A further complication arises when trying to evaluate the greenness of electricity suppliers because it is possible for them to trade in ROCs (Renewable Obligation Certificates). By signing up to a green tariff it is theoretically possible that you are simply helping to fund the purchase of the certificates which the power companies are already under a legal obligation to purchase.

It is only when a certificate is 'retired' that there is an incentive to produce more renewable electricity. The same is also true of LECs (Levy Exemption Certificates), which can be sold to commercial organisations to help them meet their obligations under the Climate Change Levy. Unless a proportion of LECs are retired when the electricity is sold under a green tariff, there is a danger that the benefit of any one unit of production of green energy will be claimed twice under the current system, which does not provide an economic incentive to increase the production of renewable power.

For further information see the comparison service at
www.whichgreen.com

REFERENCES

[1] Energy Saving Trust.
[2] Energy Saving Trust CE69.
[3] Energy Saving Trust CE70.
[4] Energy Saving Trust via Powergen.

7 WATER

Water – a scarce resource

In most countries water is treated as a precious and valuable resource. The temperate climate and more than a century of piped mains water have led to a relaxed attitude towards water consumption in the UK, but supplies are now under increasing pressure.

RAINFALL

Statistics indicate that rainfall in the UK is falling very slightly in the long term. Perhaps more importantly, an increasing proportion of rainfall is expected over the winter months and less in summer months, so in some areas it may be necessary to increase storage capacity, which will be an expensive exercise.

The frequency and intensity of rainfall is also important, as sudden heavy downpours may now be more common. The water from this kind of rainfall tends to be washed away rapidly, often causing flooding, rather than soaking into the groundwater system and replenishing underground aquifers. This problem is exacerbated if the ground is very hard after a long period of dry weather, or if the ground is already saturated.

For example, in 1998, after two very wet months, several parts of the Severn and Wye valleys were flooded when heavy rain fell and the ground could not absorb any more water. The problem had been exacerbated by

developments upstream on land which once absorbed water, so rain that fell on the hard surfaces was channelled swiftly to the rivers, which ultimately could not cope with the additional discharge.

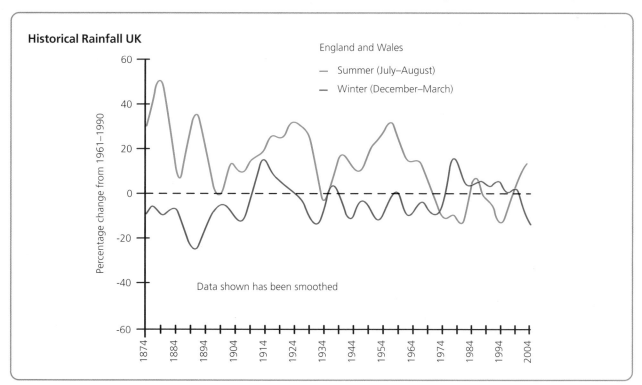

Historical Rainfall UK

England and Wales

— Summer (July–August)

— Winter (December–March)

Percentage change from 1961–1990

Data shown has been smoothed

Source: Hadley Centre / DEFRA

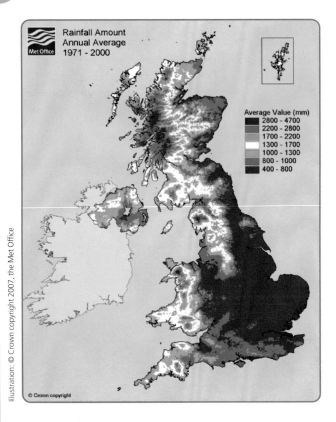

Illustration: © Crown copyright 2007, the Met Office

The rainfall pattern is skewed regionally in the UK, with the south and east receiving less water than the north and west.

DEMAND FOR WATER

Nationally, the consumption of water can be broken down into three main sectors:

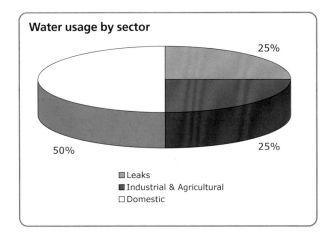

Water usage by sector

- 25%
- 25%
- 50%

☐ Leaks
☐ Industrial & Agricultural
☐ Domestic

The domestic demand for water has been rising steadily over the past century, partly due to population expansion and associated development, but also due to the increasing amount of water used daily by the average person.

Water supply companies thus find themselves having to face the dual problem of increasing demand and decreasing supply. For example, the Bewl reservoir on the

Kent/Sussex border (above) was only 37% full in February 2006, a time of year when it is normally 90% full. This was principally due to low rainfall in the winter months, but water demand per head in the South-East appears to be 10% higher than in the wetter North of the country.

The water companies themselves have a clear responsibility to reduce leaks in supply pipes and to invest in the infrastructure. The 'economic level of leakage', regulated by OFWAT, is that which is defined by comparing the cost of providing a megalitre of additional water resource with the cost of reducing leaks by the same amount. In other words, it would appear to make economic sense to accept a certain level of leakage within the distribution system. As water is no longer a public utility we are obliged to rely on government to regulate the water industry, but there is much that can be done in domestic property to reduce consumption, as the current level of demand is clearly unsustainable. However, it is curious to note that, while water bills have soared, water companies spend an average of only 11p per year per customer on water-saving initiatives.

Reducing water demand in the home

Domestic water consumption can be broken down as follows:

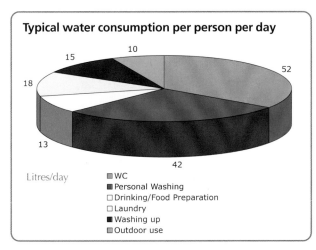

Typical water consumption per person per day

- 10
- 15
- 18
- 52
- 13
- 42

Litres/day

☐ WC
☐ Personal Washing
☐ Drinking/Food Preparation
☐ Laundry
☐ Washing up
☐ Outdoor use

These are only average figures and much depends on lifestyle and the equipment which is already installed in our houses. The increase in single-person households in the UK is also thought to have contributed to an increase in demand per person. Many of the methods by which we can save water involve simply changing the way in which we live and how we use water, rather than any costly purchase of new equipment.

METERING

If the supply is metered there will be a financial incentive to save water. It is thought that one of the most effective ways to reduce water consumption is to install a meter, as awareness that water has a cost tends to make consumers more careful.

LEAKS

Leaks account for the greatest wastage of water so, before introducing water-saving measures in a property, it is first important to address any leaks.

One drip per second	wastes	4 litres per day
Drips breaking into a stream	wastes	90 litres per day
1.5mm (1/16in) stream	wastes	320 litres per day
3mm (1/8in) stream	wastes	985 litres per day
6mm (1/4in) stream	wastes	3,500 litres per day

Stain caused by leaking overflow.

WATER WASTED BY LEAKING TAPS

If there is a meter fitted and a leak is suspected, the 'night-flow test' may prove useful: read the meter before going to bed and, as long as no water is used overnight, the meter reading in the morning will indicate whether or not there is a leak.

The supply pipe is that part of the service pipe which runs from the boundary of the property to the rising main. Technically, owner responsibility for leakage begins at the boundary of each property but most water companies offer a free supply pipe leak detection and repair service. OFWAT clearly states that it regards this as a responsibility of the water companies, especially as 75% of the water saved by *all* water efficiency measures was achieved by carrying out supply pipe repairs.[1] If the opportunity arises to replace an old lead supply pipe in the process, this will eliminate a potential source of toxins. Although this is at the expense of the homeowner, the water company will normally replace the section of the pipe (the communication pipe) which runs from the property boundary to the water main in the street at the same time, at its own expense.

TOILETS

As approximately one third of the water used in domestic property is accounted for by toilet flushing, this is a good place to start looking for savings. Cotton wool and tissues can be disposed of by means of a waste bin in the bathroom rather than using the toilet to flush them away. Older cisterns use 9 litres or more for each flush. To reduce the flush volume without changing the cistern, solid objects can be placed in the cistern to displace water which would otherwise be flushed through. It is important that an object placed in a cistern does not interfere with the operation of the flush or siphon assemblies and does not introduce unwanted chemicals into the system. Bricks placed in cisterns will eventually decompose and cause problems. However, water companies generally offer free displacement devices designed for this purpose.

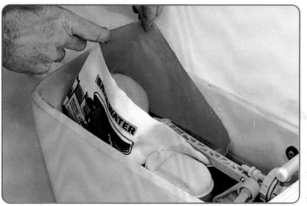

Photo: Hippo UK

Ifo Cera ES4 4.5 litre.

When replacing a toilet or fitting a new bathroom, dual flush cisterns can be installed which enable the user to select between a limited flush and a full flush. These come in either 2/4, 3/6 or 4/6-litre versions.

Flushes on new toilets are not permitted to exceed 6 litres and most now incorporate the dual flushing facility set at 4/6 litres. For siphonic toilets (compulsory in the UK until 2001) the siphon can be replaced with one which allows air into the siphon, thus reducing the flush volume. Questions have been raised about the leakage in imported valve systems, although all UK-manufactured valves will have passed the WRAS test (see below) and are of sufficient quality.

Retrofit kits are available which enable a single flush to be replaced by a variable flush. This can be achieved either by a dial change, manually setting the flush lever to control the volume used, or by the use of an interrupt button, which flushes until the handle is released. It is important to note that if a variable flush or a displacement device results in the need to flush more than once, then the saving is lost and the actual water consumption may even be increased. If this occurs, the best course of action is to revert to the previous arrangement.

For further information see 'Retrofitting variable flush mechanisms to existing toilets' (Environment Agency 2005).

The critical measure, which takes into account all these variables, is the 'effective flush volume'. When a flush volume is quoted by manufacturers it tends to under-measure the amount used. When a toilet is flushed it immediately starts to refill, so water is flowing into the cistern while it is still draining. This can be avoided by the use of a delayed action inlet valve. This type of valve has a small evacuating bowl beneath the float that operates the valve. When the flush is operated, the water level in the cistern drops but the valve is held shut by the water remaining in the bowl. As the water drains slowly, the valve can open and the cistern can refill. When used with a 7-litre cistern the valve can save about 1.4 litres per flush at 3 bar and 3.5 litres at 10 bar, when compared to the same valve without the bowl. Delayed action inlet valves are currently not available as a retrofit option but may ultimately become compulsory in new installations.

DEAD-LEGS
A dead-leg is the amount of water drawn off from a hot tap while waiting for the water to come out hot. If the distance from the cylinder (or the boiler if a combi has been fitted) to the point of use is minimised, the dead-leg will be shorter so the waste of water and energy will be reduced. Insulation of the hot water pipe that runs between the boiler and the tap may keep the water warm enough to be used without waiting for freshly heated water from the boiler or cylinder.

SINKS AND HAND BASINS
Mains pressure can run at 20L/min or more, so it is possible

In-line flow regulator suitable for basins.

to save water by restricting this flow where the full pressure is not needed – for example in hand basins. Flow restrictors are available which can be plumbed in near the point of use and smaller bore piping would reduce both the flow and the dead-leg.

Spray tap heads or aerators can reduce water flow from a tap by up to 50% while still providing an effective flow of water for washing hands. Spray taps may require more regular maintenance than conventional taps to ensure that nozzles are not blocked by soap, grease or lime-scale and that water does not become trapped.

Note, however, that 'there has been concern that spray fittings and aerators might introduce a risk of legionella. The temperature of the water is an important factor in the occurrence of legionella outbreaks. Sufficiently hot water will kill off the legionella, as they cannot survive in very high temperatures. Descaling regularly and reducing the pressure of water to taps will reduce the production of aerosol droplets, which is how legionella usually enters the body.'[2]

Taps are used for filling the sink or basin as well as rinsing so it is useful to be able to fill the basin quickly without the spray switched on. Inserts are available which

can be fitted to taps with a round outlet or standard metric thread. These inserts deliver a spray at low pressure and an unrestricted flow as the tap is opened more fully.

When fitting any kind of tap attachment it is necessary to maintain the gap between the bottom of the tap outlet and the overflow of the basin in order to guard against the risk of back contamination of the mains supply.

Some single-lever mixer taps contain a cartridge which produces resistance as the lever is lifted to a preset flow rate – 6L/min, for example. The full flow can be obtained by lifting the lever further than this stop point.

In commercial applications, sensors and push taps are effective at saving water where there is a risk that taps may be left on. Sensors are also more hygienic as they avoid the need to touch the tap with dirty hands to turn it on and then to touch it again with clean hands to turn it off. There is no reason why these should not be used in domestic applications.

Lastly, cleaning your teeth with the tap running uses an average of 9 litres of water whereas turning off the tap whilst brushing can reduce this to less than a litre.

Adopting one or more of the measures described in this section will reduce the volume of water used, but otherwise this is one example of the ways in which we may have to adjust our habits to reflect the increasing scarcity of water resources.

WASTE DISPOSAL UNITS

Waste disposal units use power and drinking quality water to dispose of food waste via the public drainage system, which seems to be a poor use of resources in every sense. In many Local Authorities, cooked food waste is now collected directly. Uncooked vegetable peelings can be added to the compost heap, saving water and energy while producing useful compost.

SHOWERS

Water-saving shower heads can deliver the effect of a power shower while using considerably less water. This effect is achieved by introducing air just before the point of delivery. They require pressure of at least 1 bar, which is usually produced by mains-fed combination boilers but is not always available from vented systems. Water-saving shower heads are not appropriate for electrically-heated showers as they can lead to overheating and the risk of scalding.

As a rough guide, most people find a flow of 10L/min comfortable for a shower, although a water-saving shower head can give the same level of comfort with a reduced flow.

Photo: H2O Building Services

Shower water use

Conventional wisdom has it that showers use less water than baths. This is not necessarily true. The average length of a shower is said to be between five and six minutes. At 9L/min, a seven-minute shower would use 63 litres whereas

	7.2kW elec	9.5kW elec	Water saver	Power shower
Flow rate*	3.5L/min	4.6L/min	4–10L/min	12L/min+
Water use for 5-min shower	17.5L	23L	20–50L	75L
% of 70L bath	25%	32%	28–71%	107%

*At 30°C rise in temperature.

a bath may use as little as 60 litres, depending on the design. Power showers consume even more than this as they are pumped from the tank at high pressure and if flow rates exceed 12L/min then technically it is necessary to inform the water supply company. On the other hand, if you share a bath, the water usage per person is halved.

BATHS

Bath sizes vary considerably. Shaped or narrow baths take less water to fill up to the equivalent height of a conventional bath. Volumes of new baths should be stated in the manufacturer's brochure and these are generally quoted to the centre of the overflow.

It is necessary to ensure that an accurate comparison can be made as some manufacturers subtract the volume of a submerged adult (usually around 70 litres) when quoting the volume to overflow level. If a bath size is quoted as 100 litres this would probably mean that the overflow is reached when adult + water = 170 litres. Available data suggests that people tend to fill the bath to approximately 40% of volume – in this example, therefore, using 68 litres

Bath sizes can be deceptive: above 290 Litres; below 185 litres.

per bath. Insulated baths keep water warm longer and reduce the need to top up when enjoying a long soak, saving both energy and water.

Technology for the extraction of energy from waste water is not yet fully developed, although trials are being carried out in the USA to make use of this recycled energy to pre-heat the incoming supply to the boiler. It has been pointed out that simply waiting for bath water to cool before disposal allows the 'useful heat' to dissipate inside the property rather than within the drainage system.

Bath water can be reused for garden watering. However, if considering doing this, it would be necessary to use soaps that contain only plant-based ingredients and to allow the water to cool before distributing it in the garden. Storing and recycling greywater raises various issues which are covered in the section on storage tanks later in this chapter.

DOMESTIC APPLIANCES

Washing machines and dishwashers are steadily becoming more efficient in terms of their water use as well as their energy use. Experts calculate that dishwashers use less water and energy than washing by hand, although they do produce noise over a more extended period. It is more efficient to avoid half loads in either machine, even if a half-load button exists, as this uses more than half the energy and water required by a full load. Water can also be saved by scraping food off dishes rather than rinsing before loading the dishwasher.

Even given the energy and water savings available from more technologically advanced machines, it usually only makes economic sense to replace a machine which is nearing the end of its life (typically eight years), due to the embodied energy of the appliance and the environmental impact of its production and disposal. Water consumption is now mentioned on the EU energy labelling of relevant domestic appliances (see the 'Appliances' section in Chapter 5). The following table illustrates the water savings to be gained by using a more efficient machine:

	Washing machine		Dishwasher	
	Old	New	Old	New
Litres per wash (full load)	100	50	25	16
Annual use (m³)*	37.4	18.2	9.1	5.8
Annual water cost**	£72.80	£36.40	£18.20	£11.60

*Based on seven full-load washes per week for both washing machine and dishwasher
**Based on combined average UK water and sewerage charges of £2.00 per m³.

REGULATIONS

The Water Fittings Regulations (1999) may soon be updated (Byelaws 2000 for Scotland). A considerable amount of useful information may be obtained from WRAS – the Water Regulations Advisory Scheme. Water consumption does not presently feature in Building Regulations, although the Building Regulations Advisory Committee is currently considering this matter.

Reducing water demand in the garden

It is possible to have a beautiful and productive garden with minimal use of mains water. The peak demand for garden watering tends to be in high summer when water supplies are under greatest pressure, so measures to reduce garden water use can have a very significant effect.

PLANTING

Examples of plants which thrive in hot and dry conditions once established include:

- African Lily (Agapanthus africanus)
- Buddleia (Buddleja)
- Californian Lilac (Ceanothus thyrsiflorus)
- Californian Poppy (Romneya)
- Catmint (Nepeta)
- Daisy Bush (Olearia)
- Evening Primrose (Oenothera)
- Foxtail Lily (Eremurus)
- French Honeysuckle (Hedysarum coronarium)
- Lavender (Lavandula)
- Peruvian Lily (Alstroemeria)
- Pink (Dianthus)
- Red-hot Poker (Kniphofia uvaria)
- Rock Rose (Cistus, Helianthemum)
- Rosemary (Rosmarinus officinalis)
- Straw Daisy (Leucochrysum Albicans)
- Thyme (Thymus)
- Tulip (Tulipa)

There are many other shrubs and herbs of Mediterranean origin which require little or no watering, although some may struggle in soils which are not well drained. Ornamental grasses come in many varieties and sizes and thrive in arid conditions.

WATERING

Most established trees and shrubs do not need watering. Vegetable seedlings need to be watered with a rose-head attachment on the watering can. For established vegetables it is more effective to water the base of the plant directly without the rose-head and to avoid soaking the leaves.

Watering in the early morning or late evening will reduce evaporation so a higher percentage of the water will penetrate to the roots. Watering cans direct water more efficiently than hoses and reduce the risk of damage to plants, which is a common problem with trigger jets on hoses. Occasional soakings are better than regular light watering as a good soaking encourages the roots to go deeper to seek out the water stored in the ground.

LAWNS

Lawns are probably the greatest cause of water wastage in a garden. A sprinkler uses as much water in an hour as the

average family uses in two days. Although lawns will turn brown during a prolonged dry spell, they will not have died; the roots are deep and lawns will quickly recover once rain returns. As with vegetables, occasional soakings are much better than regular light watering. Allowing the grass to grow longer provides shade which reduces soil temperature, cuts down evaporation and reduces the need for watering.

Photos: Kent & East Sussex Railway

SOIL AND MULCHES

Soils which contain a good quantity of organic matter will tend to hold water best. Organic matter reduces the frequency at which watering will be required, in addition to providing essential nutrients for plants.

Mulches and bark placed over the topsoil will help water

to be retained in the soil and will greatly reduce evaporation. If you are laying gravel to reduce evaporation, the use of a permeable liner avoids mixing the gravel with the soil.

HARVESTED WATER

Water butts are the most familiar form of harvested water. These are simple to install and are usually filled directly from the downpipes which convey water from the gutters to the drainage system, by means of a diverter.

The simplest form of water butt allows a watering can to be filled from a tap near the bottom of the butt. This requires mounting at sufficient height for the can to be placed easily under the tap. A stand can be made simply from old bricks and offcuts of timber and need not require a bespoke unit – but beware, water butts are very heavy when full. Butts vary in size up to 220 litres and many are made from recycled plastic. Some incorporate child safety lids.

When the butt is full – which will be the case for much of the winter when rainfall is high and demand is low – the overflow must be connected to the drainage system. It may be possible to connect into the downpipe below the overflow point, or to a drain or gully below. Submersible pumps can be installed in water butts, which means that a hosepipe can be run directly from the harvested water, even during a hosepipe ban.

Some plants will benefit from a winter soak to make use of the abundance of stored water. This is particularly important for plants that lie in a 'rain shadow' against a fence or building which shelters them from the prevailing wind and rain.

Rainwater harvesting

The basic principle behind rainwater harvesting is to collect the water which falls on the roof and store it for use in flushing toilets. It is also possible for washing machines to use harvested water – rainwater is soft and therefore ideal for clothes washing, eliminating the need to use conditioners.

If water efficiency has already been addressed and the effective flush volume of toilets has been reduced to less than 4 litres, the demand for non-potable (non-drinking) water may be so low that there is little to be gained by installing such a system. There is also at present a considerable debate about the environmental effectiveness of rainwater harvesting as it takes energy to construct, install, run and maintain a rainwater harvesting system. As has been noted, embodied energy calculations are potentially extremely complex but recent research has drawn attention to the fact that the mains water system is actually a very energy-efficient way of delivering water to

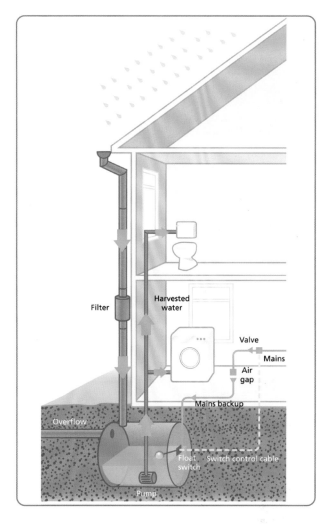

our homes and businesses. Further research is evidently needed but instinctively it feels wasteful to purify water to drinking quality and then to utilise it as a waste-disposal mechanism. If water shortages become more common as a result of climate change, this may also affect the way in which rainwater harvesting systems are assessed.

STORAGE TANKS

Rainwater storage tanks may be sited above or below ground. Above-ground systems require protection from freezing.

Communal systems (usually underground) that pool the rainfall from several properties are slightly more efficient than

Photo: Rainharvesting Systems

Photo: Rainharvesting Systems

individual systems and should require less mains backup in prolonged periods of low rainfall.

Water is pumped from the storage tank, either directly to the points of use in the property or to a secondary header tank in the loft. The main disadvantage with direct-pumped systems is that toilets have to be flushed with a bucket of water if the pump fails. By contrast, rainwater harvesting provides a source of water for toilet flushing at the very least during the occasional interruptions to the mains supply.

MAINS BACKUP

There are several ways of arranging mains backup but the most common for direct-pumped systems is to use a float switch inside the storage tank to sense when the level reaches a critical low point and then to open the mains water feed to refill with a limited amount of mains water.

As the tank only partly refills there will be plenty of room for rainwater to be collected when it starts raining again, so the system will always favour the use of harvested water. Mains backup must be correctly installed in accordance with the Water Regulations (1999) to prevent back contamination of the mains supply and there are legal standards of how pipes must be marked up to identify rainwater or greywater pipes clearly.

FILTRATION AND CLEANING

Filtration is necessary to prevent leaves and other debris from entering the tank via the gutter system. There are sophisticated filtration systems available which are self-cleaning and some even reject the first flush of water when rain commences as this tends to contain the most debris.

When the tank is full, excess water drains off to the surface-water drainage system as normal. This overflow will also remove floating contaminants, which is a good reason not to oversize the tank.

TANK SIZING

Tank sizing is subject to the law of diminishing returns. The larger the tank, the fewer the occasions when mains backup will be required, but the effect decreases as tank size is increased. A tank size of 1,500 to 2,000 litres will supply most of the toilet and washing machine requirements in the average house. As a guide to volume, one cubic metre contains 1,000 litres.

To work out the amount of water that could be collected from a domestic property, first calculate the area of the roof in plan – the effective area of the roof is independent of the slope, so it should be similar to the ground floor area of the house. Next, find out the expected annual rainfall per square metre – average rainfall figures for all areas of the country are available on the Met Office website (**www.met-office.gov.uk/climate/uk**). For example, a house in the West Midlands would receive an average rainfall of 669mm p.a. If the ground floor measured 5m x 9m the available water would be calculated as follows:

Average rainfall (m) x area of roof (m^2) = available water (m^3)

Ground floor area = 5m x 9m = $45m^2$
Available rainwater = 45 x .669 = $30.1m^3$

As some is lost to evaporation, filtration inefficiencies and overflow, not all of this water is collected, so multiply by 0.75 to gain an approximate idea of the yield ($0.75 x 30 = 22m^3$). Terraced housing with the ridge running parallel to the street will only realistically allow harvesting on one side of the property unless costly alterations are made to convey water through or under the building.

PAYBACK PERIOD

Most water bills charge for supply of water and for disposal. For metered properties, the amount billed for both supply *and* disposal is calculated from the supply meter. As the water which is harvested displaces mains water supply but is still drained eventually via the toilet, it has been argued that rainwater harvesting is unfairly depriving the water companies of revenue. On the one hand, this fails to account for the fact that the water

Wisy filter.

Illustration courtesy of Rainharvesting Systems

Discount rate p.a.	5%	
Water price escalation p.a.	5%	
Installed cost of system	£2,500	
Tank size	1,500 litres	
Mains water saved p.a.	22m³	
Combined cost per m³	£2.50	
Saving per annum	£55	
Payback period: 2,500 ÷ 55 =	45 years	

which is harvested is stored when rain falls rather than being transferred directly to the drainage system, so there is indeed a net reduction in the volume of water which is drained away. On the other hand, the amount of pollutants which water companies are required to treat remains the same.

Note that if interest rates and water price escalation are unequal over the long term this significantly affects the calculation. If water prices rise more quickly than the absolute level of long-term interest rates, the payback period for rainwater harvesting will be shorter. The calculation also ignores the cost of maintaining the system, and takes no account of the small amount of energy required to run the pump (unless the system is gravity-fed).

Payback periods will vary across the country. In the South-West, where rainfall is higher, water charges are currently double those in the South-East. This leads to the bizarre conclusion that the payback period for installations in the South-West may be far shorter than for installations in the South-East.

Rainwater harvesting also has a beneficial, if minor, effect on the drainage system as it serves to hold water when it rains, rather than conveying it directly to the storm-water drains. With the increasingly evident effects of climate change, periods of heavy rain are expected, so widespread harvesting and storing of rainwater could reduce the risk of local flooding.

For further information see: The Chartered Institute of Water and Environmental Management, **www.ciwem.org***; and The UK Rainwater Harvesting Association,* **www.ukrha.org**

GREYWATER REUSE

Greywater is defined as that which is recovered from hand basins, baths and showers and, like harvested rainwater, it is normally used for toilet flushing. Using greywater on the garden without further treatment is not recommended unless biodegradable detergents have been used, and only then in small quantities.

Unlike rainwater, greywater requires a settlement tank and filtration treatment to remove contaminants, and biological cleansing or disinfectant chemicals or UV filtration to deal with organic compounds generally. It is not recommended that greywater is stored for long periods.

PRIVATE WATER SUPPLIES

There is a common misconception that boreholes are a water-saving substitute for mains supply. Boreholes abstract water from the same underground reserves that are used for the public mains supply – 75% of the water supply in the South-East is already taken from underground reserves. Energy is also required to drill and operate boreholes, whereas the mains supply performs the same function very efficiently in energy terms. An Environment Agency licence is required for abstraction of more than 20m^3 per day.

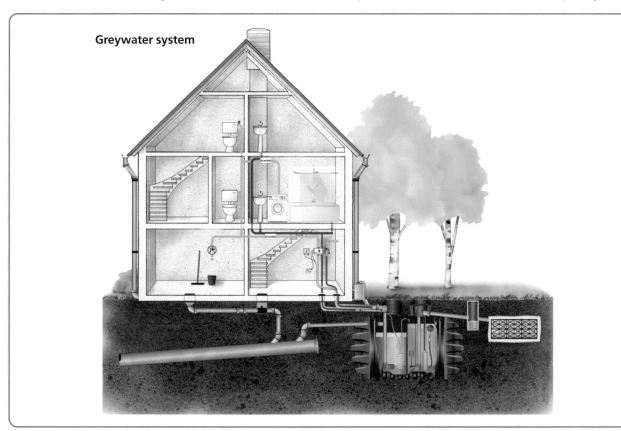

Greywater system

Illustration: www.aqua-lity.co.uk

Reed-bed systems and composting toilets

COMPOSTING TOILETS

The basic concept of a composting toilet is to allow natural processes to break waste down into a safe and essentially inert form so that it can be disposed of safely as a fertiliser. This process may need encouragement - sometimes shredded cardboard is added to the waste in order to prevent the mixture becoming too wet for the natural mouldering processes to operate properly. It is not uncommon to add tiger worms to the mixture to accelerate the process.

Two basic varieties are available – self-contained toilets are larger as the waste is stored in the bathroom. The alternative, if space and layout permit, is to collect the waste in a tank which is situated below the bathroom floor, effectively on a different level. Vent fans are fitted to most units but, at an average of 5W, their power consumption is surprisingly low (under £5 per year at 10p/kWh).

Smaller models require regular turning in order to aerate the mixture and some models even incorporate heaters to accelerate the process of decomposition. The energy consumed by heaters would partly offset the environmental benefits of using a dry toilet system.

It is possible to obtain Building Regulations approval for composting toilets. It is worth noting that as there is no connection to mains water, the Water Supply (Water Fittings) Regulations 1999 do not apply.

Compost toilets require no drainage, they are silent to operate and, thanks to the fan, they do not produce odour.

Waterless self-contained.

Waterless remote tank.

Photos: Sancor Industries Ltd

They do not freeze, which can be a great advantage in a remote location without power and even for outdoor toilets in parts of the UK. Their only disadvantage is that the compost which is produced at the end of the process will have to be removed and spread on the field or garden.

REED BEDS

Reed beds are simply ponds into which liquid effluent, such as the outflow from a septic tank, is channelled and which then convert the effluent to harmless plant material and gases. They work by using three principal methods:

- the ability of plants to convert waste matter
- the chemical properties of the gravel or soil
- the action of microbes which live in the soil

The microbes, flora and fauna in the soil are the most effective and important ingredient in these systems and the function of the reed is in part to introduce oxygen to the root system and to provide an environment for the microbes to flourish and do their work.

Ponds are generally lined in order to prevent any seepage into the adjacent ground and then filled with gravel and soil which acts as a base for the plants and reeds. The effluent is then normally delivered by means of a

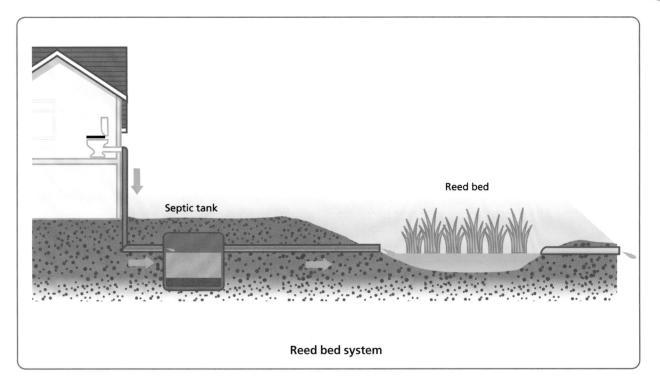

Septic tank

Reed bed

Reed bed system

feeder trench below the surface – this is known as a horizontal flow system. Where the effluent is delivered above the surface this is known as a vertical flow system, which is more common in the USA than in the UK.

REFERENCES
[1] OFWAT Security of supply, leakage and water efficiency 2005–06 report.
[2] Environment Agency Website.

Installing a Water Butt

Water butts vary in design so it will be necessary to check the installation instructions provided with any particular system. The following example is based upon the installation of a 190L recycled plastic butt and the diverter kit can be fitted to standard 68mm round or 65mm square downpipes.

THE RAIN SAVER WATER BUTT COMPRISES:
- Butt with pre-installed tap
- Diverter kit with connecting hose
- (Stand)

TOOLS REQUIRED
- Bricklaying tools
- Spirit Level
- Drill and 25mm hole cutter
- Hacksaw (plastic pipe can be cut with a wood saw but it harms the teeth so use an old one)
- Screwdriver

1 Identify a downpipe which carries the downflow from a significant portion of the roof.

2 Identify the required height of the installation – you will need to be able to get your favourite watering can under the tap at the bottom of the butt.

3 Construct a plinth for the butt to rest upon. Water butts are extremely heavy, so it is important that the plinth is strong and level.

4 Place the butt on the plinth. Some water butts come with a prefabricated stand. If using such a stand it is equally important to ensure that the stand is placed on firm level ground.

5 Measure and mark the height of the diverter. In this system, the diverter also acts as an overflow, so the height of the diverter will govern the level of water in the tank. Be careful not to set the diverter too high or the tank may overflow. For this water butt and diverter kit the cut should be made 20mm below the height of the top of the water butt.

6 Slacken off or remove the downpipe clips. Cut the downpipe and then cut off a further 30mm from what is now the lower section of the pipe.

10 Fit the lid - in this case a childproof lid has been provided.

7 Drill a 25mm diameter hole in the side of the butt, 50m below the top.

11 Sit back and wait or, if you're impatient, do a rain dance.

8 Fit the connector and washer from the inside and tighten the nut on the outside.

9 Assemble the diverter tube and the downpipe and connecting tube. Retighten or refit the downpipe brackets.

12 Enjoy your free water supply.
NB – Ensure that the overflow is working correctly when the butt is full.

Photo: Alternative Flooring Company

Carpets

It is well known that fitted carpets harbour dust mites, allergens, moulds and animal dander. In particular, the dust mite allergen triggers asthma, eczema and other allergic illnesses, affecting the health of children and other vulnerable individuals. Hard flooring does not harbour dust in the same way as carpets do.

What is less well known is that the chemicals used in many fitted carpets are a source of indoor air pollution, principally arising from the pesticides, stain inhibitors and fire retardants with which they are commonly treated. Fitted carpets can also act as a reservoir for toxic substances used in the home. Children are most at risk from this concentration of chemicals as they spend more time near or in contact with the floor and their immune systems are not fully developed.

For further information on this subject see: 'Poison Underfoot' – Greenpeace/Exeter University, **www.healthyflooring.org**. *For the carpet industry's view of this subject visit* **www.comebacktocarpet.com/ heal.htm**.

Alternative natural carpet materials are now widely available which, combined with regular cleaning, can significantly reduce this risk. In terms of hygiene they are most effective if used as rugs placed over hard flooring, as rugs are easier to remove and clean and hard flooring avoids the dirt traps which exist in the corners of carpeted rooms. It is also worth noting that natural materials do not generate static electricity in the same way as synthetic products, so they attract and retain less dust. Natural carpets are usually backed with natural latex rather than PVC or other synthetic products. If produced abroad, there is a significant embodied energy in natural carpets but this has to be offset against their many advantages and the fact that conventional carpets use a much larger amount of energy and water in their production.

JUTE

Jute is derived from the stems of the cochorus plant, a herb grown in tropical areas. At present it is mainly available in natural colour. As jute is soft, it can be closely-woven, giving the carpet a fine texture and making it ideal for use in bedrooms. Its use is not recommended in areas of heavy traffic such as entrance halls and stairs.

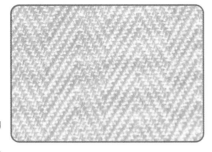

SISAL

Sisal is made from the leaves of the agave plant, which is a type of cactus. It is extremely hard-wearing and can be finely woven, making it suitable for living rooms and stairs. It accepts dye better than other natural carpet fibres so is available in a wider range of colours.

COIR

Coir consists of fibres taken from the outer husk of the coconut – the coconuts we normally see are just the inner shell of the seed pod. These fibres are soaked and softened and then spun into a yarn. It produces a rugged, tough and inexpensive flooring material.

SEAGRASS/MOUNTAIN GRASS

Seagrass is harvested from tall grass-like plants which grow in wetland areas. The weave tends to be quite coarse and open and there are plenty of natural colour variations. Grass carpets are hard-wearing and inexpensive. but they tend to have a natural sheen which makes them unsuitable for use on stairs.

WOOL

Wool is a much more familiar natural carpeting material, widely popular as it is softer than all the materials described above. Lanolin acts as a natural stain inhibitor so there is no need to add the chemical stain inhibitors used in synthetic carpets.

Photo: Alternative Flooring Company

Photo: Natural Carpets

However, wool carpets commonly have the same synthetic backing which is applied to non-natural carpet materials, which includes synthetic latex. This contains a vulcanising agent known as styrene, which is a known carcinogen.[1] Styrene is one of the chemicals responsible for the 'new carpet smell'. Many wool carpets are also treated chemically and may therefore contain some of the fire retardants, pesticides and other chemicals mentioned above.

Some of the UK's wool carpeting is made from wool which is imported from New Zealand and Australia, which greatly increases the embodied energy of the product, while there is a plentiful supply of British wool for which farmers presently receive a low return.

SOFT FURNISHINGS

Foam furnishings can add to the cocktail of synthetic substances present in the indoor environment and they give off highly toxic fumes when burnt. Polyester-filled furnishings are routinely treated with a variety of chemicals including fire retardants, which have given rise to various health concerns. Rugs and other soft furnishings manufactured in more remote areas, by contrast, contain none of these chemicals and seem to perform perfectly well without them.

Polybrominated diphenyl ether (PDBE) is one of a family of brominated fire retardants commonly used in computers and other household electronic equipment. A recent US study has shown that PDBEs are now occurring in abnormally high concentrations in breast milk.[2]

Imported traditional furnishings.

Courtesy of: Eastern Importers, Taunton

Hard flooring

WOOD FLOORING

A wide selection of wood flooring is now available. Care is needed as there are also products which imitate wood but are made from different materials – some are plastic with a photograph of wood grain printed on the top. Hybrid products, sometimes known as 'engineered boards', have a real wooden surface attached to a core of MDF or plywood (see the section on 'Composite/particle boards' in Chapter 2). These may not last as well as solid wood and are difficult or impossible to repair if a scratch occurs. Some engineered boards consist of small sections of solid wood laminated together to form a board or tile, although lamination frequently involves the use of formaldehyde resins.

The presence of the FSC (or PEFC) logo on solid wood flooring indicates to the consumer that the wood has been sustainably harvested from well-managed forests. Ash, birch, cherry, maple, oak, and beech are all used for flooring and it is possible to obtain timber which has been grown in the UK, although most of the timber available

Above: Solid oak flooring.
Below: Wood sections glued together.

is European and North American. Hardwood flooring specialists and timber merchants may be able to help if local products are not available from DIY stores.

Adhesives are frequently employed when fitting wooden floors. Many of these adhesives are toxic and continue to emit fumes for months or even years. Non-toxic adhesives have recently become available but they will need to be ordered via a builders' merchant until they are used more widely and stocked on the shelves.

Photo: Rewmar

Floor finishes are another source of concern for the environment as many substances contain VOCs (volatile organic compounds). However, natural oils or wax provide an excellent finish for hardwood floors. They are less hard-wearing than some factory finishes or varnishes and will need periodic reapplication to maintain their lustre, but they have the great advantage that scratches can be simply

Oak flooring finished with UV oil.

repaired by sanding and then adding a little of the oil/wax originally used. UV oils (made from soy and sunflower oils) harden under exposure to ultraviolet light to form a natural lacquer which is an attractive and tough floor finish. Natural oils and waxes also have a better smell than products which contain high levels of VOCs.

Photo: Western Cork Ltd

CORK

Cork is derived from the bark of the cork oak tree, mainly grown in Portugal and other parts of the Mediterranean. The bark is harvested every nine years and then grows back without harming the tree so it is a completely sustainable product. In addition to being an excellent insulator, it regains its shape well after being compressed under furniture, due to its cellular structure. Cork can also be used in bathrooms and kitchens; the natural presence of suberin, an inherently waxy substance, means that cork is resistant to water and therefore to rot. Many cork flooring products have already been sealed with PVC but it is still possible to buy unsealed cork. Alternative sealants are also available.

LINOLEUM

Linoleum was originally manufactured from linseed oil, hence the name. However, during the second half of the 20th century this natural product was often substituted by petrochemical-based plastic products (vinyls) which appropriated the name 'lino'. Genuine linoleum is still made and is rapidly regaining popularity. It is available in a wide variety of colours and textures and is made from linseed oil, wood flour, rosin, jute and limestone. The pigments used

Marmoleum.   Photo: Forbo-Nairn

are also sourced in an environmentally responsible manner.

Natural linoleum is ideal for use in bathrooms and kitchens. It needs little or no maintenance, is easy to clean, and it smells good. In terms of environmental life-cycle assessment, natural linoleum has one of the lowest environmental impacts of all flooring materials.

BAMBOO

Bamboo is a plentiful and fast-growing plant which is excellent for flooring, being very strong and hard-wearing. Bamboo is produced in thin strips which are laminated together to be used as flooring, so it may be necessary to check which chemicals have been used for lamination and for finishing.

Photo: Dain Sansome

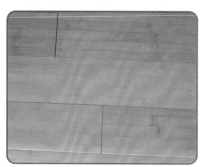

As bamboo is fast-growing it is a good alternative to hardwoods (hardwoods are extremely slow to grow and have a limited supply which cannot respond quickly to increased demand). Bamboo is grown primarily in South-East Asia, so it has a relatively high embodied energy compared to locally grown timber but its durability helps to offset the energy costs of transport to the UK.

TILES, STONE AND ADHESIVES

Ceramic tiles are generally considered to have a low environmental impact, being fired from clay, which is a plentiful resource. Tiles are also very durable and inert so they can be safely recycled as hardcore at the end of their use. Like stone, the main environmental impact of ceramic tiles is the transportation required, as most tiles sold in the UK are manufactured abroad. It is still possible, but not easy, to source locally produced stone and tiles.

Solvent-based tile adhesives, like conventional paints, contain a variety of toxic substances, including VOCs and synthetic resins. Water-based latex adhesives are not widely available in the UK at present and some water-based adhesives are not suitable for use in bathrooms. However, good quality non-toxic tile adhesives can be purchased from the USA or via the Internet.

RUBBER FLOORING

Underlay is now available which is made from recycled car tyres, or rubber crumb. Rubber underlay has excellent sound attenuation and thermal properties and can also help to prolong the life whatever carpet is laid over it, as it is more resistant to compression than many other underlays.

Photos: Interfloor

Paint issues

Paint consists of three primary ingredients – pigments, solvents and binders.

- **Pigments** are colours of either synthetic or natural origin, used in combination with white – normally titanium dioxide – which gives the paint its solidity of colour (opacity).
- **Solvents** allow the paint to be spread thinly and then evaporate as the paint dries. Water or white spirit are the most common, although turpentine, citrus oil and de-aromatised white spirit are also used.
- **Binders** are essentially glues whose primary function is to stick the paint to the surface being painted. Water-based paints commonly use petrochemical binders such as vinyls or acrylics while solvent-based paints use linseed oil or soya alkyds.

ECOLOGICAL ASSESSMENT

There are issues associated with all three of these ingredients and the ecological assessment of paints is a complex subject. Much attention has been focussed on the impact of paints on indoor air quality but the manufacturing process is equally important. Relevant factors include:

- Embodied energy and CO_2 emissions
- Volatile organic compounds (VOCs)
- Air pollution
- Land and sea pollution
- Resource use
- Environmental impact of extraction

It is important to choose the right paint for the job. If a paint does not perform as required the effort and expense has been wasted, so the environmental impact is significant. Similarly, coverage per litre and the number of coats required to achieve opacity are highly relevant, so it is only realistic to compare the impact (including labour time) of one coat of a thick paint that covers well with the impact of several coats of a translucent paint. For external paints, concerns about air quality are less pressing but performance is still important, as the longer a paint lasts – the lower will be its impact relative to products of a similar toxicity and embodied energy.

VOLATILE ORGANIC COMPOUNDS

The growing market in natural paints has arisen partly due to concerns about the high levels of volatile organic compounds (VOCs) that are to be found in the solvents in many paint products. The fact that ventilation is advised by the manufacturers during and after application, together with the appearance of reduced VOC paint in conventional paint ranges, indicates that the industry recognises that there are health problems associated with some of these compounds, especially toluene and xylene. However, it is worth noting that, including car paints and industrial coatings, paints only contribute about 10% of the solvents present in the environment.

TITANIUM DIOXIDE

It appears that the greatest environmental impact in paint production comes from the use of titanium dioxide (TiO_2). Without this chemical it is difficult to achieve opacity (solidity of colour), but TiO_2 did replace more toxic substances (such as lead oxide and zinc oxide) when it was introduced. The Ecolabel report produced for the EC states that the four environmental problems to which paints and varnishes contribute most are:

- Non-renewable resources depletion due to petroleum consumption for the production of TiO_2, resins and solvents
- Global warming through release of CO_2 and VOCs resulting from TiO_2 production and from solvents in paints and varnishes respectively
- Atmospheric acidification due to SO_2 released from TiO_2 processing
- Discharges of waste into water essentially due to TiO_2 mining

Many alternative paints are designed to have a reduced TiO_2 content or to eliminate this substance altogether. Some accept that it is a necessity for performance but reduce the content of other environmentally damaging chemicals in their paints.

PRESERVATIVES

Many paints contain preservatives. In the concentrations at which they are present even in conventional paints they are not regarded as a health hazard, but they *are* designed to be toxic to certain micro-organisms, which is the reason for their inclusion. Several brands of alternative paints are free of preservatives.

BREATHING WALLS

In addition to their reduced environmental impact, many natural or organic paints are breathable. Most old buildings and some new eco-buildings are designed to breathe. Old buildings are frequently prevented from breathing by cement renders and a variety of paint skins on both sides of walls – this can on occasion lead to damp and other associated health issues or even structural problems. The re-emergence of natural paints therefore gives homeowners the opportunity to allow walls to breathe again, as long as all the impervious material is first removed. It is worth noting that paints can be resistant to water while still being vapour permeable.

For further information see: 'Paints and Ecology' by Neil May (2005), article accessible via **www.natural-building.co.uk***; and EC ecolabel research,* **http://ec.europa.eu/environment/ecolabel/product/index_en.htm**
To recycle paint visit **www.communityrepaint.org.uk**

Alternative paints

LIME PAINT

Lime is an alternative and traditional binder used in paint. Cheap and simple to produce, lime paints are most commonly used on lime-plastered or lime-rendered walls in order to maintain breathability or vapour permeability and to ensure an effective union between paint and substrate. In some recipes a small amount of linseed oil is added to the mix in order to stabilise the finished surface.

Tallow, a type of animal fat, can be added to the limewash to increase water resistance but is rarely used anywhere now except on ancient buildings. Casein, the solid component of milk, is also sometimes added to limewash, as the resultant compound (calcium caseinate) gives better adhesion than pure limewash while retaining good porosity.

LINSEED PAINT

Linseed oil is another traditional binder for paint. Linseed paints last much longer on exterior joinery than many modern paints and limited maintenance will only be required approximately every seven years. Most traditional linseed paints currently available contain significant levels of titanium dioxide, although generally they are free of solvents and other toxic chemicals. Linseed-based paints have a longer drying time than 'conventional' paints. Although normally used on woodwork, they can be mixed with water into an emulsion for use on walls and ceilings.

SILICATE MASONRY PAINT

Previously unpainted mineral surfaces such as cement render, lime render or stone are ideal for the application of silicate paints, which are based upon stabilised sodium silicate. The paint forms a chemical bond with the substrate, which makes it extremely hard-wearing and resistant to weather and ultraviolet light, so it is most useful as an exterior masonry paint. Available silicate paints are non-toxic and free from solvents and biocides; surprisingly they are also vapour permeable, which helps to prevent the accumulation of moisture.

DISTEMPER

Distemper is an ancient paint formulation. The principal traditional ingredients are powdered chalk and animal skin glue, although modern mixes use linseed oil in place of the glue. It is still used today, as very subtle colours may be obtained from this base. However, it is not hard-wearing and is ineffective on damp surfaces. The addition of oil as a binder and borax as an emulsifier improves its durability while reducing its porosity – these are known as oil-bound distempers.

CLAY PAINT

Natural clay can also be used as a base for paint. Clay paints are breathable and contain mainly natural ingredients, although vinyl acetate is normally used as a binder. They are slightly different to apply in comparison to conventional paints and can result in a more textured surface.

WAXES, OILS AND VARNISHES

The main function of wax, oil or varnish is to protect timber while enhancing the grain. Lacquers and varnishes became popular because they appeared to offer more durability than wax or oil, but once a lacquered surface has been scratched or dented it is more difficult to repair than wood treated with natural coatings. Many lacquers and varnishes also contain a high level of VOCs and other synthetic materials.

There are plenty of natural oils and waxes which will perform the same function as a varnish while penetrating into and enriching the wood rather than simply coating it. Oils can be combined with vegetable wax and beeswax to form highly durable surface finishes.

DIY PAINTS

Using the base paints outlined above you can mix your own paints by adding pigments; these are becoming more readily available in shops and online. Natural pigments produce a much more natural tone than synthetic pigments and, if the paint is not mixed absolutely perfectly, there will be slight variations in the finished colour, which many people find more attractive and interesting than large areas of perfectly consistent colour.

PAINT STRIPPERS

Most paint strippers are highly toxic and do not biodegrade. The alternative method of dipping doors in sodium hydroxide can cause damage to the door as it has been known to raise the grain and can also dissolve whatever glue may remain in the joints. However, a new product has recently become available which is water-based, solvent-free and biodegradable. The manufacturers claim that it can even be washed down the drains safely, but of course if the stripper is contaminated with the removed paint material then this may not apply.

Wax finish.

Home Strip.

PROPRIETARY PAINT BRANDS

Eco-friendly paints vary widely so it is necessary to mention some proprietary brands which are more similar to conventional paints than those outlined above but which, in varying ways, have a greatly reduced environmental impact compared to conventional paints. Bearing in mind the issues raised in the preceding section, the following information is provided by manufacturers or distributors of leading natural paint brands:

■ 'Natural Building Technologies trade emulsions have been reformulated to have at least 30% less embodied energy (and 30% less CO_2 emissions) than similar conventional trade emulsions. This is mainly achieved by reducing TiO_2 content, the ingredient with most embodied energy and having greatest impact on resource use, habitat destruction and pollution, by over 25%. NBT trade paints are also manufactured in the UK, thus minimising transport CO_2 emissions. All NBT paints are designed to have minimum health impact. Indoor air quality is now a major factor in health and is the cause of many allergic and auto-immune problems. NBT trade emulsions are genuinely solvent free, virtually zero VOC free paints with no chlorinated preservatives, and no hormone mimics. They are also highly vapour permeable, thus assisting moisture control in buildings.'

■ 'Green Paints are produced for the Green Shop in the UK to exacting industrial standards, they can be used in virtually any situation to replace conventional emulsion and gloss paints both inside and out. Although modern technology is employed in their production, they contain no petroleum solvents, vinyl, or other toxic components. Instead they are based on a resin made from soya bean oils, water and renewable raw materials. Due to safe ingredients Green Paints create a safer environment for children and allergy sufferers.'

■ 'AURO decorating products are good for you and good for the environment. We stand out among manufacturers of natural paints and wood finishes because we have always been totally committed and uncompromising in our environmental standards. It goes, almost without saying, that we do not use petrochemicals in our products. We also ensure that natural raw materials come from environmentally managed sources and are produced using a sustainable ecological cycle. For example, much of the raw linseed oil used in our paints is organically grown close to the factory and any waste product and excess paint can be composted. Our paints are breathable and are based on natural ingredients and plant and mineral pigments. Our wood finishes are microporous so they don't flake, peel or blister and are easily maintainable. Our use of natural and plant based ingredients means that allergy sufferers and people who are chemically sensitive are more able to tolerate our products.'

■ 'Biofa natural paints not only perform as well, if not better, than your standard pot of chemical soup, they cost no more than other premium paints and won't damage your health. Biofa natural paints can help people with allergies and the paints smell of bergamot and citrus oil – much nicer than conventional paints! Your home will also appreciate natural products which allow buildings to breathe, being microporous. By allowing a surface to breathe properly, this discourages the build-up of condensation and resulting mould and allows the walls to naturally expand and contract as the temperature rises and falls within the house.'

■ 'Aglaia paints and decorating products have been manufactured since 1968 using only natural ingredients. These high performance products are based on traditional formulations that have been further developed to minimise the impact on the environment, to have no adverse impact on our health, and allow buildings to breathe more easily. Aglaia natural paints are made from abundant minerals and renewable crop sources, where *all* of the manufacturing waste goes to the municipal composting facility. Modern petrochemical-based paints produce toxic waste and, once applied, release dangerous volatile organic compounds that can be seriously damaging to our health. Aglaia natural paints are non-carcinogenic and do not encourage allergic reactions, as they contain no synthetic chemicals and attract little dust build up.'

Photos: The Green Shop

ALTERNATIVE PAINT BRANDS
www.natural-building.co.uk (NBT own range)
www.greenshop.co.uk ('Green Paints' and others)
www.auro.co.uk (Auro)
www.villanatura.co.uk (Biofa)
www.naturalpaintsonline.co.uk (Aglaia)
www.ecospaints.com (Ecos)
www.holkham.co.uk/linseedpaints (linseed oil-based)
www.realpaints.com (distemper, lead, oil etc)
www.earthbornpaints.co.uk (clay-based)
www.stastier.co.uk (lime paints)
www.limeearthpaints.com (lime earth paints)
www.osmouk.com (Osmo) natural wood finishes
www.ecosolutions.co.uk (less toxic paint strippers)

This list is by no means exhaustive and is only intended to give the reader an initial guide.

Kitchens

The kitchen is a great consumer of energy in the house. Electrical appliances are discussed in some detail in Chapter 5 so this section will focus on design and on the materials used to build kitchens.

LAYOUT

The layout of a kitchen can have some effect upon energy consumption. Good daylighting is useful for preparing, cooking and for washing up and can reduce electricity consumption. It therefore pays to design to make the best of the available windows (or skylights). Task lighting for the remainder is usually more effective than central lighting.

Fridges and freezers work more efficiently together if the freezer is below the fridge. This also reduces the need to bend down as fridges are opened more often than freezers. It makes sense to position fridges out of direct sunlight if possible and not to site them next to the boiler, the cooker or a radiator, as they would have to consume more power to maintain a low temperature.

CARCASSING

Carcassing is the kitchen manufacturer's term for the basic structure of wall- and floor-mounted cupboards which typically make up a kitchen. It does not include doors or worktops. Normally the material used for carcassing is chipboard or MDF. In addition to the health issues raised in connection with these materials in Chapter 2, they have the great disadvantage that they swell up when in prolonged contact with water. Chips and scratches are also difficult to repair.

It is an unfortunate fact of life that leaks occur from time to time and there is often more than one potential source of leaks in a kitchen. It is a considerable waste of resources to have to throw away base units as a result of leaks, so when replacing a whole kitchen a tougher material such as (certified) plywood or softwood should be considered. Beech ply and birch ply provide an attractive and hygienic finish and need only occasional oiling. Natural materials such as these are also easier to repair if scratches or dents occur – simply sand, fill any deep dents and then re-oil.

For existing kitchens which have become 'tired' or simply unfashionable, the major visible items such as worktops and doors can be changed without having to throw away the carcassing, as long as it is in reasonable condition. Often this can be done without major disruption, depending on how tiling has been fixed and the presence

Chipboard swollen by water.

of any services penetrations through the worktops.

Freestanding kitchen units are generally more expensive than fitted kitchens but last considerably longer. They can also be removed when a house is sold and be taken to the next property.

Plywood carcassing.

WORKTOPS

The most common construction for worktops is a thick layer of MDF or chipboard finished (usually only on the top) with a thin layer of formica. As with carcassing, the MDF and chipboard do not stand up well to water ingress.

Damaged worktops are a common reason for complete kitchen replacement, which is an expensive and energy-intensive exercise. Conventional worktops also combine materials with glues, which makes them extremely difficult to recycle.

Polished granite or smooth slate worktops are tough and durable and, if sourced from the UK, have a relatively low embodied energy. They are extremely hygienic and require little or no maintenance. Mosaic tiled surfaces are somewhat less hygienic as dirt often gets trapped in the grout joints.

Above: Chipboard.
Below: Polished granite.

Wooden worktops such as beech have low embodied energy and, if the timber is sustainably harvested, are probably the most eco-friendly worktops currently available. Whether it is the end grain or the side grain which is left exposed, the timber used is in small sections, so this can be an excellent use of offcuts which are not suitable for structural or joinery work.

Solid wooden worktops can be sanded and refinished if the surface becomes damaged, which is why they are more durable than other types of worktop. Danish oil is a well-recognised treatment for solid wood kitchen worktops but

there are other natural products such as tung oil, boiled linseed oil and teak oil that will all do a similar job. Beech, cherry, walnut, iroko, maple and oak can all be used for worktops.

Side grain (above) and end grain (below).

RECYCLING FACILITIES

In the course of everyday living, the majority of waste produced by a home is generated in the kitchen. This waste stream can be reduced by choosing products that have less packaging, choosing paper rather than plastics (especially hard plastics), and purchasing vegetables loose rather than in packets.

Photo: The Bin Company

By providing convenient recycling storage facilities in the kitchen for fruit and vegetable peelings, cardboard, paper, glass, cans and recyclable plastics (usually milk and drinks containers), the weekly task of recycling can be made much simpler and more efficient.

Generally the small kitchen storage facilities can feed the larger recycling boxes kept outside or in porches. Uncooked fruit and vegetable matter can be added to the compost heap along with modest amounts of cardboard. Paper, glass and cans are increasingly disposed of via kerbside recycling collections and schemes to recycle plastics are developing.

Home office

An increasing number of people have the opportunity to work from home either full or part time. Working from home has the huge advantage of cutting out the commute, for some or all of the week, saving time, money, stress and pollution (car sharing schemes and community car clubs can reduce the environmental cost of personal transport).

Timing of work can also become more flexible and allow other domestic responsibilities to be undertaken at the same time as putting in a full working day.

To set up a home office, all that is required is enough space for a desk, some shelving, a computer and printer, power and a telephone connection. The provision of a home office need not require the sacrifice of an entire room, as the office can also be used as a guest room or dining room. It is even possible to fit a home office into a cupboard that can be closed when not in use.

The advent of portable computers, bluetooth data exchange and wireless internet connection means that the home office can function without power or a telephone connection, although power is useful for task lighting and for connecting printers.

A home office could also be set up in a bespoke building sited in the garden. Planning permission may be required for garden buildings over a certain size and it is important that services connections to exterior buildings are carried out by suitably qualified professionals. Considerable thought must also be given to the heating strategy for independent home office buildings in order to avoid heating badly insulated buildings with fossil fuels for long periods.

The internet is changing the way in which we do business, enjoy our leisure, order goods and even conduct relationships. Without doubt its full potential has yet to be realised but it may hold the key to more sustainable living in the future, so it is likely that a home study area will become an increasingly important feature of modern living.

Photo: Oak-Apple Frames

For further information see the Working from Home Manual *by Kyle MacRae, Haynes (2006).*

REFERENCES

[1] www.osha.gov/SLTC/styrene/index.html.
[2] *Environmental Health Perspectives*, volume 111, number 14, November 2003, 'Polybrominated Diphenyl Ethers (PBDEs) in U.S. Mothers' Milk' by Arnold Schecter, Marian Pavuk, Olaf Päpke, John Jake Ryan, Linda Birnbaum and Robin Rosen.

9 WASTE AND POLLUTION

"When you build a thing you cannot merely build that thing in isolation, but must also repair the world about it, and within it, and the thing which you make takes its place in the web of nature." *Christopher Alexander* (A Pattern Language)

Construction waste

32% of the UK waste stream is generated from the process of construction and demolition. This constitutes over 90 million tonnes of waste per annum.

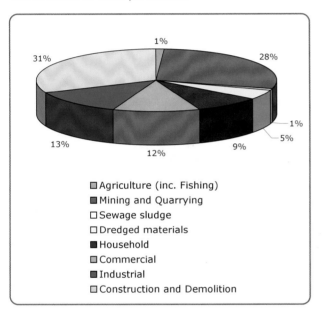

- ☐ Agriculture (inc. Fishing)
- ■ Mining and Quarrying
- ☐ Sewage sludge
- ☐ Dredged materials
- ■ Household
- ☐ Commercial
- ■ Industrial
- ☐ Construction and Demolition

Approximately 50% of construction and demolition waste is currently recycled, mainly in the form of hardcore which is crushed and reused, for example as road base. The UK has excellent resources of aggregates but it is less energy intensive to use recycled materials for aggregates than to mine and transport them afresh.

WASTE HIERARCHY
The environmental impact of available means of dealing with waste can be ranked as follows:

Reduce
13% of waste generated on building sites is made up of materials which pass directly from the manufacturers to the waste stream without ever being used. While it may be more efficient to order a small amount more than the estimated requirement – to avoid having to leave a job unfinished through lack of materials and deal with the consequent delays to other trades – the sheer size of this wastage implies that manufacturers or merchants cannot deal with returned items cost-effectively.

Packaging also forms a high percentage of materials on building sites, which implies that much packaging is not easily returnable or recyclable. Under the Producer Responsibility Obligations (Packaging

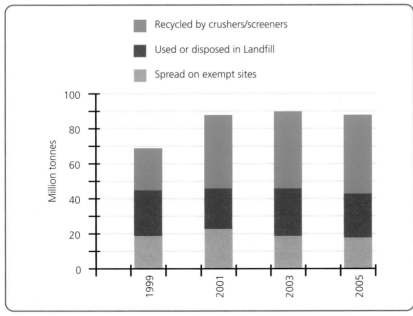

- ▨ Recycled by crushers/screeners
- ■ Used or disposed in Landfill
- ▨ Spread on exempt sites

Source: Department for Communities and Local Government

Regulations) which came into force in 2005, businesses over a certain size are now obliged to recover and recycle specified amounts of packaging waste each year and to certify that this has been achieved. In the domestic renovation sector, the main contribution that can be made by householders or small contractors is to select products which have the minimum of packaging and to order the correct amount of materials.

Re-use

Waste bins made from reclaimed timber.

The re-use of materials does not require energy to transform them into other materials, which is why re-use is above recycling in the environmental impact hierarchy. To encourage re-use, it is important to avoid spoilage by storing goods safely on site until they are needed. (It is also helpful to keep on good terms with the local builders' merchant, in order to be able return surplus materials in good condition, and to accept any percentage restocking charge which may be applied.)

Surplus timber can be re-used in any number of ways

either inside or outside the home although, as with all plans for re-use, the ability to store materials until the need arises is critical.

It also pays to see what materials can be re-used locally. For example, waste topsoil is usually generated when constructing a patio. By talking to neighbours, it is often possible to establish that someone in the district has a need for topsoil. It would cheaper for both parties to dispose of top soil in this way and saves on the transportation. Keeping it local also makes ecological sense as topsoil varies so much even over comparatively short distances.

The demise of local reclaim yards (often in favour of housing development) makes this kind of re-use more difficult to achieve, but the internet is an ideal method of advertising the availability of materials and a network of locally based sites would be a good way to promote low-energy re-use.

Recycle

Municipal household waste facilities now encourage recycling, after decades of dumping unsorted waste into landfill.

All waste sorted into the following categories can be recycled so, when carrying out renovation projects, householders can reduce the amount of waste which goes into landfill by keeping waste separate:

- Hardcore
- Timber
- Garden waste
- Metals
- Cardboard
- Plastics
- Electrical
- Batteries
- Paper
- Textiles
- Tyres

The Waste and Resources Action Programme (WRAP) is responsible for a range of innovative schemes which make use of recycled material. WRAP also works to promote waste minimisation through home composting, the real nappy programme and a range of other initiatives. Through their website it is possible to research the various uses for materials which are collected via recycling centres. For example, recycled glass is currently used for bricks, grit blasting, sports turf, container glass, water filtration, aggregate in concrete products, and fibreglass insulation. New uses for recycled products are being developed all the time. This represents a fundamental and welcome change of attitude – from viewing waste as a problem, to considering its potential as a resource.

For further information visit **www.wrap.org.uk***;* **www.wastewatch.org.uk***; and* **www.salvo.co.uk**.

Paint recycling
Each year approximately 80 million litres of paint are stored in garages and sheds or simply thrown away. In some parts of the country there are now schemes to enable the recycling of paint. To find out whether there is a paint recycling scheme in your area visit **www.communityrepaint.org.uk**.

Skips and segregation
At present the municipal waste facilities are not generally open to building contractors, so if you are planning a larger renovation project it is likely that you will need to hire a skip. Although different types of waste are mixed together in skips, the skip hire company will take the waste to its own transfer station and segregate it there. This is achieved by a combination of hand and mechanical sorting, all of which takes energy. Builders can take pre-sorted waste directly to skip companies' transfer stations, where they are charged by volume or weight.

Just as car breakers (scrap yards) store, dismantle and ultimately recycle cars, the same can be done with

Segmentation process for waste from mixed skips. Mechanical sorting through to hand sorting.

construction waste. Schemes are just beginning to develop to allow contractors to take pre-sorted waste to local holding areas. A pilot scheme in Peterborough (The Ecotrade Centre) has proved to be a great success so this could be repeated across the country. The cost of disposal at such sites will be less than the equivalent cost of skip hire, although the additional cost of transport and time for the builder has to be factored in so it is important that there is a wide network of holding sites. The accrued waste can also be sold on cheaply for direct re-use, such as topsoil or timber, or added to the waste stream for recycling, such as glass or aggregates.

For larger construction sites it is more efficient not to mix the waste but to segregate it as it arises on site. Skips filled with only one type of waste can be cheaper than mixed-waste skips.

The Building Research Establishment has set up the SmartWaste programme to help managers in construction and other industries to audit and improve their waste-handling procedures.

For further information visit **www.bre.co.uk**

Designing to minimise waste
Ideally, waste is best recycled and reused where it is generated, in order to reduce transport costs. Developers and renovators can assess the probable waste generation at the start of a project and design to reuse some of the materials in the finished building. Heavy items such as hardcore and bricks provide the best opportunities for reuse on site and the reuse of old bricks helps to keep the building consistent with its environment, for example when building an extension where outbuildings currently exist.

Composting
Composting is discussed in more detail in the section on 'Eco-friendly gardening' in Chapter 10. Composting releases methane (a potent greenhouse gas) but is otherwise an efficient way to recycle household and garden green waste. Home composting also avoids the energy consumption involved in transporting green waste to the local municipal site.

Incineration
Incineration is the next-to-last resort when handling large amounts of waste. It has the advantage that it reduces the volume of waste but, despite measures to reduce emissions, a variety of toxins is still released into the atmosphere. Approximately two million tonnes (9% of the total) of municipal solid waste is presently incinerated at 13 sites in the UK each year.[1] The environmental impact is somewhat reduced as the heat created is used either to generate electricity or for district-heating.

Landfill
Landfill is the last resort for waste disposal. The UK is running out of landfill space in many areas and the present rate of landfill is unsustainable. Leachate (liquid leaking) from active or closed sites poses a considerable threat to groundwater as it contains high concentrations of heavy metals, ammonia, toxic organic compounds and pathogens (organisms which cause disease).[2] Modern landfill sites are engineered to prevent contamination of groundwater, and methane can be collected and used for power generation and district-heating.

Above: Methane capture from landfill site.
Below: Power generation plant at landfill site.

The EC landfill directive was introduced in 2002. The new regulations aim to reduce the impact of landfill by reducing the amount of waste disposed of in this manner, by banning certain substances from landfill altogether, and by classifying landfill sites according to what type of waste they are permitted to accept. Attitudes towards landfill are finally beginning to change but perhaps one day we will dig up old landfill sites to recover anything from precious metals to bricks.

Electronic equipment and vehicles

When renovating property it is not uncommon to dispose of out-of-date electronic equipment. The average age of electronic equipment when it is discarded is as follows:

Electric cookers	12 years
Refrigerators and freezers	11 years
Televisions	10 years
Washing machines, dishwashers and tumble dryers	9 years
Hi-fi and stereo	8 years
Vacuum cleaners and carpet cleaners	8 years
Microwave ovens	7 years
Video equipment/radio, personal stereo and CD	6 years
Home and garden tools	6 years
Telephones, faxes, answer machines	4 years
Computers/small work or personal care appliances	4 years
Mobile phones and pagers/toys	2 years

Given the short life of these items, their collection and recycling will have to be improved markedly, especially in the light of the following items of EC legislation:

WEEE

The Waste Electrical and Electronic Equipment (WEEE) Directive aims to minimise the impact of electrical and electronic goods on the environment by increasing reuse and recycling and by reducing the amount of WEEE going to landfill. The directive seeks to achieve this by making producers responsible for financing the collection, treatment, and recovery of waste electrical equipment, and by obliging distributors to allow consumers to return their waste equipment free of charge.

ROHS

The Restriction of Hazardous Substances (RoHS) is an EC directive which came into force in the UK in July 2006. This directive restricts the use of heavy metals and flame retardants in electrical equipment, thereby aiming to reduce their environmental impact. Products placed on the European market on or after 1 July 2006 may not contain more than the specified limits of lead, cadmium, mercury, hexavalent chromium, polybrominated biphenyls (PBB) and polybrominated diphenyl ethers (PBDE).

BATTERIES

Increasingly, domestic and automobile batteries can be disposed of via kerbside recycling or in special bins at municipal sites as they contain a variety of heavy metals and other toxic substances. The 2006 EC Batteries Directive requires a gradual increase in the percentage which must be collected, thereby avoiding disposal in landfill sites, but also prohibits the sale of batteries which contain more than specified limits of mercury and cadmium.

END-OF-LIFE VEHICLES

Approximately two million vehicles are scrapped every year in the UK, of which over a million go to dismantlers in the first instance. Vehicles which have reached the end of their life were at one time worth something for scrap value. More recently it has frequently cost owners a small amount of money to dispose of them.

From January 2007, as a result of the EC ELV directive, vehicle producers are required to provide facilities where the last owners of their brands of vehicles may take them free of charge for recycling and disposal at the end of their lives.

Pollution

AVOIDING POLLUTANTS

When refurbishing or upgrading property it is likely that a variety of toxins and pollutants will be introduced into the home environment. Chapter 2 highlights some of the issues relating to the manufacture and use of building materials, while issues relating to interior furnishings are discussed in Chapter 8. It is also possible that toxins are released during the manufacture or disposal of products and, while their impact on the home environment is negligible, the pollution occurs elsewhere.

Two DIY retailers came in the top ten in Friends of the Earth's 2004 survey of 28 major retailers who are making efforts to reduce the number of hazardous chemicals in their products. Although it is incomprehensible that most of these substances were ever introduced into products in the first place, it is still worth finding out your local supplier's policy on selling toxic chemicals to the general public.

For further information see: **www.foe.co.uk/campaigns/ safer_chemicals/news/league_table2004.html**; *the*

World Wildlife Fund (WWF) Public Information Leaflet 'Chemicals and Health in the Home'; Greenpeace's 'Human Impacts of Man-made Chemicals' (2003); and Ecolabel's website at **http://ec.europa.eu/environment/ ecolabel/index_en.htm***.*

CLEANING PRODUCTS

Having gone to the effort of refurbishing your home with healthy materials, maintaining it and keeping it clean runs the risk of introducing a new set of toxins which can be found in everything from air fresheners to oven cleaners. In many cases, the chemicals in the cleaners are more toxic than the dirt at which they are aimed. Older products such as vinegar are surprisingly effective cleaning agents, and bicarbonate of soda is a useful oven cleaner. There are plenty of alternative ways of dealing with household cleaning and there is a growing range of products which are both biodegradable and much safer for humans to handle.

ACCIDENTAL POLLUTION

Carrying out refurbishment work can itself give rise to pollution. Care needs to be taken with the use of construction materials to prevent contamination of the dwelling being refurbished, or of neighbouring properties. Hazardous substances such as brick acid or paint strippers need to be handled and stored with great care. Nature is no respecter of property boundaries, so products used or spilled in one garden may soon leach out and pollute another.

Cement and lime-based mixes (mortar, render, concrete) should be thoroughly diluted when being washed out as they can cause visible staining if allowed to set on hard surfaces or cause damage to plants and trees if washed out over soft landscaping.

White spirit, which contains toluene and xylene, has gradually replaced turpentine (a natural product distilled from the sap of pine trees) as a thinner and brush cleaner. White spirit should not be added to the drainage system but disposed of safely at the local municipal refuse site. Another natural solvent which is less damaging to the environment is d-limonene, a common constituent of eco-paints which is distilled from the peel of citrus fruit.

RADON

Radon is a radioactive gas which comes from uranium and exists naturally in very small quantities in soils and rocks. In certain areas of the UK, particularly in parts of Cornwall, radon readings can be abnormally high; if an individual property is tested and found to have a high radon level, the Health Protection Agency recommend a series of remedial measures, depending on the ground-floor construction. If the construction is solid then the recommendation is to build a radon sump. The radon is then extracted by means of a fan. If there is already a sub-floor void, mechanical ventilation will suffice provided that all the vents are open and unobstructed.

In areas where the risk is significant, new buildings are required to incorporate a damp-proof membrane which is vented to the outside via a cavity tray. In high-risk areas, sumps and mechanical ventilation may also be required. The same precautions should be followed for extensions or whenever a ground floor is completely rebuilt.

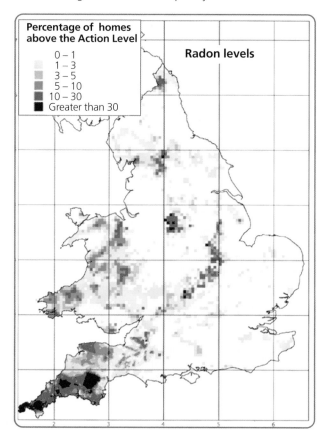

Radon levels

Percentage of homes above the Action Level

0 – 1
1 – 3
3 – 5
5 – 10
10 – 30
Greater than 30

For further information visit **www.hpa.org.uk/radiation/radon/index.htm**

CLEANING UP CONTAMINATION

Refurbishment work provides an ideal opportunity to atone for the environmental recklessness of the industrial and post-industrial age. Small concentrated pockets of polluted soil are best removed altogether but lower-level more widespread pollution can be cleaned up by a variety of methods – physical, chemical, thermal and biological.

Biological methods of decontamination are often the

most environmentally sustainable and best suited to renovation projects as they take longer to achieve the desired result than other methods. For new development, time is of the essence and there is usually insufficient time available to allow biological methods to work fully before the property is sold on.

Bioremediation techniques include adding a mixture of compost and minerals to the soil. This can 'fix' heavy metals within the soil so that plants, vegetables and trees may be grown safely on the site in the future. Preventing take-up of such substances into the food chain is technically known as breaking the pollutant-receptor pathway.[3] The action of composting can also break down some pollutants and the presence of compost in the soil introduces micro-organisms which can further break down certain chemicals.

Fungi have the capacity to break down a wide variety of substances including fuel oils and PCPs – biocides which were once widely used but are now banned. This technique is known as mycoremediation.

Oyster mushrooms.

Phytoremediation involves growing plants specifically to deal with certain types of contaminants. This works either by the plants breaking down the pollutants into less harmful compounds or by taking the pollutants up into the part of the plant which is above ground. The plant can then be harvested (in some cases used for biofuel) and the contamination then removed from the residue rather than having to transport or lift and treat the soil. Willow, reeds and some species of rye, among other plants, are often used for this purpose. Phytoremediation is far cheaper than soil removal but potential for its success varies from site to site depending on the other conditions required by the relevant plants and their ability to withstand the toxins.

Soil chemistry is a specialist subject and professional advice should be sought. However, it is clearly more environmentally beneficial to clean soil than to dispose of it and bring in fresh soil, as transportation is avoided and the problem is eliminated rather than transferred to a landfill site, with all the associated risks of leaching and contamination in the future.

Willow.

For further information see: Contaminated Land: Applications in Real Environments (CL:AIRE), **www.claire.co.uk**; *Contaminated Land Assessment & Remediation Research Centre,* **www.clarrc.ed.ac.uk**; *The Environment Agency; and The Scottish Environment Protection Agency (SEPA).*

OTHER FORMS OF POLLUTION

We tend to think of pollution as the presence of toxic substances in the ground, in the atmosphere, or in watercourses, but there are other forms of pollution which relate to buildings and construction work. Dust arising from refurbishment work is easily carried from one property to another so measures to reduce dust plumes will minimise risks both to the builders and to the neighbours. Noise pollution can also be managed and minimised – the theory of eco-building recognises that everything is connected, so good planning and consideration for neighbours is simply an example of the consideration to be shown for the environment in which we all live.

Light pollution is also a growing concern, as the view of the night sky from within our towns and cities is reduced or sometimes obscured by artificial lighting. The view of towns at night from nearby hills indicates just how much energy is being used to light nothing in particular. On a smaller scale, permanently lit

Dust control equipment in use.

security lights and other outdoor space-lighting can cause nuisance to neighbours while often adding little to security or safety. Simply walking or driving past some properties can trigger a series of security lights, which is not only pointless but also a waste of energy.

REFERENCES

[1] POST.

[2] Naturegrid.

[3] 'How to Remediate Heavy Metal Contaminated Sites with Amended Composts' by René van Herwijnen, Vishnu Priya Gadepalle, Tony R. Hutchings, Abir Al-Tabbaa, Andy J. Moffat, Mike L. Johns and Sabeha K. Ouki1.

Photo: Chris Gibson, Natural England

In urban areas, gardens act as corridors for wildlife while creating pockets of eco-diversity in an otherwise sterile environment. By absorbing CO_2 and rainwater, gardens soften the environmental impact of city living while providing a place to relax or to take some exercise in the fresh air.

Property renovators have a tendency to concentrate on the main dwelling and ignore the garden, or at best leave it right until the end, by which time the money has usually run out. Starting with the garden, on the other hand, allows neglected soils to recover and gives new plants and trees the chance to get established while the rest of the work is carried out.

PROTECTED SPECIES

Gardens which have been neglected for many years and left to grow wild can have a high ecological value and there may be legally protected species present. Bats may of course be using the building itself and particular care must be taken to avoid disturbing bat roosts. A neglected garden may have become home to slow worms, dormice, grass snakes, great crested newts, badgers and many other species which are protected by law so it may be necessary to carry out surveys before clearing what may appear to be waste land. Wherever possible it is best to maintain and work around existing features such as mature trees and hedges.

BIKE PARKING

Making provision for bike parking is also important when renovating a property. As much as 61% of journeys made by car in the UK are under five miles. Short journeys to school or to the shops can usually be made by bike instead; congestion would be reduced and we would all get fitter by trading four wheels for two as often as possible. However,

roads and houses have been developed for decades with little thought given to public transport or bike use, so this may not be possible for all properties. Ideally, direct access is best so that muddy bikes do not have to be wheeled through the house, causing inevitable damage to carpets and furnishings. Most Victorian terraces have access to the rear, originally for coal deliveries. This access can be used for bikes, and a shared entry gate adds extra security. Much semi-detached housing has side-alley access, which is ideal for bikes.

Many bike thefts from sheds are reported every year. If using a shed to store bikes it is wise to lock the bike to a

secure fixing set in concrete and to have a good lock (not just a padlock) on the shed itself. Where a garage is planned, bike access is made easier by having a separate side door so that the main door does not have to be opened just for a bike journey. In garages which are wide enough to get past the car without damaging it, bikes can be stored by being hung from hooks or racks fixed to the wall or ceiling.

CLOTHES DRYING

Drying clothes in the garden saves money and energy. If there is not sufficient space to erect a clothesline, a rotary dryer (whirligig) will do the job just as well. Rotary dryers are easily removable when not in use, as a short length of pipe can be driven (or concreted) into the ground to act as a sleeve for the post.

Hard landscaping

The same principles apply to materials used in the garden as apply to any other construction materials, namely:

- Use reclaimed or recycled products where possible
- Source locally produced items
- Avoid materials which can cause pollution

The garden is a good place to reuse material which has been rejected from the fabric or interior of the house. Reclaimed materials also tone in much better with older properties – railway sleepers make ideal borders for raised beds, although for an organic garden an untreated sleeper would be best. The creosote in sleepers makes them unsuitable (in fact against EU law) for use in situations where there is a risk of frequent skin contact, such as tables or children's play areas.[1]

SURFACING MATERIALS

Paving materials vary widely in terms of their cost, environmental impact and raw material. Concrete slabs are very effective but, as with all concrete products, they have a high embodied energy and may have travelled a long way before reaching the local merchant. If laid continuously and drained to the surface water system, slabs add considerably to the load on the drains, although this can be reduced by allowing gaps between the slabs and inserting low-growing plants so that water can drain through. Failure to insert plants will simply encourage weeds. Alternatively, a fine gravel can be used for the same purpose.

Cars can be parked on most paving materials as long as the sub-base is sound – it is certainly not necessary to concrete over the front garden to provide good hardstanding. Solid materials such as concrete and tarmac have a high environmental impact, add to the drainage problem and can also contribute towards the 'heat island' effect in cities, as they absorb excessive amounts of heat during the day. In extreme cases, impermeable landscaping materials have even been held responsible for subsidence as clay subsoils can shrink if they dry out, which is more likely if rainwater is prevented from entering the adjacent ground.

Blocks are more porous than slabs – clay blocks have a lower embodied energy than cementitious blocks and

encourage a wider variety of lichens and small plants but they are expensive if purchased new and reclaimed paviors can be difficult to find.

Gravel is completely porous (unless laid on an impervious membrane) and has a low embodied energy – for more information on the importance of the porosity of hard landscaping materials see the section on 'Sustainable urban drainage systems' later in this chapter. If using gravel in a garden it may be necessary to lay it over a sheet of porous membrane to discourage weeds.

Beech/Yew hedge: Above, winter; below, summer.

BOUNDARY PROTECTION

For security, longevity, cost and wildlife attraction, the most effective form of boundary protection is a hedge. In urban

environments, hedges can also be very effective at reducing traffic noise.

The main disadvantage with hedges is that they take a while to grow so they have fallen out of favour with a house-renovating public who require instant results. Hedges also take up more space than a fence, which may be an issue in small or narrow gardens; they do require some maintenance, although small clippings of most hedges provide good fuel for the compost heap.

To maintain privacy in all seasons, evergreen hedges are preferred, although it is possible to achieve excellent results by mixing deciduous and evergreen species to give year-round cover and changing colours through the seasons.

Fencing can be divided into three main groups: post and rail (or wire); closeboard; and post and panel.

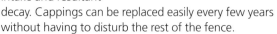

In just the same way that timber for structural use should be carefully selected, timber used in the garden should be certified as having come from a sustainable source (see the section on 'Sustainable timber use' in Chapter 2), and while treatment may be necessary this should be carefully selected to avoid introducing toxins into the outdoor environment. Local timber mills might not be certified by a major scheme but may still be able to provide reassurance that their timber is sustainably harvested and that trees are being replanted. The embodied energy of locally produced timber will be much lower and choosing local goods helps to boost the regional economy.

Post and wire fencing can be used as an initial support for living fencing. Willow is a good example of a plant which does not take up much room but grows rapidly to form a visual screen. If land drains are present, care must be taken with the planting as willow roots can cause serious damage to drains; regular pruning will also be required.

Photo: www.westwaleswillows.co.uk

All softwood fence posts should be treated and, if they are set in concrete, their life can be extended significantly by good concreting techniques:

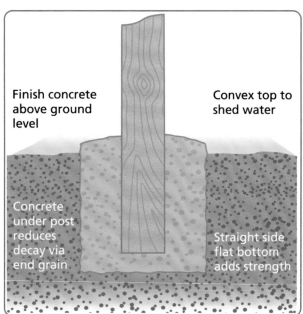

Finish concrete above ground level

Convex top to shed water

Concrete under post reduces decay via end grain

Straight side flat bottom adds strength

Closeboard fencing should also be treated to prolong its life and the end-grain capped to prevent excessive water intake and resultant decay. Cappings can be replaced easily every few years without having to disturb the rest of the fence.

Post-and-panel fencing is usually the cheapest form of fencing and the fastest to erect. It does not last as long as any of the others mentioned as the softwood panels tend to rot or become damaged more quickly. The life of the fence can be extended by using a solid wooden gravel board at the base – firstly this will last longer than the fence panel when in contact with moisture and secondly the gravel board can be replaced in due course without having to disturb the fencing material above (although sometimes the panels will have slumped onto the gravel board).

Concrete gravel boards are also available, but they are a higher energy product and tend to outlast the rest of the fence (ie posts and panels) for which they are designed. They are perhaps best used where concrete posts have been used, as these normally last longer than wooden posts.

Panel fencing is often associated with larchlap or similar products, but many other types of panels are available, although they may take a little more effort to locate. The use of locally grown materials for panel fencing also adds local character to the garden, whereas larchlap is used throughout the country.

Sustainable (urban) drainage systems (SUDS)

There is a dawning realisation that we have concreted over much of our urban environment and that most of the problems faced by our partly Victorian drainage system are due to the massively increased area which it is required to drain, and not simply to the increased frequency of heavy rainfall. Rainwater which used to soak into fields, gardens and lawns now lands on car parks, drives, roads, roofs and patios, from where it is channelled directly to the drainage system. Where rivers are used, the problem is gradually transferred downstream, with occasionally catastrophic results.

Photos: Hugh Hamner

Sustainable (urban) drainage systems (SUDS) is a relatively new science and at present it is largely directed towards new housing although there is no reason why many of the techniques which constitute SUDS should not be used in renovation – in other words, once people are aware of the issues they can avoid adding to the problem. In Scotland it is already a requirement for all new development to have a SUDS strategy in place.

SUDS has three main aims:

1. To reduce or delay the discharge of rainwater into the drainage system
2. To enhance the quality of the water which is released into the drainage system
3. To improve the environment and provide habitats for wildlife

Conventional approach   **Integrated approach**

Quantity   Quality   Quantity   Quality   Amenity   Amenity

The SUDS 'triangle'

Above: Ecoblock grid to stabilise grass or gravel.

Photo: Cooper Clarke Civils & Lintels

PERMEABLE SURFACES

Permeable surfaces allow water to permeate and soak through to the underground aquifers, replenishing the water table and reducing the burden on the drains. A solid concrete surface – including imprinted concrete – allows no water to pass through and, furthermore, it has a high embodied energy in comparison to gravel or block paving. Some forms of block paving are more porous than others, mainly dependent on the size of gaps between the blocks. Ribbed blocks are specifically designed to allow the maximum amount of water to permeate through.

Not all sites are suitable for permeable surfacing – if the subsoil is impermeable the water will not drain away. If the

subsoil contains pollutants, rainwater may transfer those pollutants elsewhere within the ecosystem.

HARVESTING WATER

Harvesting water for WCs and washing machines and rainwater harvesting in the garden (see Chapter 7) are both examples of water collected and stored for later use.

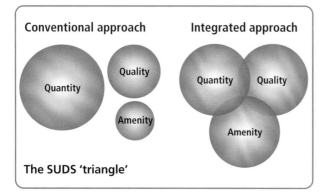

HOLDING PONDS

Ponds, drainage ditches (swales) and wetlands can all be used to store water so that it can be released gradually when the burden on the drainage system is reduced. This is known as attenuation. When rain falls on roofs or

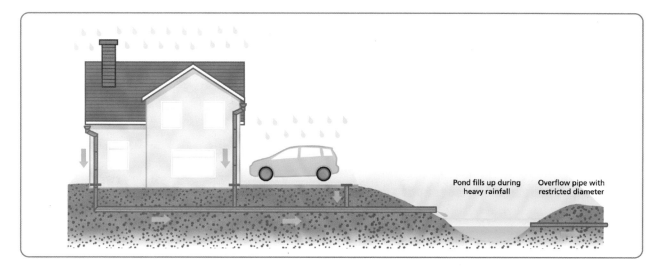

Pond fills up during heavy rainfall

Overflow pipe with restricted diameter

impermeable hard surfacing it is collected and then held in a pond or a series of ponds before being released into the drainage system in a controlled manner.

Attenuation pond. Doubles as play area.

WATER QUALITY

Rainwater often gathers pollutants such as oils, salts, litter or even sediments during its journey from the ground to the drainage system. Water quality is now a recognised concern for housing developments and SUDS techniques are increasingly used to clean the run-off from commercial property. An extreme example is the petrol interceptor tank commonly used on filling station forecourts, but reduced quantities of impurities can be dealt with by more natural techniques such as bioremediation. In general, SUDS techniques are most effective when used in combination, especially when the principal aim is to improve the quality of water discharge.

GREEN ROOFS

Green roofs not only use rainwater to feed the plants in the vegetative top layer but also act to slow down the release of water into the drainage system, as the layer of soil and gravel that forms the bed for the plants can absorb a significant quantity of water (see the 'Roofing' section in Chapter 2).

Photo: David Michael

Photo: Blackdown Horticultural Consultants

RECREATION AND WILDLIFE

Depending on topography, larger ponds can be created for existing developments as a shared community resource, acting as a holding pond for rainwater but also providing an amenity and a wildlife attraction. Native planting and careful design can therefore transform a potential flooding problem into an environmental asset.

For further information visit **www.sepa.org.uk/wfd** *and* **www.ciria.org.uk/suds**

Eco-friendly gardening

Most gardeners prefer to work with nature rather than against it and are consequently eco-friendly by default. Gardening is a huge subject so this section will only focus on gardens insofar as they affect the wider environment.

ORGANIC GARDENING

The key to organic gardening is soil quality. If the soil is healthy and well drained with plenty of organic matter, plants will be healthier and less prone to disease. Disease-resistant varieties of many vegetables are available where soil quality is poor but the best thing to do in such cases is to improve the soil. The main strategies for gardening without chemicals might be summarised as follows:

'Digging in' the compost.

- Enrich the soil with manure or compost rather than chemical fertilisers
- Grow green manures to protect and improve the soil
- Use companion and sacrificial planting to ward off pests from vegetables
- Encourage natural predators by providing suitable food and habitats
- Use barriers to stop pests attacking young and tender plants
- Prune and dispose of diseased plants or parts of plants
- Pick off and dispose of slugs, snails and other pests (best done at night)
- Rotate crops, even in small vegetable gardens
- Choose species appropriate to the soil and other conditions
- Hoe, mulch and dig to control weeds, even perennials
- Protect plants from stress by good husbandry

By using these strategies it is possible to create an environment in which plants can be grown successfully without damaging or polluting the soil or the wider environment.

AVOIDANCE OF CHEMICALS

Chemicals are easily transported through the action of wind and rain, so may end up affecting areas some distance from their intended location or – worse – in neighbouring gardens. Pesticides have a tendency to affect a much wider variety of creatures than their intended victims – the widespread decline in butterflies and moths is in great part due to the indiscriminate use of pesticides.

Some otherwise organic gardeners are prepared to countenance the use of glyphosate to kill perennial weeds such as couch grass, dock, thistle, bindweed and ground elder. However, Friends of the Earth have carried out a study of this chemical.

For further information on this subject visit
www.foe.co.uk/resource/reports/ impacts_glyphosate.pdf.
For further information on all aspects of organic gardening visit 'Garden Organic', formerly The Henry Doubleday Research Association (HDRA), at **www.gardenorganic.org.uk**

PEAT

Peat is produced over thousand of years as dead plants build up rather than decay due to acidic waterlogged conditions. In addition to their importance as a historical record, peat bogs are a unique habitat and several rare plants depend on them for their survival.

Forestry and agriculture have already accounted for much of our peatland but commercial extraction of peat for nurseries and gardens is now the major threat to the little peatland which remains. 94% of lowland raised peat bogs in the UK have already been lost. Large-scale harvesting of

Photo: K Denham

peat for horticultural purposes only commenced in the 1950s as the result of a successful marketing campaign by peat producers. The harvesting method used causes destruction of the bog, as it is deep-drained and the plant layer is stripped off.

Reducing peat consumption can be achieved not only by using more traditional alternatives such as compost or leaf mould but also by selecting plants grown in peat-free materials. The Government's Biodiversity Action Plan has

set a target of 90% reduction in peat use by 2010. Peat has been cut for fuel for centuries but hand-cutting of peat does allow for partial recovery of the bog and may be sustainable on a small scale in the future.

For further information visit **www.peatlandsni.gov.uk** *and* **www.wildlifetrust.org.uk/facts/peat.htm**.

GROWING VEGETABLES AND FRUIT

Fruit, vegetables and herbs grown organically in the garden are cheap and any produce grown at home has zero 'food miles'. In addition, the pleasure of growing and eating your own food is impossible to describe.

Even small gardens can yield surprising amounts of produce but, for people with no gardens who would like to grow food, there are plenty of allotments available in many towns in the UK – local councils usually have a register of allotment areas and contact details for each. If there are no allotments and sufficient people register an interest, the local authority is obliged to provide land under section 23 of the 1908 Allotment Act (as amended).

INVASIVE NON-NATIVE SPECIES

The cultivation of non-native plants is in a sense what ornamental gardening is all about and non-native plants can enhance any garden. However, a minority of non-native species have escaped from the garden and are causing considerable environmental damage and becoming a threat to a number of native plants. Schedule 9 of the Countryside and Wildlife Act 1981 lists plants which cannot be planted or caused to grow in the wild but it is now seriously out of date, although consultation on a new list is expected soon. In 2005 the list was updated for Scotland and 13 plants were added to the original schedule:

■ *Terrestrial plants*
   False-acacia (Robinia pseudoacacia)
   Few-flowered Leek (Allium paradoxum)
   Hottentot Fig (Carpobrotus edulis)
   Shallon (Gaultheria shallon)
   Giant Hogweed (Heracleum mantegazzianum)
   Japanese Knotweed (Fallopia Japonica)

■ Aquatic plants
Curly Waterweed (Lagarosiphon major)
Floating Pennywort (Hydrocotyle ranunculoides)
Giant Salvinia (Salvinia molesta)
Water Fern/Fairy Fern (Azolla filliculoides)
Fanwort (Cabomba caroliniana)
Australian Swamp Stonecrop (Crassula helmsii)
Parrot's-feather (Myriophyllum aquaticum)
Water Hyacinth (Eichhornia crassipes)
Water Lettuce (Pistia stratiotes)

■ Seaweeds
Giant Kelp (Macrocystis pyrifer)
Japanese Seaweed (Sargassum muticum)

In addition to the plants on this list, several others are causing widespread problems. Spanish Bluebells are invading woodland and cross-breeding with our native bluebells, causing them to lose their distinctive characteristics. Rhododendron (ponticum) is spreading in acid woodland and shading out native plants, causing particular problems in the west of Scotland and Snowdonia. Botanists have also warned that the 'Tree of Heaven' (Ailanthus altissima) may become a serious problem, as it spreads rapidly and prevents other species from germinating and establishing in its vicinity by leaking toxins into the ground.

For further information visit **www.defra.gov.uk/wildlife-countryside/non-native/index.htm**. For an alternative plant list see the European and Mediterranean Plant Protection Organisation (EPPO) website at **www.eppo.org/QUARANTINE/ias_plants.htm**

COMPOSTING

Composting turns a problem into an asset. If there is sufficient space in the garden for a good compost heap, garden waste (and some household waste) can be broken down into soil-enriching organic matter, all without the trouble and expense of removing waste and importing compost. The keys to good composting are to have a good mix of soft and woody materials and to have sufficient size (around 1m³) to make the heap work properly. Temperatures in a well-designed compost heap can reach 70°C and, in general, the warmer the heap, the faster will be the microbial action that breaks down the organic matter. Turning the heap speeds up the process by introducing air and helps to ensure that material which might otherwise be left at the edges of the heap is also composted.

Compost these
Dead leaves
Lawn mowings
Soft hedge clippings
Shredded paper (not magazine paper)
Old bedding plants
Uncooked vegetable peelings and trimmings
Tea and tea bags, coffee and filters
Eggshells
Annual weeds
Pond weed
Cotton and wool

Don't compost these
Food scraps
Meat or bones
Diseased plant material (unless the heap is hot)
Soil pests
Any weeds with seed heads
Perennial weeds
Dog or cat faeces and litter
Synthetic material
Cardboard in large quantities
Nappies

Shredders
Woody material such as thicker prunings and stems of vegetables may need shredding first before adding to the heap. These materials will break down eventually but may need several passes through the composting process. It is a nuisance to have to pick out uncomposted material each time so shredding is the most efficient option. A shredder is a good example of a resource which is best shared between several households, as it would otherwise only be used for a few hours each year. Sharing a resource such as this enables a larger and more robust machine to be purchased at a reduced cost to everyone.

Moisture content
Composting needs some moisture to get started but too much moisture will stop the process so there is a balance to be struck between the two. Generally there is enough moisture in the materials which have been assembled but when building a heap after a prolonged dry spell it may be necessary to add a little water. To avoid the heap getting too wet, covering it with a scrap of carpet or a tarpaulin will prevent it from absorbing too much rainwater.

For further information visit **www.recyclenow.com/ home_composting/index.html***; call the WRAP (Waste & Resources Action Programme) composting helpline on 0845 600 0323 or see the Composting Association at* **www.compost.org.uk** *or call 0870 1603270.*

Community composting
There are a number of advantages to organising composting on a community basis – for example, an individual garden might not produce the right kind of mix of constituents to build a successful heap. By pooling resources (and also expertise) there is a much better chance of getting a good result. There may also be social benefits to be gained from getting small groups of people to work together towards a shared goal.

To find out how to set up a composting club in your area or for further information visit **www.communitycompost.org**

Encouraging wildlife

By planting a variety of perennials, shrubs and trees in the garden, wildlife will be encouraged to visit or to make a home there. These plants do not have to be native, it is more important to provide a good structure with as many layers of vegetation at different heights as possible. In larger gardens, leaving an area wild or uncut will encourage a wide variety of helpful creatures. Hedges are particularly welcome as they provide nesting opportunities for birds and shelter for voles, hedgehogs and many useful insects.

Bees are the gardener's best friend, as they perform a vital role by pollinating plants – yours and your neighbours'. 25% of native bee species are now thought to be endangered. There are many plants which are rich in nectar and pollen and bees are best attracted to gardens where

Photo: Chris Gibson, Natural England

Photo: Tony Lush

they have flowers to visit for as much of the year as possible. Mason bees can be encouraged by providing nesting cylinders which can be bought or made simply from bamboo canes and attached to a tree or a solid garden structure.

Butterflies and moths will be attracted by a range of plants, especially those which are rich in nectar. Herbs and flowers planted in sunny positions are best at encouraging these welcome visitors and some species will come to particular plants. It is equally important to provide plants which caterpillars like to feed on. At all costs avoid the use of pesticides. A healthy population of moths can also bring bats to the garden to feed on them (six of the 16 species of bat in the UK are endangered or rare).

Birds will visit if food (and water) is provided – cats and dogs permitting – and will repay the gesture in many ways, including pest control. Thrushes, for example, feed on slugs and snails. If there is space, plant a tree in the garden – birds will be grateful for the perch and might even make a nest there one day. If a suitable tree already exists, a nesting box can be erected (taking care not to damage the tree) to encourage small birds to nest. For houses or flats with little or no garden, nesting opportunities for swifts can be provided by holes in the structure of the house itself or by fixing boxes to the wall. Swift nesting bricks can even be inserted into walls.

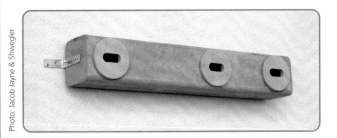

Photo: Jacob Jayne & Shwegler

For further information visit **www.rspb.org.uk/gardens**

Insect Hibernacula.

Photo: Tony Lush

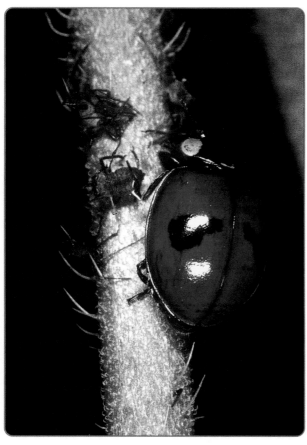

Photo: Dr. Roger Key, Natural England

Ladybirds and lacewings (and their larvae) devour aphids, so they can be used as a natural form of pest control and reduce reliance on chemical methods. They can be attracted to the garden by planting pollen-rich plants such as angelica, dill, parsley, caraway, catnip, lemon balm and thyme. They can also be imported as larvae from specialist suppliers. Hoverflies are also beneficial and are attracted to open-structured plants of the daisy family.

Hedgehogs can eat up to half their bodyweight in slugs, snails and caterpillars every day so they are a very welcome garden resident. They can be encouraged by putting out food during periods of shortage (cat or dog food in jelly is recommended) and piles of brush or leaves make ideal places for hedgehogs to hibernate. Shrews and voles need to eat through the winter so they can be helped by making protected feeding areas for them near to the base of hedges, where they prefer to live for safety.

Probably the biggest wildlife asset you can add to your garden is a pond. This is a great way to attract frogs, newts, toads and a whole host of water insects.

Lastly, it pays not to be too tidy because wildlife thrives in the unkempt margins of the garden. If you can resist 'doing the garden' until the warmer weather arrives, it will give hibernating invertebrates a chance to wake up and move out of their winter retreats.

For further information visit Natural England (English Nature) at **www.naturalengland.org.uk** *and see 'Nature in the Garden' or visit* **www.plantpress.com/wildlife/home.php***; to find lists of plants that attract each of the groups of wildlife mentioned above visit* **www.englishplants.co.uk***; for further information on conserving wildflowers, fungi and lichens visit* **www.plantlife.org.uk/uk/index-uk.html***; and for further information on wildlife and habitats in general contact your local wildlife trust.*

REFERENCES
[1] www.hse.gov.uk/pesticides/creosote.htm

Building a Compost Heap

There are plenty of purpose-made compost heaps on the market, but if you would like to build one out of recycled materials, here's how.

TOOLS REQUIRED
- Spade
- Wire cutters
- Spirit Level
- Hammer

1 Find 4 pallets from a local building yard or other commercial enterprise. Pallets should be at least 1m square in order for the heap to generate sufficient heat to work properly. It's much easier to build the heap if pallets are of the same size.

2 Identify a suitable area for the compost heap. If this is on a slope then you'll need to level the ground first with a spade. It's not necessary to put anything on the bottom of the heap – leaving it open makes it easier for tiger worms to find it and accelerate the composting process.

3 Ensure that the sides are level – this will make it much easier to attach the back and front sections.

4 Set 2 pallets at right angles to each other. Pallets generally have more timber on one face than the other, so have the side with the most timber facing inwards.

5 Connect these two pallets together with strong wire. This can also be achieved with screws or bolts but it requires a little more work.

6 Repeat the process to form the other side of the heap.

7 Composting does require oxygen to work properly. However, if your material is small pieces and you're worried about it falling through the sides of the heap, chicken wire can be attached to the inside of the pallets. Measure the rear of the heap and add the two sides to work out the total length of mesh required.

8 Measure the full length of the three sides and mark the roll of wire mesh.

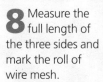

9 Cut the mesh with tin snips or electrical wire cutters

10 Fix the mesh to the inside of the pallets using galvanised staples

11 Construct a removable front for the heap. This can be done using a fourth pallet. Being able to remove the front section makes it easier to dig out the heap at the end of the process. More sophisticated versions use planks which are dropped into slots at the front of the side pallets.

12 Fill the heap (see main text section for guidance on what can and can't be composted) and cover to keep the majority of the rain off. An old piece of carpet can be used, or a sheet of polythene as long as it's weighted down. Sit back, relax, and let nature do the rest.

13 For the really efficient composter, it's easy to add a feeder heap and a finished storage heap either side of the main heap, simply by adding more pallets. A feeder heap is useful as it helps to achieve a good mix of rich and woody materials ready for the main cooking heap. A finished storage heap may not be required if your compost goes straight back onto the garden as soon as it's ready.

GLOSSARY

Accumulator – Device used to store the heat produced by a wood burning stove and release it in a controlled manner.

Acid rain – Rain or other precipitation which has been contaminated with sulphur and nitrogen compounds in the atmosphere, largely released from the combustion of fossil fuels, leading to a weak acidity which can have a significant cumulative effect on living organisms and on building materials such as limestone.

Air conditioning – Changing the quality of internal air to the desired levels of temperature, humidity and purity.

Back boiler – Device fitted to the rear of a solid fuel stove which heats water for space heating or domestic use.

Ballast – Material used to hold down or add weight.

Batt – Semi-rigid form of insulation material that will not slump in vertical applications.

Binder – Any substance that adheres material together or, when added to loose aggregate, forms a solid mass when activated.

Biodegradable – Able to be decomposed by biological agents such as micro-organisms.

Biodiesel – Oil for heating or other combustion consisting of mono-alkyl esters of long chain fatty acids produced from processed plant matter such as soybeans. Raw vegetable oil must first have glycerin removed to be termed biodiesel.

Biogas – Gas (often largely methane) generated by the bacteriological degradation of biological material in the absence of oxygen (anaerobic digestion).

Biomass – Fuel derived from non-fossilised organic material. (Also 'biofuel', 'bioenergy'.)

Blinding – Layer of fine aggregate (usually sand) laid over coarse aggregate to provide a smooth surface.

Blockwork – Sections of walls constructed from cementitious blocks.

Breather membrane – Membrane which is porous to air and water vapour but impervious to water.

Breathing wall – Form of wall construction that allows air and water vapour to pass through the structure, primarily from inside to outside.

Car club – Arrangement by which a group of people own or lease a vehicle or series of vehicles in common, thereby sharing the fixed costs and making more efficient use of resources and space.

Carbon cycle – The fundamental chemistry of all living material on earth. The main transmission compound is CO_2 (Carbon Dioxide) which is emitted (through respiration and burning) and then absorbed in oceans, or is chemically changed, for example via photosynthesis.

Carbon neutral – Any process or material which takes up as much CO_2 as is released over its life cycle; fuel which is grown and burnt and re-grown may be said to be 'carbon-neutral'.

Carcassing – Manufacturer's term for the main body of kitchen units, excluding doors and worktops.

Carcinogen – Substance which causes cancer.

Casement – Inner section of window carrying the glass, hinged on one edge and designed to open inwards or outwards.

Cavity wall – Modern form of construction whereby two leaves or skins of brickwork or blockwork are built with a gap between them, and the two leaves are connected together with wall ties. More recently the cavity has been widened to accept insulation during the construction process but a gap is still maintained.

Cellulose – Carbohydrate forming the chief component in cell walls of plants and trees. Wood pulp is almost pure cellulose.

Cement – Binder made from clay and calcined limestone.

Cladding – Timber used to provide a rain screen on the outside of a building.

Closeboard – Form of fencing where vertical overlapping feather-edged boards are fixed to horizontal bearers.

Combined heat and power – Plant which has the capacity to generate electricity while the heat produced is used for space heating

Communication pipe – The section of a water pipe running from the mains supply in the street to the property boundary. It is the responsibility of the supply company.

Concrete – Solid mass formed by combining aggregate of differing sizes with a binder such as cement.

Condensing boiler – A boiler that recovers and uses some of the heat present in the flue gases, causing water vapour in those gases to condense.

Counterweight – Attached to the other end of a sash cord, a counterweight is designed to balance a sliding sash window and make it easier to open and to keep in position. Rarely seen.

Creosote – Formed in chimneys and flues when wood is incompletely combusted. Fine particulates in the smoke condense to form creosote, which is flammable. Creosote may be dry and flaky or tarry and wet in appearance.

Cylinder – Vessel for storing hot water or for heating water.

Damp-proof membrane – Impervious layer of polythene or bitumen laid under, over or within a concrete ground floor slab to prevent rising damp.

Dead leg – Length of pipe through which water must pass from boiler or cylinder to taps (or the amount of water which must pass) before the water at the tap becomes hot.

Decrement delay – The time taken for changes in external temperature to affect internal temperature, passing through the building structure.

Dew-point temperature – The temperature at which condensation forms, given the humidity level. If the temperature is relatively warm on one side of a wall and below the dew-point temperature on the other, there is a risk that the moisture-laden air will reach the 'dew-point temperature' within the wall and liquid water will form and be deposited at this point.

Dichroic lamp – see *Halogen lamp*. In this context dichroic means the property of reflecting different colours of light when viewed from different angles.

Dry lining – The use of plasterboard, sometimes insulated, to form the finished inner surface of a wall. plasterboard may be fixed to battens or glued directly to the wall.

Dry rot – *Serpula lacrymans*, fungus that attacks and destroys timber in the presence of moisture, especially in unventilated situations. Dry rot can also spread through masonry, although it does not attack it directly. It has several forms or stages, ranging from a white cotton-like sheet appearing on affected surfaces, to dark strands (hyphae) through which it travels, and yellow fruiting bodies that turn red as spores are released.

Dual flush – Mechanism on WCs which allows the user to choose the flush volume.

Ecology – The study of organisms in terms of their relationships with other organisms and with their local environment.

Economy 7 – Electricity pricing structure whereby different prices are charged according to the time of day the electricity is drawn from the grid. The timing of the cheaper tariff normally starts at 12:00 midnight and ends at 8:00am.

Floating floor – A timber or laminate flooring surface that is not mechanically fixed (such as glued or nailed) to the subfloor in any way.

Floor slab – The concrete slab that is commonly poured directly on the ground to form the ground floor construction of a property.

Fossil fuel – Fuel derived from the remains of prehistoric plants and animals that did not decay into carbon dioxide due to anaerobic conditions. Once buried, exposure to heat and pressure within the earth's crust produced coal, oil and gas, the main 'fossil fuels'.

Gravel board – Concrete board placed horizontally at the base of a fence to prevent timber fencing from coming into contact with damp ground and suffering decay.

Grid connection – Where embedded renewable energy generating technology, such as PV or a wind turbine, is connected to the mains electricity supply.

Halogen lamp – A lamp which consists of a tungsten filament in a sealed chamber containing a halogen gas such as iodine or bromine.

Hardcore – Aggregate of relatively large size used as the base for roads or concrete.

Hardwood – Timber obtained from broad-leaved, deciduous flower-bearing trees. The term does not strictly indicate the hardness of the timber, although in general hardwoods are much harder than softwoods.

Heat exchanger – Device designed to transfer heat from one substance to another such as air-to-air, air-to-water, water-to-water etc, without mingling the two.

Heat island – Effect noticed in cities when the sun's warmth is absorbed by the dense masonry of buildings and roads, then radiated back out, leading to warmer temperatures than in the surrounding areas. The energy burnt in cities adds to this effect.

Heat pump – Pump that drives a circuit capable of transferring heat from one body to another. A heat pump may provide cooling or heating, depending upon the configuration of the pump within the vapour compression cycle.

Heat recovery – The extraction of heat from air or water that is expelled from a building and the reuse of this heat within the building.

Heavy metal – Metal with relatively high density (atomic weight). Mercury, cadmium and lead are the most widespread heavy metals with potential toxicity to humans.

Hemp – Plant grown for a wide variety of purposes, including fibres for paper and cloth.

I-beam – In cross-section, an I-beam has wide top and bottom sections and a narrow separating section, like a capital letter 'I'.

Import/Export meter – Meter which measures the net electricity generated from micro-renewables such as PV or wind turbines and also the incoming energy received from the grid.

Joinery – Generic term for windows, doors and other timber items assembled and substantially finished prior to fixing.

K-glass – In a double-glazed k-glass unit, the surface of the inner pane of glass which faces into the air gap is coated with a microscopically thin film that reduces its emissivity. The heat absorbed by this glass from within the property is inhibited from radiating across the air gap, improving the insulative value of the glass.

Landfill – Disposal of waste by means of transportation to and burying in low-lying areas of land.

Levy Exemption Certificate – Certificates are awarded to generators in proportion to the amount of renewable power which they produce. LECs can be traded separately from the power itself, which means that companies can theoretically claim to have produced green energy simply by purchasing LECs.

Light-emitting diode – Solid state light source that emits light or invisible infrared radiation when electricity is passed through it.

Light pollution – Glow from multiple light sources in towns and cities that alters the visual landscape at night and prevents the night sky from being fully visible. Can be reflected back to earth in cloudy conditions, leading to a coloured glow.

Lime – Calcium hydroxide (slaked lime) is either dried to a powder or preserved wet as lime putty. Used extensively in the building industry as a binder in mortars and renders.

Lintel – Horizontal bearing member, usually formed from timber, stone or steel, that accepts the loads above a doorway or window and transfers them to the supporting structure either side of the opening.

Masonry – Anything made principally from stone, brick, sand and gravel.

Mechanical ventilation – Fan-driven ventilation, whether individual room fans or a whole-house system.

Membrane – See *Breather membrane*, *Damp-proof membrane* and *Vapour control layer*.

Mortar – Combination of fine aggregate (such as sand) with a binder (lime or cement) to form thin adhesive joints between masonry elements such as bricks and blocks.

Net metering – see *Import/Export meter*.

Neutraliser – Device introduced into a heating system where more than one boiler is present to ensure that one boiler, when in operation, does not supply another boiler with hot water when it is not in operation.

Passive infrared – Sensor which operates by detecting the heat given off by a body that passes through its 'field of vision'. When motion is detected, a message is relayed to the control panel.

Passive ventilation – Ventilation drawn through a building by a combination of the stack effect and wind pressure, assisted by natural leakage or purpose-designed ventilators.

Payback period – The time it takes for an investment in any form of resource-saving device to pay back in the form of reduced bills, with allowance for the effect of interest rates.

Phenolic foam – Type of cellular plastic insulation.

Pigment – Substance used to give colour to another substance (paint, plaster etc).

Plasterboard – Rigid gypsum board faced with paper, primarily used to cover walls and ceilings prior to a skim finish.

Pollutant-receptor pathway – Means by which contaminants in the ground or air are collected, concentrated and transferred into the food chain or other vegetation.

Polyisocyanurate –Type of cellular plastic insulation.

Potable – Fit to drink.

Purlin – Major roof member running horizontally between walls or major trusses, used to support rafters mid-span.

Rafter – Sloping roof member running from apex to eave or valley.

Reclaim – To use an item (especially a building material) again in the same function or a different one, without reprocessing.

Recycle – To gather the waste at the end of life of a material (empty glass bottles, for example), reprocess it, and produce a new product from the resulting raw material (such as insulation).

Render – Sand and cement/lime mix applied externally to walls of buildings, primarily to protect them from the weather.

Renewable – In this context energy that can be reproduced by the same method, such as wind, solar or biomass, in contrast to fossil fuels.

Renewables Obligation Certificate – Certificate that proves that energy has been generated from a renewable source. Power companies are obliged to generate an increasing proportion of their energy from renewable sources each year.

Resistance (in the context of insulation) – The thermal resistance of a given thickness of a material is its ability to prevent heat from passing through. Measured in m^2K/W.

Resistivity (in the context of insulation) – The thermal resistivity of a material is the ability of that material to prevent heat transfer. Measured in mK/W.

Resource depletion – The gradual consumption of the earth's raw materials and sources of energy.

Reveal – The side and top sections of an opening in a wall where a window or door is inserted.

Riser – The vertical section of a staircase between each tread.

Road miles – The distance that a building material has to travel from mining or harvesting through processing and ultimate delivery to the merchant or place of use.

Sash box – Hollow section of a sash window frame that contains a counterweight to assist the operation of vertical sliding windows.

Screed – Smooth finish coat on top of a solid floor slab, usually comprising sand and cement.

Segregation – Keeping waste separate by type, so that recycling becomes easier.

Service pipe – The section of a water pipe that runs from the water main to the stopcock serving a building. See *Supply pipe* and *Communication pipe*.

Sick building syndrome – Generic term used to describe the cumulative effects of poor ventilation, inadequate daylight levels and toxic building materials, leading to noticeable effects on the health of the occupants.

Siphon – The key part of the flush mechanism within a cistern; a bent tube whereby water may be drawn off over a higher point to a lower level.

Softwood – Timber produced from trees bearing needles or cones, generally evergreen.

Solar gain – The heat from the sun that is able to enter a building, primarily through windows where the resistance is lowest.

Solvent – A liquid that is capable of dissolving another substance.

Stud – Vertical member of a timber wall.

Supply pipe – The section of a water pipe that runs from the property boundary to the stopcock serving a building.

Suspended floor – Floor normally constructed from timber and spanning from wall to wall with an air gap below, rather than resting on the ground.

Sustainable – Being able to meet present needs without compromising the ability of future generations to meet their needs.

Swale – A shallow linear depression in the ground, used for storing and dispersing rainwater.

Thermal break – An element of low conductivity placed within material of higher conductivity in order to reduce heat transfer.

Thermal bridge – A conductive material that bypasses an insulation system.

Thermal mass – Dense material within the insulated shell of a building, capable of accepting and storing significant amounts of heat.

Thermal resistance – See *Resistance*.

Thermostat – Temperature-sensitive device that sends a signal to the control switch on a heating or cooling system when it reaches a specific level.

Timber frame – Type of building in which the primary vertical loads are borne by a timber construction.

Toluene – Aromatic hydrocarbon widely used as a solvent. It is readily absorbed by contact, ingestion or inhalation and considered to be a toxin.

Transmission loss – Energy lost during the transmission of electricity, mainly due to heat production as a result of resistance in the transmission wire.

Turbine – Device to create rotary mechanical power from a stream of air or fluid.

Two-way metering – See *Import/Export meter*.

Useful heat – Heat produced by electrical appliances designed for other purposes, but which contributes towards the thermal comfort of the occupants.

Vapour compression cycle – Process whereby a substance changes state from a liquid to a gas and back again, absorbing and releasing heat energy as it passes around the loop.

Vapour control layer – Sheet material that does not allow water vapour to pass from the inside of a building into the wall and roof structure. 1,000 gauge polythene is often used for this purpose.

Virgin aggregate – Sand or gravel freshly mined, as opposed to recycled aggregate.

Woodchip – Logs or sawmill offcuts which have been processed down to a small size to make them suitable for use as fuel, horse bedding, path surfacing, etc.

Woodworm – Wood-boring larvae of a number of beetles including Common Furniture Beetle, House Longhorn Beetle, and Deathwatch Beetle.

Xylene – Aromatic hydrocarbon widely used as a solvent. It is readily absorbed by contact, ingestion or inhalation and is considered to be a toxin.

Abbreviations

BFRC	British Fenestration Rating Council
BRE	Building Research Establishment
CCA	Copper chromated arsenic
CFC	Chlorofluorocarbon
CFL	Compact fluorescent lamp
CHP	Combined heat and power
CO_2	Carbon dioxide
CoP	Coefficient of performance
CSA	Canadian Standards Association
DIY	Do-it-yourself
DPM	Damp-proof membrane
EA	Environment Agency
EC	European Community
ELV	End-of-life vehicles
ESCO	Energy Services Company
EST	Energy Saving Trust
FENSA	Fenestration Self-Assessment Scheme
FoE	Friends of the Earth
FSC	Forestry Stewardship Council
GJ	Gigajoules
GSHP	Ground source heat pump
GWP	Global warming potential
HCFC	Hydrochlorofluorocarbon
HETAS	Heating Equipment Testing and Approval Scheme
IARC	International Agency for Research on Cancer
kW	Kilowatts
kWh	Kilowatt-hours
kWp	Kilowatt peak
LCA	Life cycle analysis
LEC	Levy Exemption Certificate
LED	Light-emitting diode
LPG	Liquefied petroleum gas
LSOH	Low smoke zero halogen
MDF	Medium density fibreboard
MTCC	Malaysian Timber Certification Council
NOABL	Numerical objective analysis of boundary layer
ODP	Ozone depleting potential
OSB	Oriented strand board
PEFC	Program for the Endorsement of Forest Certification
PIR	Passive infrared
PVC	Poly vinyl chloride
PVC-u	Unplasticised PVC
PV	Photovoltaic
ROC	Renewables Obligation Certificate
RoHS	Restriction of hazardous substances
SFI	Sustainable Forestry Initiative
SPAB	Society for the Protection of Ancient Buildings
SUDS	Sustainable Urban Drainage System
TRV	Thermostatic radiator valve
uPVC	Unplasticised PVC
WEEE	Waste electrical and electronic equipment
WHO	World Health Organisation

INDEX

Further reading

BOOKS

The Whole House Book - Cindy Harris & Pat Borer - Centre for Alternative Technology Publications 2005
Natural Building: A guide to materials and techniques - Tom Woolley - The Crowood Press 2006
Green Building Bible Vols 1 & 2 - Ed: Keith Hall - Green Building Press 2006
The Water Book - Judith Thornton - Centre for Alternative Technology Publications 2005
The Energy Efficient Home: A Complete Guide - Patrick Waterfield - Chelsea Green Publishing Company 2000

MAGAZINES

Green Building Magazine
Permaculture
Green Futures

DISCUSSION FORUMS

www.greenbuildingforum.co.uk

ORGANISATIONS

Association of Environment Conscious Builders
Centre for Alternative Technology
National Green Specification
Friends of the Earth
Greenpeace

Author:	Nigel Griffiths
Project Manager:	Louise McIntyre
Copy Editor:	Ian Heath
Design/layout:	James Robertson
Illustrations:	Rob Loxston & Matthew Marke
Architect's drawings:	Alan Coles
Index:	Peter Nicholson